World War I and the Origin of Civil Liberties in the United States

THE NORTON ESSAYS IN AMERICAN HISTORY
Under the general editorship of
HAROLD M. HYMAN
William P. Hobby Professor of American History
Rice University

World War I
and the Origin of
Civil Liberties in
the United States

~~~~~~

Paul L. Murphy

W · W · NORTON & COMPANY · *New York* · *London*

W. W. Norton & Company, Inc., 500 Fifth Avenue,
New York, N.Y. 10110

W. W. Norton & Company Ltd., 37 Great Russell Street,
London WC1B 3NU

Library of Congress Cataloging in Publication Data
Murphy, Paul L   1923–
    World War I and the origin of civil liberties
in the United States.
    Bibliography: p.
    Includes index.
    1. Civil rights—United States—History.
2. European War, 1914–1918—Law and legislation—
United States.   3. European War, 1914–1918—
United States.   I. Title.
JC599.U5M833   1979   323.4'0973   79–9519

ISBN 0-393-95012-3

4 5 6 7 8 9 0

For my graduate advisees, who have taught me fully as much as I have taught them.

Contents

Foreword

RECALLING HIS World War I experience, John Haynes Holmes noted in 1959 that with the war declaration in 1917 "disarmament was a lost cause, but . . . there suddenly came to the fore in our nation's life the new issue of civil liberties." Roger Baldwin, writing in 1970, indicated that the organization of the Civil Liberties Bureau in 1917 marked "the first time that the phrase 'civil liberties' had been so used in the United States." "It was borrowed," Baldwin stated, "from a British war-time Council for Civil Liberties, whose leaders we knew."

Regardless of the authenticity of such retrospective efforts to validate "firsts," the fact remains that in the vital area of constitutional politics prior to American entry into the First World War, controversies regarding Bill of Rights freedoms occurred infrequently in judicial halls and in the public forum. Indeed, in 1941 Henry Steele Commager felt no qualms in contending that

[the record] discloses not a single case, in a century and a half, where the Supreme Court has protected freedom of speech, press, assembly, or petition against congressional attack. It reveals no instance . . . where the court has intervened on behalf of the under-privileged—the Negro, the alien, women, children, workers, tenant-farmers. It reveals, on the contrary, that the court has effectively intervened again and again to defeat congressional efforts to free slaves, guarantee civil rights to Negroes, to protect workingmen, to outlaw child labor, assist hard-pressed farmers, and to democrati-cize the tax system.[1]

1. Henry Steele Commager, *Majority Rule and Minority Rights* (New York, 1943), p. 55.

9

Such a view was recently reiterated by Stephen W. Gard in his "The First Amendment Prior to 1919: 140 Years of Silence."[2]

This study asks, and attempts to answer, a number of questions about this phenomenon. Why had the politics of civil liberties not been a factor in the shaping of public policy in the years prior to 1917? Why did the few judicial rulings in this area from 1790 to 1917 produce so little in the way of public reaction? What was unique about national developments after April, 1917 which suddenly catapulted the civil liberties issue into the public consciousness? What were the immediate results of this development? How did different groups and individuals align themselves on civil liberties issues? Once the issue was brought to the nation's attention, what made it an increasingly significant factor in public policy considerations? Today, scarcely a party platform emerges which does not contain planks on one or more central issues in the civil liberties field. Indeed, there have been few national elections since the late 1940s in which one or more civil liberties issues have not been hotly debated. Why has this increasingly come to be the case in our own times, when it seemed not to be a major concern to Americans for approximately the first 130 years of the nation's history?

Any venture into civil liberties history is replete with a variety of land mines which are frequently avoided only with the assistance of academic friends and colleagues.[3] My path has been greatly eased and my perceptions sharpened invaluably by a number of people. To all I express my gratitude. Former

2. Stephen W. Gard, "The First Amendment Prior to 1919: 140 Years of Silence" (Master of Law Thesis, University of Chicago, 1972). In a convention paper, read at the 1979 Annual Meeting of the Organization of American Historians (Alexis J. Anderson, "State Courts and Free Speech during the Formative Period of First Amendment Theory"), a variation on this same theme was fruitfully explored.

3. I have addressed some of these problems in an article, "Dilemmas in Writing Civil Liberties History," *The Civil Liberties Review* 5 (May/June 1978): 16–22.

students James McCarthy and Erik Monkkonen offered a variety of fresh and stimulating insights which helped shape central assumptions in the study. John Townsend graciously shared his very deep and perceptive knowledge of the IWW and the radical suppression syndrome. Carol Jensen similarly broadened my understanding of the Non-Partisan League. Colleagues Phil Shively and John Thayer both offered valuable suggestions, the pursuit of which proved very fruitful.

I profited from the work of Herman Belz of the University of Maryland and Stephen Vaughn of Indiana University and appreciate their sharing research findings with me. Colleagues at the University of North Carolina, Charlotte—especially Paul Escott, Harold Josephson, and Mary Kelley, now of Dartmouth College—offered provocative and useful suggestions, as did members of the history department at the State University of New York, Albany, and the University of Georgia to whom I presented some of the preliminary findings of this study. A number of friends offered intellectual and moral support at several vital points which kept the project going. Here my appreciation goes out to Robert Kaczorowski, Kermit Hall, Sandra Van Burkleo, Kim Rogers, and Clark Miller. Harold Hyman and Robert Kehoe improved the work appreciably by perceptive and pithy criticisms.

Finally, as in prior projects, I am indebted in countless ways to Helen Murphy and to Pat and Karen Murphy for support, re-enforcement, tolerance, and patience—qualities which they not only express toward me (for which I am grateful) but, as civil libertarians themselves, manifest in their lives.

World War I
and the Origin of
Civil Liberties in
the United States

1

Introduction

〰〰〰〰〰〰〰〰〰〰〰〰〰〰〰〰〰〰〰〰〰〰〰〰〰〰〰〰〰〰〰〰〰〰〰

THE STORY OF civil liberties during World War I is a dreary, disturbing, and, in some respects, shocking chapter out of the nation's past. Americans, committed through their president, Woodrow Wilson, to "make the world safe for democracy"—a phrase which implied that the nation and its allies bore a responsibility to free the world to adopt America's traditional "liberal" commitment to liberty and justice [1]—stood by on the domestic scene and saw liberty and justice prostituted in ways more extreme and extensive than at any other time in American history. The various aspects of this development have been explored frequently by popular writers, participants, and a number of distinguished scholars. Indeed, the historiography of this subject reflects the civil liberties views of those who have analyzed it and forms a useful chapter of civil liberties history in itself.

Given the dimensions of civil liberties violations in the war period, it is not surprising that there would be early attempts, especially on the part of those involved, to explain and rationalize their behavior to a postwar audience.[2] John Lord O'Brian,

1. William L. O'Neill, *The Progressive Years* (New York, 1975), p. 141, points out the further irony that Wilson knew full well that other Allied nations in the "concert of free people" had no intention of freeing the hundreds of millions of people in their colonial empires, no matter how the war came out.

2. The historian, William A. Dunning, was one of the first of his profession to assess the civil liberties aspects of the war, comparing Wilson favorably with Lincoln and commending his restraint in internal security procedures and their enforcement. "Disloyalty in Two Wars," *American Historical Review* 24 (July 1919): 625–30.

the special assistant to the attorney general for War Work in charge of prosecution under the Espionage Act, is a case in point. Properly considered a sensitive civil libertarian in the context of those days, O'Brian, after resigning from office, denounced continued operation of wartime statutes. Nonetheless he felt compelled, in April 1919, to justify the Justice Department's repressive actions during the war as proceeding from a sincere commitment to the protection of the constitutional and civil rights of the citizen. "The policy," wrote O'Brian,

was based upon the confidence felt in the law-abiding character of our citizens, and in the conviction that, in this country, it was very generally recognized that liberty meant obedience to law, self-control, and self-restraint, and that in every part of the country the strongest deterrent influence against disloyalty was neighborhood public opinion.

It was the view of the department, he concluded, that there should be no repression of political agitation, "unless of a character directly affecting the safety of the state"; that the constitutional guarantees protecting life and property must be strictly enforced; and that under no circumstances should the military or naval authorities be permitted to perform any act which would arbitrarily interfere with the life and habits of the individual citizen.[3] While acknowledging that absurdities were carried out, particularly as a result of the "spy mania," by "organizations and societies created for the purpose of suppressing sedition," [4] O'Brian argued that "the American spirit of fair play did not permit excesses to occur, with the exception of certain groups whose activities constituted willful attempts to interfere with conduct of the war."

George Creel, the bombastic and impetuous head of Woodrow Wilson's Committee on Public Information, an agency

3. John Lord O'Brian, "Uncle Sam's Spy Policies: Safeguarding American Liberty during the War," *The Forum* 61 (April 1919): 407–16.

4. The allusion here was to such groups as the American Defense Society, the National Security League, and others like them. See H. C. Peterson and Gilbert C. Fite, *Opponents of War* (Madison, Wis., 1957), pp. 18–19.

devoted to making winning the war dominate the thought and activity of every American, struck a similar note in his immediate postwar assessment of wartime civil liberties. In his 1920 book, significantly entitled *How We Advertised America: The First Telling of the Amazing Story of the Committee on Public Information that Carried the Gospel of Americanism to Every Corner of the Globe,*[5] Creel sharply assaulted critics who charged that the Committee on Public Information (CPI) had engaged in the careful construction of hysteria in order both to support the war effort and to suppress those who opposed it. A similar focus marked his book, *The War, The World & Wilson,* published the same year [6]; and in his memoirs, published in 1947, he was still protesting in a similar vein, denouncing the "censorship myth" which had grown up around his wartime activities and contending that although freedom of the press was a right that did suffer a few abuses, "better abuses than the evils of a deadening and autocratic control" [7] imposed by Old World tyranny.

The most perceptive of the immediate postwar evaluations, however, was *Freedom of Speech,* by Zechariah Chafee, Jr., of the Harvard Law School, also published in 1920.[8] Chafee had developed an abstract interest in civil liberties, and particularly freedom of expression, immediately before the war, when he had inherited Roscoe Pound's third-year equity course. Pound had shortly before sought to enliven the material by introducing considerations on the law of libel, and Chafee, uncertain as to the meaning of freedom of speech, had read every pre-1916 case on the subject, with singularly unrewarding consequences. Not only were there few cases, but most of them had results unsatisfactory to one seeking precedents for free-speech protection.[9] Within months of American entry into the war and

5. (New York, 1920).

6. (New York, 1920).

7. George Creel, *Rebel At Large: Recollections of Fifty Crowded Years* (New York, 1947), p. 157.

8. (New York, 1920).

9. Quoted in Jerold S. Auerbach, "The Patrician as Libertarian:

the enactment of stringent new espionage and sedition laws, Chafee suddenly found himself confronted with law being made "before his eyes" and with a wave of persecution in the wake of this new legislation. Realizing that it would be necessary for lawyers to begin searching quickly for new boundaries regarding freedom of expression and that the public would have to be apprised of the importance of this need, he began injecting articles into the popular press [10] as well as in law journals.[11] One of the first to recognize that civil liberties was not only a matter of legal doctrine, but of politics as well, he both encouraged popular concern with the issue and deplored those who would turn the question into a smoke screen behind which to hide their selfish purposes. As such, his work tended to be more purist and descriptive than exhortatory and prescriptive, even though conservative critics railed against its revelations and its tone, which implied that wartime government officials had departed with distressing frequency from a consistent commitment to the rule of law in the civil liberties area—and had done so in spite of the fact that they should have known that they were corrupting liberal democratic principles and procedures.

Further writing on World War I civil liberties did not occur, however, until the late 1930s—the issue of wartime limitations on personal freedom being one which Americans of the late 1920s and early 1930s found neither interesting nor relevant.[12]

Zechariah Chafee, Jr., and Freedom of Speech," *The New England Quarterly* 42 (December 1969): 514.

10. The most famous and influential was an article in the *New Republic*. Zechariah Chafee, Jr., "Freedom of Speech," *New Republic* 17 (November 16, 1918): 66–69. The article was requested by the editor, Herbert Croly, partly to calm dissension in his staff, who felt that his opposition to suppression of war criticism was not sufficiently vigorous. See Fred D. Ragan, "Justice Oliver Wendell Holmes, Jr., Zechariah Chafee, Jr., and the Clear and Present Danger Test for Free Speech: The First Year, 1919," *Journal of American History* 58 (June 1971): 37.

11. See Zechariah Chafee, Jr., "Freedom of Speech in War Time," *Harvard Law Review* 32 (June 1919): 933–61.

12. The one important exception was Ray H. Abrams, *Preachers Present Arms* (New York, 1933), a revealing study by a University of

Then, with Europe on the brink of a second war, a spate of works appeared, assessing the threat which a wartime period might again produce if the example of World War I were to be followed. In 1939 James R. Mock and Cedric Larson published a detailed and critical (although not hostile) evaluation of the Committee on Public Information entitled *Words That Won The War,*[13] spelling out the favorable and unfavorable aspects of the work of Creel and of the various segments of the committee. Mock followed up this work two years later with a study entitled *Censorship, 1917* [14] which probed that issue in detail. The year 1939 also saw the release of H. C. Peterson's *Propaganda for War: The Campaign Against American Neutrality.*[15] James M. Read followed in 1941 with *Atrocity Propaganda, 1914–1917.*[16] Both explored propaganda and its manipulation, as well as its contribution to the intolerance of the wartime period. In 1941 Chafee brought out a second edition of his earlier work. This volume, entitled *Free Speech in the United States,*[17] reexamined World War I and explored what had happened in the free speech area in the succeeding twenty years. He left no doubt that in writing the work he was responding to his own sense of the "growing danger of the recurrence of the conditions" [18] which he had deplored in his 1920 work and of the importance of avoiding the wartime mistakes of Woodrow Wilson, particularly in the civil liberties area. All of these works were period pieces, reflecting the attitudes of the pre– World War II period and generally coming from an essentially libertarian perspective.

The post–World War II period saw two sharp articles by

Pennsylvania sociology professor deploring, with lengthy and revealing examples, the ways in which the clergy caved in before national patriotism and hysteria in the first war.

13. (Princeton, 1939).

14. (Princeton, 1941).

15. (Norman, Okla., 1939).

16. (New Haven, Conn., 1941).

17. Zechariah Chafee, Jr., *Free Speech in the United States* (Cambridge, Mass., 1941).

18. Ibid., p. xi.

Ora A. Hilton [19] contrasting the overall good civil liberties record of the Second World War with the excesses of World War
I and generally assailing Woodrow Wilson for World War I
violations. But Cold War tensions and the McCarthy loyalty
hysteria apparently dimmed this interest, and it was nearly ten
years before the subject was again tackled. In 1957 H. C.
Peterson, in a work completed after his death by Gilbert C.
Fite and entitled *Opponents of War, 1917–1918: The Story of
the Persecution of Anti-War Groups,*[20] provided the most complete overview yet of the various dimensions of World War I
civil liberties violations. Old-left conflict history in a consensus
decade, the work stressed the quasi-conspiratorial aspects of the
anti–civil liberties activities, arguing that repressive programs,
particularly those directed against the Socialists, the IWW, and
the Non-Partisan League, were fostered by conservative power
groups and more conservative progressive leaders in a deliberate
attempt to utilize the hysteria of the war period to wipe out
critics of the capitalist system. Thus, in the eyes of Professor
Peterson, wartime repression was at least partially planned and
carried out to cleanse America of radicalism, a policy which
earlier progressives had favored but could not implement without the excuse of wartime exigency.

Harold M. Hyman in his 1959 volume, *To Try Men's
Souls: Loyalty Tests in American History,*[21] and in a subsequent
1963 work, *Soliders and Spruce: Origins of the Loyal Legion
of Loggers and Lumberman,*[22] subscribed to the same theory.
Hyman acknowledged the pressures placed on the Wilson administration to move against disloyalty from superpatriots and
chauvinistic groups. He also emphasized the willingness of administration leaders to act on the excuse of public hysteria,

19. Ora A. Hilton, "Public Opinion and Civil Liberties in Wartime,
1917–1919," *Southwestern Social Science Quarterly* 27 (December 1947):
201–24; "Freedom of the Press in Wartime, 1917–1919," *Southwestern
Social Science Quarterly* 27 (March 1948): 346–61.

20. (Madison, Wis., 1957).

21. (Berkeley, 1959).

22. (Los Angeles, 1963).

which they did nothing to reduce, and to support fully, if clandestinely, private repressionist groups set up to intimidate and harass war critics.

Donald Johnson, in a 1962 article [23] and in a subsequent book, *The Challenge to American Freedom: World War I and the Rise of the American Civil Liberties Union,*[24] afforded a similar emphasis, coming down particularly hard on Attorney General Thomas Gregory and the Justice Department. Johnson saw Word War I civil libertarians as upper-class reformers and generally as opponents of big business who wanted to mitigate the evils of industrial capitalism by softening inequities within the law. Johnson, however, writing in 1963—before the federal government's questionable use of its power in Vietnam and Watergate, and before recent CIA and FBI revelations of their violations of civil liberties—did not look at the World War I situation through lenses ground by those experiences. In fact, in 1963 liberal Americans were cheering the growing intervention of federal authority into the area of race relations as an overdue step toward the achievement of civil rights. As a result, Johnson did not see, as Roger Baldwin and other civil leaders did in 1917 and 1918, the ominous threat inherent in the startling new relationship of government to the individual which came with federal criminalization of aspects of both speech and written expression, and its accompanying proscription of unwarranted opinion, and association. Neither did he see the potential for civil liberties violations which the nascent bureaucratic institutions created during World War I would have when they fell into the hands of highly insensitive people.

In this respect his work failed to recognize the prescience of early civil libertarians in realizing that what was happening in the First World War was not simply a matter of the Wilson government using its power inequitably and unfairly to benefit

23. Donald Johnson, "Wilson, Burleson, and Censorship in the First World War," *Journal of Southern History* 28 (February 1962): 46–58.
24. (Lexington, Ky., 1963).

some as opposed to others.[25] This was especially true of their concern with the impact of such developments upon the democratic process and on public values. The shift of power to new central agencies, with heavy discretion for its use no longer determined democratically, was particularly troubling, especially when agency officials assumed "emergency" discretion over the forms and degression of permissible nonconformity in people's attitudes and behavior.

Johnson's work complemented a range of early 1960s studies. These included Harry N. Scheiber's *The Wilson Administration and Civil Liberties, 1917–1921*,[26] which also castigated Wilson but emphasized that civil liberties violations could more often be laid to exuberant subordinates than to cabinet officials such as Attorney General Gregory who were charged with initial implementation. Out of the same milieu came Richard P. Longakers' *The Presidency and Individual Liberties*,[27] which stressed Wilson's carelessness in failing to restrain repression, rather than his instigating of it, and John P. Roche's *The Quest for the Dream*,[28] which viewed wartime repression as an attempt at homogenizing a set of pluralistic communities through enforced patriotism.

This theme was also elaborated on in the most recent general synthesis, an extended essay in the 1974 *Wayne Law Review*, by Thomas A. Lawrence.[29] This study argued that the climate of repression during the First World War was fed most strongly by nativist impulses. These, in turn, arose from traditional native-born Americans' growing fear of the rising political power of immigrants—and particularly those whom the melting pot had not sufficiently melted. In addition, Lawrence emphasized the public's identification of "nefarious doctrines"

25. Ibid., p. 201.
26. (Ithaca, N.Y., 1960).
27. (Ithaca, N.Y., 1961).
28. (New York, 1963).
29. Thomas A. Lawrence, "Eclipse of Liberty: Civil Liberties in the United States during the First World War," *Wayne Law Review* 21 (1974): 33–112.

such as socialism, pacifism, radicalism, bolshevism, syndicalism, and even unionism with immigrants from the "central powers," who were now seen as subversives and even fifth-columnists. Thus, the wartime civil liberties situation was tied up with attempts to Americanize alien elements, a process which necessitated the suppression of alien propaganda and the destruction of alien ideologies. Here Lawrence viewed the courts as willingly collaborationist, turning the law into a "codification of intolerance, war-time policy and political expedience."

William Preston's *Aliens and Dissenters: Federal Suppression of Radicals, 1903–1933*,[30] published in 1963, added a new perspective. Setting the wartime suppression of radicals in a broader context, Preston struck a sharply new posture, which he extended further as the 1960s progressed and new-left history came into its own.[31] For Preston civil liberties were generally a deception at the outset. Rather than being a central aspect of American values, and thus something worth fighting for—a view which pervaded the earlier works of Chafee, Peterson and Fite, Hyman, and Roche—the idea of civil liberties was simply a trick which the power elite played on the American people to hold out some ray of hope as an alternative to standard repression. As such, civil liberties were part of the ideology of the middle class, which could be waived at any time. The power elite extended these liberties to other Americans only when the use of such liberties in no way threatened the status quo. This created the image of an open society behind which it could hide and rule. For those middle-class citizens who, in their naïveté, worked for the protection and expansion of civil liberties, in the wartime period and after, their actions were meaningless gestures made to assuage their guilty middle-class consciences. As such, civil liberties violations in World War I were not unusual or any departure from the norm. The war

30. (Cambridge, Mass., 1963). A similar tone pervaded Richard Harris, *Freedom Spent* (Boston, 1974).
31. On Preston's later work see Arthur M. Schlesinger, Jr., "An Uneven Chronicle," *The Civil Liberties Review* 4 (Summer 1975): 135.

merely called forth the kind of overt repression which the "establishment" was prepared to use anytime its power or authority was challenged. Such a new-left view of civil liberties was possibly carried to its logical extreme in a 1963 article in which Marc Schleifer argued that the only thing of any significance that the New Deal did was to enact the Smith Act.[32]

Joan Jensen's 1968 study of the most virulent of the private wartime suppressionist groups, the American Protective League,[33] was more in the Hyman and Johnson tradition, again stressing Wilson's shortcomings but trying hard to explain them as well. According to Jensen, Wilson must be given some points for his consistent opposition to military trials and military intervention into civilian loyalty matters. On the other hand, she faulted him for not insisting that those nonmilitary officials who acted for the government be held clearly responsible to it. Here Wilson failed in not seeing to it that the home-front war fought by his subordinates did not degenerate into guerrilla warfare, ranging dissenter against conformist, pacifist against militarist, and radical against conservative. However, she did see the wartime excesses giving birth to a new concern for the defense of civil liberties against the federal government, a development which she viewed as positive.

Finally, the anti–Vietnam war movement of the late 1960s and early 1970s produced further studies reevaluating the antiwar movement of the World War I period and the frequent violation of the rights of those involved in it. Here the works of Charles Chatfield,[34] Roland Marchand,[35] and Blanche Wiesen Cook [36] explored aspects of World War I in which pacifists and

32. Marc Schleifer, "A Socialist Plea for Black Nationalism," *Monthly Review* 15 (September 1963): 225.

33. Joan M. Jensen, *The Price of Vigilance* (Chicago, 1968).

34. Charles Chatfield, *For Peace and Justice, 1914–1941* (Boston, 1971).

35. C. Roland Marchand, *The American Peace Movement and Social Reform* (Princeton, 1972).

36. Blanche Wiesen Cook, "Woodrow Wilson and the Anti-Militarists, 1914–1917" (Ph.D. dissertation, Johns Hopkins University, 1970).

antipreparedness types suffered the sting of civil liberties deprivation.

This study makes no pretense of covering the previously plowed ground of the civil liberties story. Rather, it addresses certain basic but significant questions about these developments. Why did they take place, and why, particularly, did they take place at this time? And, perhaps more importantly, what immediate and long-range reactions and implications in doctrinal, attitudinal, and behavioral terms did this development produce in American history?

What happened during World War I in the civil liberties area was a new and disturbingly different development in American history. The utilization of the federal government as an active instrument for social control was itself a twentieth-century phenomenon, one identified with the Progressive movement, which advocated a newly centralized, paternalistic regulation of the nation's public policy. But now government was recruited as an instrument for rationalizing and carrying forward desirable social policies which private power groups could no longer successfully effectuate independently, thereby achieving a type of modernization which involved new relations between citizens and government.[37] This took the form of curtailing "evil" behavior by "evil" individuals—whether these were purveyors of impure food, narcotics, or obscenity, exploitive employers of women and children, despoilers of the nation's natural resources, or corrupters of the political process. But a progressive spokesman like George Creel would have extended the positive government process to encompass federal employment bureaus, industrial courts, government loan agencies for farmers, national health insurance, and even educational support through federal instrumentalities.

Prior to the war, however, national progressive leadership, although to a degree doctrinally antiindividualist, was still re-

37. Robert H. Wiebe, "The Progressive Years, 1900–1917," in William H. Cartwright and Richard L. Watson, Jr., eds., *The Reinterpretation of American History and Culture* (Washington, D.C., 1973), p. 434.

luctant to utilize government to repress individual freedom—speech, press, the right to engage in legitimate, if controversial, social and political activity—unless that activity took the form of illegal actions punishable through traditional types of predominantly local criminal sanctions. Clearly, members of the Industrial Workers of the World (known as Wobblies) who were disturbing the peace or urging others to engage in violence could be charged with violating local criminal statutes and be indicted for their actions. But the general expression of dissident viewpoints, while sometimes deplored, was not formally made criminal by progressive leadership. Rather, if such behavior seemed a threat to social stability and to the "establishment" generally, it was contained through a variety of more subtle private sanction available to those in positions of power. Dissident behavior was handled prescriptively through various manipulative techniques designed to encourage acceptable comportment. In education, Americanization programs and a variety of forms of socialization led toward the goal of greater "reconciliation" and assimilation.[38] The traditional view that the federal government represented the gravest threat to personal freedom, which had led to the initial adoption of the Bill of Rights, had pervaded American thinking through the nineteenth century. The unique departures of the Reconstruction in attempting federal extension of rights to the freedman had run afoul of this tradition, but the older view was left in place and widely embraced until the eve of American entry in 1917 into the war. As long as such a view prevailed, the enactment of federal legislation restrictive of traditional Bill of Rights freedoms was largely precluded.

With the war, vital new developments took place. To assure patriotism and wartime victory, and to support Wilson's crusade abroad for proper progressive and democratic values, a new policy of formal and prescriptive federal governmental action

38. Don S. Kirschner, "The Ambiguous Legacy: Social Justice and Social Control in the Progressive Era," *Historical Reflections* 2 (Summer 1975): 85.

was adopted to repress individualism and diversity of opinion in order to secure the unwavering allegiance of immigrants, hyphenates,[39] and a wide range of other Americans whose loyalty was in any way suspect. This meant not only persuasive Americanism campaigns but also vigorous action through federal espionage, sedition, sabotage, and revised immigration laws against those who seemed to offer any resistance to these campaigns, or whose general public posture advocated an alternative approach to what rapidly became official wartime orthodoxy. Contributing to the acceptance of the legitimacy of such an approach was the general progressive sense that sufficient steps had been taken during the previous dozen to fifteen years to liberalize social conditions within the American system, to eliminate its evils, and to create a society based upon social justice and new opportunities for depressed groups. With the system now more liberal and socially responsible, criticism of it was all the more suspect and unjustified. To its defenders, the anticapitalistic postures of the Socialists, the Wobblies, the Non-Partisan League, or others working to discredit the system and tear it down had even less claim to the protections of Bill of Rights guarantees such as freedom of speech and press than they might have had twenty years earlier. Thus, Wilsonian leaders had few misgivings about extending Progressive forms of social control into wartime restraints, and in fact manifested a growing impatience with those in society who in any way objected to or criticized this process.

But the implications for those thus victimized—whether they were Socialists, Wobblies, Non-Partisan Leaguers, antipre-

39. The term "hyphenate" is formally defined as "those immigrants and their descendants who, either of their own choosing, or as a result of outside pressure, link their American nationality with that of their ancestral land." See Louis L. Gerson, *The Hyphenate in Recent American Politics and Diplomacy* (Lawrence, Kan., 1964). In the everyday parlance of the World War I period, the term took on a more pejorative meaning, implying, especially in the case of German-Americans and Irish-Americans, a suspicious divided loyalty between the country of origin and the United States.

paredness advocates, hostile to conscription, or pacifists (opposed to war generally)—were ominous. Progressive leadership, in an earlier day, had utilized the federal government as an instrument to regulate and rationalize the behavior of private economic interests, and especially to strike at "unwarranted" behavior. This generally had involved a process of defining as "criminal" the actions of entrepreneurial groups or other powerful economic bodies which exercised power in such a way as to damage or injure the public interest. This process touched the practices of the trusts, the abuses of railroads, the exploiting techniques of unconscionable employers, and the deception of the public through mislabeled drugs or impure foods by those who would cash in on public gullibility for the profit of a corporation. To the degree that distinctions were drawn between permissible limits of freedom of economic activity and the right of the public to be protected against abuses of power, they involved fairly clear delineations between recognizable abuse and the legitimate profitable activity of various organizations. However, the government found that enforcement was frequently a problem in dealing with these power groups. Such groups were not reluctant to seek exemption from rigorous application of laws by bringing well-financed test cases to essentially sympathetic, property conscious, laissez-faire-oriented courts; nor did they hesitate to forestall effective enforcement by influencing regulatory agencies or, if relief was not possible this way, to seek legislative relief in getting laws modified which they considered too punitive and too restrictive to business generally.

The government's wartime program, which placed sharp limitations on individual actions previously considered permissible and even protected by the Bill of Rights, constituted the application of new normative rules. This action presented its victims and its critics with a unique challenge. With freedom of speech and freedom of the press sharply restricted, with conscription imposed, and with the right to diversity of individual action sharply impeded (whether that be the right to teach or speak German, the right to publish foreign language newspapers, or the right to engage in unpopular political activity and campaign for office on an essentially anticapitalist platform), constructive avenues of alternative action posed a serious dilemma. Lawmakers had been persuaded to criminalize aspects of individual action, thereby placing clear operational limits upon personal freedom. Admittedly, some overtones of group liability were involved in this policy—an anarchist, for example, made himself suspect by affiliating with a suspect group—but generally the government was marking out new lines between where personal freedom stopped and restriction, in the name of the public or national interest, legitimately began. Clearly, there was some calculated risk involved, since the government was obliged to show the necessity for a policy restrictive of liberties previously thought to be beyond federal tampering or reap the wrath of public apprehension and hostility. This possibly explains the chest-thumping Americanism and superpatriotic justifications of those in the government who called for this kind of temporary suspension of traditional rights in the name of total wartime victory.

But despite the potential tactical advantage of having the American tradition of the Bill of Rights on their side, the protective instrumentalities open to the victims of repression, as essentially powerless and frequently unpopular individuals, differed sharply from those available to regulated power groups. Such beleaguered individuals, and often the groups with which they were affiliated, were not in a position to seek the easing of enforcement procedures. They had few resources with which to challenge laws in courts and little hope of relief there, even if hearings were obtained. For despite a tradition of economic laissez-faire, prior practice had resulted in little judicial support of civil liberties unless civil liberty was directly an aspect of property rights. Further, such individuals and organizations had a limited capacity to persuade bureaucrats to look the other way in enforcing such laws against them. In contrast with business regulation, there was always the possibility that if bureaucrats did look aside, irate local patriots might take it upon themselves to enforce the law in their own way. Finally, war further dramatized the inability of such victims to gain legislative relief without the economic or political power with which to carry their case to their representatives. Thus, although their cause was fairly persuasive from a traditional Bill of Rights perspective, their ability to invoke successfully the symbolism of American freedom to protect the rights of unpopular Americans was virtually nonexistent once America entered the war. The wartime period persuaded them, and other Americans sympathetic to their cause, that if big government was indeed to utilize its power in this way, it might well constitute a continuing threat. Thus, the wartime experience drove those concerned and apprehensive for the future of civil liberties to begin more organized activities in their behalf, activities geared toward inducing Americans in the future to strike the balance between freedom and order more clearly on the side of freedom.

Civil liberties emerged from this controversy as a relatively significant issue in public policy for the first time in American history. Where a previous generation had thought that the abstract issue of defining and affording rights to American citizens posed no serious doctrinal question of substantial concern to any great number of average citizens, now the argument over the nature and the dimensions of that process began to elicit public controversy. While civil liberties did not become a partisan issue or split major parties during World War I, it nonetheless produced public debate, from the halls of Congress, down to various local forums, and through the press. This encouraged Americans to explore the idea that the protection of civil liberties was a serious public responsibility in a democracy and that the shaping of proper public attitudes on pertinent issues was essential if responsible civil liberties practice was to occur.

The government's wartime behavior, and that of various quasi-vigilante bodies supporting government policies—and frequently using them as excuses for a repression far beyond any contemplated by the lawmakers—produced one other new development. Through all of prior American history, the group which had drawn the line between liberty and license, between the permissible limits of individual freedom and the point at which that freedom had to be curtailed had been the traditional propertied class, and increasingly in the late nineteenth and early twentieth century, the great entrepreneurs and financiers of the nation. Their decisions on such matters, while at times criticized by small vocal minorities, had not generally undergone successful challenge. Neither had the practices which supported their policies—private forms of sanction or coercion carried out informally—and at times extralegally—by local leadership. Now the issue of the permissible limits of the restriction of freedom, as a matter of definition and implementation, emerged as a public question. The politics of civil liberties was thus born. New civil liberties groups emerged with the deliberate purpose of shaping public policy regarding who had the right to claim liberties and why, how, and on whose terms. Such groups insisted that the government's civil liberties policy be established openly by the electorate through its representatives, and not informally and subtly by unaccountable bureaucrats and paternalistic judges who might impose their own values and criteria on society.

Thus, an issue which previous generations did not feel was a public issue emerged out of the World War I experience—an issue which over the next half-century, with the massive growth of federal involvement in the lives of citizens, became increasing vital and central in American political life.

2

The Civil Liberties Tradition in the Progressive Years

~~~~~~

CIVIL LIBERTIES, as a public policy issue in American history had surfaced only on rare occasions prior to World War I. During the brief "half war" with France in 1798–1800, the Federalist party of President John Adams had turned to war-justified repression as a deliberate partisan act to strike at Jeffersonian Anti-Federalists.[1] Jefferson and Madison, through the Kentucky and Virginia Resolutions, sought to rally their supporters and the nation against this policy, on the grounds that the Federalist Alien and Sedition Acts constituted unwarranted repression not only of personal freedom but of that political autonomy encompassed in states' rights and local self-determination. The controversy had found its way into election politics in 1800, with the Jeffersonian posture partially validated by the Anti-Federalist victory at the polls. President Jefferson's efforts to defuse the issue as a public question were generally successful, even though Jefferson's behavior did not always square well with his professed civil liberties ideology. Further, as Leonard Levy has shown, the darker side of Jefferson's civil liberties record, particularly during his Presidency, involved considerable departure from an abstract civil liberties posture. It certainly did not seem to involve general indulgence for deviant

1. James Morton Smith, *Freedom's Fetters: The Alien and Sedition Laws and American Civil Liberties* (Ithaca, N.Y., 1956).

views, and particularly tolerance for "the ideas we hate." [2] Nonetheless, Jefferson's opponents did not mount sufficient contemporary public criticism of these practices to turn them into a public issue, and the politics of civil liberty did not again surface in this early era.[3]

In fact, meaningful civil liberties politics flared up only briefly and sporadically during the remainder of the century, despite some efforts to provoke them. Northern abolitionists, as Russell B. Nye has demonstrated,[4] worked hard to rally Northern opinion against the "slave power conspiracy" by continually charging Southern leaders with following a deliberate program of repression of freedom of speech and of the press, "gagging" petitions sent to Congress, interferences with the mail, and even assaulting academic freedom in order to protect the evil institution of slavery. But no antebellum political platform, and few candidates for public office, embraced this charge as a political posture guaranteed to win wide support from the electorate. During the Civil War some Northern Democrats, called Copperheads, attempted to discredit the Lincoln war government on grounds that it was autocratic and repressive in areas ranging from the suspension of habeas corpus to infringements on freedom of the press.[5] But while antiwar militancy was surprisingly widespread and virulent, the Copperheads' attempts to foster Northern opposition to the war were unpopular enough to preclude the civil liberties issues from gaining wide sympathy.

Possibly the most overt, and temporarily successful, example of the constitutional politics of civil liberties involved Reconstruction-era developments. As a result of coercive Republican

2. Leonard W. Levy, *Jefferson and Civil Liberties: The Darker Side* (Cambridge, Mass., 1963).

3. On nineteenth-century antiwar protest, See Samuel Eliot Morison, Frederick Merk, and Frank Freidel, *Dissent in Three American Wars* (Cambridge, Mass., 1970).

4. Russell B. Nye, *Fettered Freedom: Civil Liberties and the Slavery Controversy, 1830–1860* (East Lansing, Mich., 1949).

5. Frank L. Klement, *The Limits of Dissent* (Chicago, 1970). Cf. Harold M. Hyman, *A More Perfect Union* (Boston, 1975), esp. Chaps. 5, 23–26.

Reconstruction policies, former confederate leaders were subjected to martial law and frequent denials of civil liberties guarantees by military tribunals. While these actions were all allegedly taken as steps essential for the protection of the civil rights of newly freed blacks, the broader constitutional issue underlying such a policy was raised by opponents from President Andrew Johnson down to local spokesmen for the occupied South.[6] Conversely, when the Ku Klux Klan emerged in the late 1860s with a self-appointed assignment of intimidating newly enfranchised blacks and those Southern citizens, black or white, who cooperated with northern "carpetbag" leaders gone south, such behavior raised sufficient public outcry that Congress enacted the Ku Klux Klan Enforcement Acts. In this instance governmental intervention was designed to restrain the activities of a particular group in order to protect American citizens in their freedoms to the franchise and to general expression and association.[7] With the collapse of the early Klan, however, the perceived need for federal intervention to protect the rights of citizens declined in the public mind and in 1876 the Supreme Court effectively removed the issue from the political scene by ruling key sections of the Klan Enforcement Acts unconstitutional as a form of nonpermissible federal activity.[8]

Such developments generally turned around single-issue situations involving limited and definable groups of Americans. What was being restricted was a kind of behavior which was potentially disruptive to society. Groups from former confederates to the Klansmen were temporarily deprived of their rights as an expedient means of getting at a particular problem. Few, if any, nineteenth-century Americans saw such immediate crash solutions, even though they did involve temporary curtailment of certain civil liberties, as either a threat to their own rights or

6. For Johnson's statement on black rights, see James M. Smith and Paul L. Murphy, *Liberty and Justice* (New York, 1968), pp. 250–51.

7. J. G. Randall and David Donald, *The Civil War and Reconstruction* (New York, 1969), pp. 577–78, 683–85.

8. United States *v.* Reece, 92 U.S. 214 (1876); U.S. *v.* Cruickshank, 92 U.S. 542 (1876). See also U.S. *v.* Harris, 106 U.S. 629 (1883).

a massive precedent from which the government would expand its power to cover the behavior of all citizens.

The same was true with the initial movement against labor leaders and "foreign" agitators in the late nineteenth century. When vocal spokesmen for working-class people protested against the overt and covert repression imposed upon them, limiting their freedom to organize, publicize, strike and picket, their inability to make their situation into a national civil liberties issue again reflected certain nineteenth-century values and circumstances.[9] While particular Americans were momentarily distressed by the vehemence of the repression meted out to such people, from the Haymarket agitators [10] and the Pullman Strike [11] leaders to local organizers and left-wing labor sympathizers, few saw such incidents as a cause for public concern. It was felt that in utilizing libertarian principles and appeals to justify their general assault upon the capitalistic system, these people were attempting to camouflage disruptive action and questionable motives by public appeals to civil liberties principles. Again this was a single-issue situation involving a definable group of have-nots within a society and as such was hardly appealing to majority interests as a question of public policy around which citizens should be induced to rally. Similarly, Populist rhetoric was filled with allusions to the violation of the basic rights of Populist leaders and their followers.[12] However, it produced little in the way of refutation, or even acknowledgment, by a society unprepared to dignify such charges with a serious response.

The progressive years, 1900–17, did not see this pattern altered appreciably. The attitudes of the effective wielders of private and public power in these years toward the utilization

9. For a good general overview, see Lillian Symes and Travers Clement, *Rebel America* (Boston, 1972).

10. On Haymarket see Henry David, *The History of the Haymarket Affair* (New York, 1958).

11. On the 1890s see Almont Lindsay, *The Pullman Strike* (Chicago, 1942).

12. Norman Pollack, *The Populist Mind* (Indianapolis, 1967).

of civil liberties were sharpened with the turn to active government and social control through a range of programs regulating aspects of human behavior. But despite some faltering beginnings by comparatively obscure Americans to force public consideration of civil liberties issues or to cast social questions as civil liberties issues, civil liberties politics remained largely the concern of such a minority, and not one of any substantial number of the American people. Only when American entry into World War I produced a new type of repressive governmental action affecting the personal freedom of many people did any significant number of Americans begin to react to the civil liberties implications of public policy. This development took place within the spirit of the progressive era and is fully comprehensible only within the context of the civil liberties values of these years.

Recent American historians have generally turned away from talking about progressives, progressivism, and the progressive movement, on the grounds that these are clichés describing nothing precise either in activity or in time. But there is no question that Americans of the first two decades of the twentieth century who were neither radical nor conservative but considered themselves in some ways what a midcentury American generally would call a liberal used the term "progressive" to describe themselves.[13] The term was broad, embracing all sorts of people, from politicians and social reformers, to labor leaders, journalists, and academics, to small, and even big, businessmen. Being broad, it becomes imprecise and insensitive as a way of sorting out people, ideologies, programs, policies, and postures in these years. Nonetheless, it is still possible to talk about doctrines, attitudes, and behavior regarding civil liberties in this period. It is essential to attempt to sort out popular attitudes regarding who should and should not have civil liberties, what form civil liberties should take, how they should be effectuated, and on what terms civil liberties should be extended. Here, a

13. William L. O'Neill, *The Progressive Years* (New York, 1975), p. x.

broad consensus seems to have existed among the effective wielders of private and public power at this time. That general set of attitudes toward operational civil liberties was translated into behavior revealing of the values of the age. It also produced criticism and disagreement, in some cases from people deliberately disassociating themselves from programs, policies, and actions labelled progressive. Thus, there existed in the years prior to the outbreak of World War I a sufficiently identifiable set of doctrines, attitudes, and behavioral patterns in the civil liberties area that one can both talk about the nature of the abstract issue and understand why it was a public policy nonissue at this time.

For purposes of this study, the terms "doctrine," "attitude," and "behavior" are being used fairly precisely. Civil liberties is definable most centrally as an aspect of law. Law operates at three levels in a society. The doctrinal level involves the rules of behavior set down by authoritative and legitimate institutions in response to majority imperatives regarding desirable human relationships. These may be set forth in formal documents, such as constitutions and statutes, or in the formal rulings of courts interpreting those doctrines. In civil liberties law, those doctrines are evolving and fluctuating in that both legislatures and courts tend to be continually deciding whether certain human activities fall within or exceed the parameters set by the rules. Thus, for example, in the progressive years, vigorous criticism of the president was in no way to be proscribed; yet World War I doctrine drew new restrictive lines regarding the permissible limits of such criticism, both in the form of federal and state statutes, and in judicial actions interpreting those statutes.

The degree to which such doctrines are operational, however, depends largely upon people's attitudes toward them. If they enjoy broad popular support compliance will normally follow. Prohibition in the United States, on the other hand while a doctrine with legitimate constitutional and statutory implementation, was not successful, largely because people's attitudes toward such denial of freedom of choice were negative and frequently defiant.[14] Americans generally respect free speech. But the most resolute and unanimous judicial statement of doctrine supporting the right to dissent will not alter popular hostility or strict popular action toward the speech of those whom a majority of the people finds unacceptable. This suggests that the attitudes of those who implement doctrines can and will be affected by the attitudes of those to whom the doctrines are applied. The complexities here are great. Whose attitudes count most? How seriously must policy makers and enforcers take the attitudes of militant dissenters, whose view are generally unpopular with the rank and file of majority Americans? Conversely, how far will majority Americans allow sitting executive, legislative, or judicial officials to extend civil liberties to the "wrong" people, to those not ready for them, or to those who might abuse them, before such citizens revert to overt or covert noncompliance or actively demand a change of officials, of policy, and, therefore, doctrine? How long will vigilante-minded patriots tolerate what, in their eyes, is too lenient a government policy toward those suspected of disloyalty or un-American behavior? When civil liberties become a public policy issue, the resolution of that issue is determined ultimately by a broad range of attitudes toward the policies that comprise the government's response. In the civil liberties area, however, this is made more complex by the fact that the federal Bill of Rights, and the bill of rights of the states assume that the limits of majority rule are reached when minority rights are unjustifiably threatened or abused by that majority.

Civil liberties law is also affected by behavior. People respond to what actually happens to other people far more readily than to doctrines regarding what should happen to other people. When an American of the progressive era thought about permissible limits of freedom of speech, what he reacted to was what society was doing to socialists, Wobblies, militant labor leaders, and dissenters generally when their speeches produced

14. Norman Clark, *Deliver Us from Evil: An Interpretation of American Prohibition* (New York, 1976).

definable and recognizable action. Should a labor leader either through oral exhortation or through the pages of a labor journal, encourage his followers to engage in boycotting of goods? Should IWW efforts to publicize its cause be allowed to tie up communities with "free-speech fights" in which soapboxes were set up and the police were goaded into making arrests in the name of public safety? Did a person on a public platform turn liberty into license in advocating the desirability of planned parenthood? And when the United States government enacted repressive wartime legislation sharply limiting First Amendment freedoms and pacifists and conscientious objectors were harrassed by officials charged with enforcing it, that behavior also produced popular responses in the civil liberties area. In this case some Americans were concerned because what was happening to a great many young men opposed to conscription could well have happened to any rank-and-file American who opposed the government's authoritative wartime programs. In the years from 1900 to late 1918, the government's behavior in enforcing stringently the limits of personal freedom did change significantly. It changed even more dramatically with American entry into the war. That in itself brought new concern for the civil liberties issue, a concern which projected the issue into the public conscience in ways never before seen in the American experience.

Before April 1917 Progressive-era doctrines in the civil liberties areas were relatively clear, if relatively simple, legally unsophisticated, and frequently lacking in detailed specificity. Certainly, the law on civil liberties was not well and precisely defined until the war period. The United States Constitution contained a Bill of Rights, as did every state constitution. Yet Congress had seldom legislated in such a way as to define or restrict those rights since the 1798 Sedition Act. Nor, for that matter, had the states, at least where white males were concerned. New York, in 1902, had enacted the first Criminal Anarchy Law aimed at securing convictions against radical agitators who were American citizens and were, therefore, ineligible for deportation.[15] But with the exception of a 1904 case in which an anarchist was accused of slander,[16] the measure went unenforced. The federal Comstock Law of 1873 had closed the mail to all "obscene, lewd, or lascivious material," but no one at the time considered such expression any more subject to Bill of Rights protection than profanity, blasphemy, libel or slander.[17] Statute law, and even city ordinances, generally did not formally restrict civil liberties, per se. Therefore case law was sparse as well. Courts called upon to interpret civil liberties issues frequently found no statutes pertaining to free speech, free press, assembly, or the rights of a citizen charged with a crime. Civil liberties raised complex questions involving far more than simply personal freedom considerations. And when public safety or local social control came in conflict with claims of individual rights, especially the rights of controversial or "undeserving" persons, such rights were to be sublimated.[18]

The attitude of a majority of public and private leaders of the late nineteenth and early twentieth centuries toward civil liberties, as well as the attitude of great numbers of rank-and-file Americans who supported those leaders, held that such liberties were only to be protected for those citizens who had demonstrated, both by their attitudes and their behavior, that they were prepared to utilize those freedoms in positive and constructive ways. The decision as to whether a citizen deserved to have his civil liberties formally protected was to be made by those responsible elements within the society that were knowledgeable in the proper use of personal freedom. Liberty, in short, was a condition conferred by the community at its discretion, usually only to "good people" who had earned their prerogatives. Blacks, Indians, Orientals, aliens—particularly those from Eastern Europe—women, or people espousing

15. Julian F. Jaffe, *Crusade against Radicalism* (Port Washington, N.Y., 1975), p. 198.

16. Van Gerichten *v*. Seitz, 94 N.Y. App. Div. 130 (1904).

17. James C. N. Paul and Murray L Schwartz, *Federal Censorship* (New York, 1961), pp 18–34.

18. See, for example, Twining *v*. New Jersey, 211 U.S. 78 (1908).

radical and destructive economic and political theories, clearly were not ready for the full utilization of their constitutional liberties. General doctrines guaranteeing freedom to such citizens were suspect and had to be tempered in subtle ways by those in a position to implement those doctrines.

In the late nineteenth century, the Supreme Court, in the *Hurtado* v. *California* decision which became ruling case law until well into the 1930s,[19] validated such relativity of rights. Due process of law (that is, equal justice in the courts), the justices held, was not a fixed principle. "It would not be wise for the states to be bound by any fixed set of procedures in criminal cases," ruled Justice Stanley Matthews. Matthews was really saying that state courts could modify and shift their rules in dealing with criminal suspects to insure that the right people got due process; due process was not to be wasted on the wrong people or extended to those who might abuse it. Justice John Marshall Harlan dissented vigorously, maintaining that the due process clause of the Fourteenth Amendment imposed traditional common-law procedures on the states on all criminal matters. The purpose of the clause, Harlan argued, was to impose the same restrictions on state courts in respect to proceedings involving life, liberty, and property which had been imposed upon the general government. To leave it to state officers to determine who did and who did not qualify for civil liberties was improper doctrine, perverting the intentions of the framers of the Fourteenth Amendment.

The 1908 Twining case saw the Progressive-era Court embracing the same majority position. The case involved the Fifth Amendment's provision against compulsory self-incrimination. The judge in the lower court had instructed the jury that if the plaintiff refused to answer certain kinds of questions (that is, if he did claim this constitutional right), this could clearly be interpreted as tacit admission of guilt. The Supreme Court really ruled that it was up to the state courts to decide whether or not to respect this provision of the federal constitution, and, by

19. Hurtado *v.* California, 110 U.S. 516 (1884).

inference, any consitutional provision which impeded their authority. In practice this meant that the criterion by which a citizen got civil liberties could legitimately include the attitude of the judge toward the person.

Again, Harlan offered the only protest to such a view, maintaining in a lone dissent that the due process clause of the Fourteenth Amendment incorporated the whole Bill of Rights as a check on the states. To leave the proper methods of procedure to the discretion of the states and state officials he contended, was to deny citizens basic constitutional protections and civil liberties.[20] Clearly, this was true. But equally clearly, to leaders of the Progressive era, this was as it should be. Blanket extension of all civil liberties to all citizens at all times, without provision for attitudinal modification based on the circumstances, was not a Progressive attitude.

The same pattern is clear in the area of freedom of speech and freedom of the press. One of the few significant cases involving those principles occurred in 1907, when a defendant was convicted for publishing articles and cartoons critical of Colorado's Supreme Court.[21] The defendant maintained that the statements in the articles were true and that under the First Amendment to the Constitution truth was a defense for an alleged libel. Justice Oliver Wendell Holmes, however, rejected this contention. Turning to an ancient principle of William Blackstone, that "if a man publishes what is improper, mischievous, or illegal, he must take the consequences of his own temerity," Holmes argued that freedom of speech and press were a relative freedom, subject to whatever limitations society wished to impose upon them. In the Colorado situation, Holmes argued, the main purpose of the First Amendment was to prevent prior restraint of publication by government. But once printed, statements "deemed contrary to the public welfare" might be punished, whether true or false. Again, as Justice Harlan pointed

20. Twining *v.* New Jersey, 211 U.S. 78 (1908). See Bernard Schwartz, *The Great Rights of Mankind* (New York, 1977), pp. 210–17.
21. Patterson *v.* Colorado, 205 U.S. 454 (1907).

out in his dissent, this constituted the validation of judicial discretion whereby speech by proper individuals could be sanctioned, while speech by improper ones could be punished. To Harlan this further violated the principles of the Fourteenth Amendment which, he contended, sought to incorporate speech and press against the states by prohibiting the states as well as the Congress from abridging in any way those rights which constituted "essential parts of every man's liberty." [22] The case did not sharpen the criteria regarding permissible limits of free speech and press other than to leave it to the courts' discretion to draw that line on a case-by-case basis. Property rights remained the dominant consideration for judges who were free to impose their own attitudes and prejudices as they evaluated individuals and circumstances.

In many respects that criterion was bound by traditional assumptions and values central to classical liberal beliefs regarding the relationship between personal rights and property rights. In nineteenth-century America, the free man was one who was master of his own destiny. This meant that he was a man of some substance. From the time of the First Continental Congress, the rights of "life, liberty, and property" were inextricably interwoven as the basis for American public doctrine.[23] Daniel Webster reiterated that view, stating at one point, "Property is the fund out of which the means of protecting life and liberty are usually furnished," [24] thus restating a position earlier expressed by John Adams that "Property must be secured, or Liberty . . . [could] not exist." The association of property and liberty was so close that men classified property among their other fundamental "unalienable rights." [25] Further, they viewed "the freedom of property from the indefinite despotism of

22. Ibid., at 465.
23. See the Declaration and Resolves of the First Continental Congress, in Smith and Murphy, *Liberty and Justice,* pp. 38–40.
24. Quoted in Paul A. Freund, *On Understanding the Supreme Court* (Boston, 1950), pp. 15–16.
25. John Adams, *The Works of John Adams,* Charles F. Adams, ed. 10 vols (Boston, 1852), 6:280.

sovereignty . . . [as] the best security to be found against those laws by which social liberty was so often injured." [26] But while the concepts of private property and liberty were closely allied, pre–twentieth-century rules guaranteeing the rights of property did not result in increased individual liberty; they merely identified the individuals who would enjoy it. For every person who gained liberty by obtaining protection of a property right, some other person frequently lost a portion of his liberty. Therefore, the property base for liberty, while persuasive in doctrine and argumentation, was not in and of itself a device for enhancing the civil liberties of any substantial number of Americans. Granted, the opportunity was there. The road to civil liberties was through acquiring a stake in the system, embracing its values and principles, and accepting their assumptions. The recent immigrant who had worked hard, saved his money, and acquired a business, property, and status within the society was—assuming he was a WASP male—deemed ready for its rewards. But those who had not gone this route—and in early industrial America, an increasing number were unable to go this route—clearly did not yet deserve those rewards. Their very impoverishment demonstrated their lack of moral character and sense of responsibility. Civil liberties were a fringe benefit for the successful, gained with the acquisition of power and status.

The other side of the coin was clear also. If civil liberties were extended to the undeserving—those whom John Stuart Mill referred to as "those human beings not in the maturity of their faculties" or those in the "backward states of society"—or if those undeserving claimed and sought to utilize those rewards

26. John Taylor, *Construction Construed and Constitutions Vindicated* (Richmond, 1820), p. 78. See also Richard Schlatter, *Private Property: The History of an Idea* (New Brunswick, N.J., 1951), esp. pp. 188–95, 199–200; Gordon S. Wood, *The Creation of the American Republic, 1776–1787* (Chapel Hill, 1969), pp. 218–19, 404–05, 410–11, 503–04; and William B. Scott, *In Pursuit of Happiness: American Conceptions of Property from the Seventeenth to the Twentieth Century* (Bloomington, Ind., 1977).

on their own terms, abuse of such rewards would almost certainly occur. "Liberty, as a principle," Mill wrote in his famous essay "On Liberty," "has no application to any state of things exterior to the time when mankind have become capable of being improved by free and equal discussion." [27] Henry Pratt Fairchild captured this sentiment well in his influential volume, *The Melting Pot Mistake*:

There is full justification for a special application of the principles of freedom of speech to aliens, differing widely from the interpretation in the case of citizens. [28]

The influential educator, Ellwood P. Cubberley, took the next step, stressing the need

to assimilate and amalgamate these people as a part of our American race, and to implant in their children, so far as can be done the Anglo-Saxon conception of righteousness, law and order, and popular government, and to awaken in them a reverence for our democratic institutions and for those things in our national life which we as a people hold to be of abiding worth. [29]

Then, and only then, would they be ready to enjoy the benefits of the Bill of Rights.

Thus, when courts in the Progressive years were called upon either to protect or to deny civil liberties, judges essentially had to decide whether the individual seeking those liberties was sufficiently committed to American values to insure that extension of civil liberties to him would not basically threaten society. Even more precisely, what judges had to decide was whether the utilization of civil liberties presented a sufficient threat to property interests to warrant their curtailment. [30] The view that

27. John Stuart Mill, *On Liberty* (Library of Liberal Arts ed., Indianapolis 1956), pp. 13–14.

28. (Boston, 1926), pp. 255–56.

29. Ellwood P. Cubberley, *Changing Conceptions of Education* (Boston, 1909), pp. 15–16.

30. A classic statement of this occurred in the nationally famous case of Benjamin Gitlow in New York, when the "silk stocking" Judge Bartow S. Weeks berated the defendant from the bench as a person with no moral character and deserving of no consideration, since he was a

the criterion should entail whether or not the utilization of free speech and free press, for example, served the general welfare of the whole human community was a decidedly minority one at that time, held principally by a few liberal legalists and radical reformers.

But to such classical values and traditional attitudes, Progressive-era developments added further considerations. The period was a highly dynamic one. Recent American historians have seen it as an era of dramatic modernization, with a growing mechanization of production and distribution and increasing impersonality in social relations; as an era marked by a growth in size and power of large bureaucratic organizations and the centralization of power both in government and in private power structures, from corporations and businesses to labor and farm organizations; as a period of development of sophisticated new forms of mass communications, with increasing uniformity of attitudes; as a period of secularization of popular thought; and as a period of rising faith in the scientific solution of human problems. All of these general trends had subthemes. Among the most dramatic developments for civil liberties history was the tendency, typified by the growing authority of the office of the presidency, for political power to be concentrated in national hands, with policymaking carried out by a small directing elite. At the same time, a quite different tendency toward the centralization of values was gaining momentum. Apprehensions about unassimilable immigrants were leading to a type of anti-pluralism which produced Progressive demands for aggressive Americanization programs to screen out both undesirable "foreign" attitudes and suspected undesirable "foreign" behavior.

Simultaneously, and in sharp contrast, the same period saw an intellectual revolt against formalism and a shift to relativism, with an accompanying new emphasis among liberal intellectuals on the value of dissent, particularly intellectual iconoclasm. This new departure stressed the importance of personal expres-

person of no property. Benjamin Gitlow, *I Confess: The Truth about American Communism* (New York, 1939), p. 73.

sion, including sexuality, as basic to the newly self-conscious drive for modern freedom. It thus added a further dimension to the controversy over the permissible and proper limits of human expression.

These developments led the directing elite to new levels of anxiety regarding the imposition of social control. To the extent that the elite shared civil liberties attitudes, it embraced the old Puritan view of "freedom through submission to authority." But new groups were challenging the legitimacy of that concept and claiming civil liberties in order to assail many aspects of the American way. Did freedom now mean new rights for such have-nots, who had not earned their place within the structure? Did freedom mean the right of an anarchist to assault the capitalist system? Did freedom embrace the right of Wobblies, socialists, and agrarian radicals to force their views into the public debate regarding proper public policy in this new modernizing society? And what was the appropriate reaction to a new and disturbing bohemianism which was producing a revolt among young intellectuals who were filled with contemptuous assaults on conventional American values?

The proper attitude toward these questions, and the proper role of the government in coping with civil liberties problems, was not clear in the Progressive years. Were private power's earlier forms that subtly contained deviant expression and action still capable of producing the proper balance between freedom and authority? Was it time for new forms of social control of deviance, especially with socialism growing, IWW militancy increasing, and intellectual protests against the system gaining new adherents? Wasn't there a legitimate fear that these new, troubling forces could not be controlled adequately by traditional, informal, local techniques? Since many Progressive leaders took the view that government should take on new roles and functions in order to rationalize the desirable competitive struggle which capitalism inspired, possibly, it was time to apply progressive efficiency, social engineering, or a new technology to the solution of civil liberties tensions. Possibly, the new bureaucratic structure should be called in to work on the dissent problem, the loyalty problem, or the Americanization problem. Possibly, it was time for the federal government to resort to techniques of surveillance and suppression in order to contain forces rapidly getting beyond the control of local or private directing elites. On the other hand, there was a minority of elite leaders who questioned whether it might not be time to consider exploring new ways of protecting the citizen's rights from violation by the community or by individual members of the community. This sentiment was particularly prevalent among leaders of groups such as the NAACP, and the American Jewish Congress. Clearly, these dilemmas troubled a number of thoughtful Americans.

But the Progressive era did not offer any strongly embraced consensus solutions. It took the urgency of war to bring Progressive-era leaders to take that step and rethink their attitudes sufficiently to come up with new, concrete approaches for confronting this situation.

Until then a number of essentially "informal social controls" and restraints were imposed by the private sector.[31] When some element of the government was brought in, it was usually at the behest of private citizens, to enable them to implement private programs. A troublemaker in a community could be silenced or censured by economic sanctions, social ostracism, pressures on his family by employer, teacher, minister, or ward-heeler. If unwarranted, deviant behavior continued, a battery of breach of the peace, trespassing, or even vagrancy statutes could be turned to in order to impose criminal sanctions. The press of the period, and particularly the local press, while in no way inhibited from muckraking evildoers and exposing graft and corruption within the establishment, was still sufficiently committed to the purification and maintenance of the system through

31. The concept refers to Ferdinand Tonnies, *Gemeinschaft und Gesellschaft* (East Lansing, Mich., 1957). For its application in the civil liberties area, see Paul L. Murphy, "Sources and Nature of Intolerance in the 1920's," *Journal of American History* 51 (June 1964): 68–69.

the proper means that if troublemakers appeared they could quickly be designated in the public mind as "bad" people whose actions and views good citizens should either reject or ignore. This system was not overtly repressive but it was highly efficient. When it was not, as militant members of the IWW were to learn when strikes and free-speech fights were mounted, vigilante actions, private detectives, company guards, and, in scattered instances—as in the coal fields of Pennsylvania or Colorado— state troopers and even federal militia would suppress violent actions with violent retribution. Pennsylvania's Coal and Iron Police were notoriously successful in this regard.[32] The famous Ludlow Massacre in Colorado in 1914 shocked a number of otherwise placid Americans when forty-five people—striking miners or their wives and children—were killed and many more wounded when their tent village was attacked and burned by the state militia. The episode was eventually investigated by the Senate Industrial Relations Committee later in the same year.[33] A few other scattered such incidents demonstrated that when the use of certain personal freedom threatened the power structure, public or private, little time would be lost in clarifying the limits of personal freedom by direct and often harsh action.

Thus, the Progressive civil liberties world of the years up until 1914 was rather benign. Critics did exist. Theodore Schroeder, along with a number of opponents of the era's rather suffocating Victorian oppressiveness, organized a Free Speech League in 1913.[34] Victims of overt repression seldom lost an opportunity to point out the ways in which they, as Americans, were being deprived of their basic birthright of civil liberties.

32. John P. Guyer, *Pennsylvania's Cossacks and the State Police* (Reading, Pa., 1924).

33. On Ludlow see James Weinstein, *The Corporate Ideal in the Liberal State, 1900–1918* (Boston, 1968), pp. 193–95. On the Industrial Relations Committee, see Graham Adams, Jr., *The Age of Industrial Violence, 1910–1915* (New York, 1966).

34. On Schroeder see David Brudnoy, "Theodore Schroeder and the Suppression of Vice," *Civil Liberties Review* 3 (June–July 1976): 48 ff.

Critical reaction, particularly to the Ludlow Massacre or the troubled Patterson strike of 1913 [35] showed that the consciences of some Americans were touched by the extremes to which the power group would go when it was threatened. But before 1914 none of these reactions produced sufficient demands for public consideration of civil liberties questions to involve any substantial number of people in a serious consideration of civil liberties issues. Only with the outbreak of war in Europe, and Americans' focus on the new relationships which a war-torn world suddenly produced, did that monolith begin to undergo some serious reconsideration.

35. On Paterson see Morris Schonbach, *Radicals and Visionaries: A History of Dissent in New Jersey* (Princeton, 1964), pp. 57–66.

3

The Emergence of the Civil Liberties Issue

THE IDEA OF the federal government suppressing public expression in the Progressive period had generally been precluded by a variety of factors. Private power was in a position to keep the dissenters from getting too far out of line. If private power alone was insufficient, the authority of the states could be invoked up to and including the utilization of force where necessary to deal with overtly disruptive and dissident elements. With the acceleration of the war in 1915 and 1916, and with the growing inevitability of American participation on the side of the Allies, signals began to come from the White House, indicating that federal authority would be used, when and if the time came, to muster the American people behind an actual war effort. Further, there was little question in Woodrow Wilson's preliminary statements and actions that if events unfolded as expected, government actions would not warrant any wholesale public debate as to their desirability as proper public policy. In fact, the president and prominent members of his cabinet worked to prepare the nation for the possibility that domestic dissent might have to be curbed in wartime. In so doing they revealed an early concern to forestall a public controversy over the civil liberties of Americans.

One of the early manifestations came as the outbreak of the European war and American actions on the Mexican border raised the question of the necessity of censorship to preserve national security. As these developments threatened to involve

Americans directly, and create controversy, administration officials expressed concern that "they had not laws adequate to
deal with the insidious methods of internal hostile activities." [1]
The only federal statute on the books which seemed at all
appropriate was the Alien Enemies Act of 1798, which gave
the president the authority to imprison dangerous enemy aliens
without trial. Attorney General Thomas W. Gregory, whose
department was to become an instrument for repressive activity,
stressed the need to criminalize a variety of forms of protest
and dissent, contending that new ways had to be evolved to
contain America's enemies use of "warfare by propaganda." [2]

The president's involvement reflected his early desire to
define loyalty and Americanism in such a way as to exclude
certain forms of dissent from government protection. While
acknowledging the value of the foreign-born in enriching American life in a speech to the annual meeting of the Daughters of
the American Revolution the president hinted strongly that a
small minority of aliens and naturalized citizens were not committed to this nation. "I am in a hurry," he stated, "to have a
line-up, and let the men who are thinking first of other countries stand on one side, and all those that are for America first,
last, and all the time, on the other side." [3]

Two months later the president's position hardened notice-
ably. In delivering his third annual message to Congress, which
included an armaments program, Wilson no longer implied that
the number of disloyal foreign-born was insignificant. Foreign-
born opponents of his policies, he charged, were "pouring the
poison of disloyalty into the very arteries of our national life." [4]

1. John Lord O'Brian, "New Encroachments on Individual Freedom," *Harvard Law Review* 66 (1952): 8–9.

2. *Annual Report of the Attorney General, 1918* (Washington, D.C.,
1918), pp. 16–17. Gregory, a Texan, was particularly interested in Mexican matters.

3. Ray Stannard Baker and William E. Dodd, *The New Democracy:
Presidential Messages, Addresses, and Other Papers* (New York, 1962),
3:377.

4. Ibid., 423.

In addition to an extensive rearmament program, the president cited the need for legislation to suppress disloyal activities. He implied not only that the behavior of such disloyal elements was indefensible, but that it was not a subject on which there was room for any public debate, since they had sacrificed their right to civil liberties by their own behavior. His posture cast suspicion on the loyalty of all foreign-born. On the following day the cabinet asked Attorney General Gregory to begin drafting security legislation, a task which the Texan undertook with relish.

This move to raise suspicions about the loyalty of opponents of government policy intensified steadily during the presidential campaign of 1916. The preparedness issue was clearly before the country. Many Americans, both hyphenates and native-born, questioned this preparedness posture, fearing involvement in Europe's affairs. These included large numbers of Irish- and German-Americans, Socialists and other political radicals, as well as pacifists and a number of progressives, who feared that shifting national priorities toward involvement in a foreign war would inevitably result in downgrading further domestic reform. Preparedness advocates, particularly those drawn from the business community, were quick to lump such people together as a "common enemy," questioning their patriotism and their commitment to the nation's highest values.[5] Wilson, as he confronted both his Republican opponent, Charles Evans Hughes, and the vociferous and popular Theodore Roosevelt, now back in Republican ranks, took much the same line. Thus, the number of those being placed on the side of the line where their loyalty was suspect was gradually increasing.

In 1916 the president seemed to become more and more obsessed with the stepping up of this process. As Democratic leaders developed campaign strategies, the president insisted that Americanism be a major theme. He took special interest in the drafting of the party's plank on loyalty, which condemned

5. C. Roland Marchand, *The American Peace Movement and Social Reform, 1898–1914* (Princeton, 1972), pp. 97–98, 177.

every group or organization, political or otherwise, that has for its object the advancement of the interest of a foreign power, whether such object is promoted by intimidating the government, a political party, or representatives of the people, or which is calculated and tends to divide our people into antagonistic groups and thus to destroy that complete agreement and solidarity of the people and that unity of sentiment and purpose so essential to the perpetuity of the Nation and its free institutions.[6]

Implicit in this statement was the note that these matters were not debatable.

The indivisibility and incoherent strength of the nation is the supreme issue this day. . . . all men of whatever origin or creed who would count themselves Americans [should] join in making clear to all the world, the unity and consequent power of America. This is an issue of patriotism. To taint it with partisanship would be to defile it.[7]

Wilson's statement in a Flag Day address expressing his anxiety over the propagandistic activities of "hyphenated groups," and contending that "every effort must be exerted to secure unity of opinion as a basis for unity of action" [8] was formalized in the Democratic party plank. In the subsequent campaign, Wilson played upon this theme heavily. Questioned at one point as to "tolerance," the president made clear that there should be no tolerance for those who would "inject the poison of disloyalty into our own most critical affairs." Americans, he argued, should "teach these gentlemen once and for all that loyalty to this flag is the first test of tolerance." [9]

Accompanying the president's bombast were supportive cabinet-led efforts to enact into law what the president was calling for rhetorically. Although measures framed by the cabinet, and introduced into the Congress in mid–1916, calling for sharp curtailment of freedom of speech and press were not

6. Ray Stannard Baker, *Woodrow Wilson: Life and Letters* (New York, 1939), 6:256.

7. Kirk H. Porter and Donald B. Johnson, *National Party Platforms* (Urbana, Ill., 1973), p. 195.

8. Baker and Dodd, *New Democracy,* 5:67.

9. Ibid., 4:209, 283.

acted upon prior to that body's adjournment, they were re-introduced, at administration urging, at a special session of the Congress in early 1917 as the Webb-Overman bill—a measure defining and punishing espionage. Although the measure did pass the Senate in February, the House adjourned before voting on it. Thus, espionage legislation was on the agenda prior to the nation's entry into the war on April 2, 1917, and quickly became one of the first objectives of the Wilson administration's domestic wartime program.[10]

One measure was passed in this period which signaled the road ahead. On February 14, 1917, with the attorney general's approval, the Congress passed a Threats Against the President Act, providing federal criminal penalties ($1,000 fine and up to five years' imprisonment) for persons who "knowingly and willfully" made written or spoken statements threatening the life of or bodily harm to the president.[11] This constituted a potential first step to "criminalizing" expression, foreshadowing the further curtailment of First Amendment freedoms. Little controversy was aroused as to whether such a public policy of abrogating certain civil liberties was justifiable.

Wilson's pre-entry attitudes and behavior were carried to their logical extreme when war came. The president was a man who could tolerate little criticism of himself or his policies at any time. Anticipating the necessity for coercing total national unity if a national emergency occurred, he began eliminating criticism by screening out people whom he was convinced the majority of Americans would feel had no business expressing strong, controversial views on the proper course for the nation. Recent immigrants, hyphenates, particularly German-Americans, Irish-Americans, and others not fully identified with and unquestioningly committed to the Allied cause, had

10. Homer Cummings and Carl MacFarland, *Federal Justice: Chapters in the History of Justice and the Federal Executive* (New York, 1937), pp. 414 ff.

11. 39 *Stat.* 919 (1917). Sixty cases were prosecuted under this act before June 1918; of these, at least thirty-five resulted in convictions. *Report of Atty. Gen., 1918*, p. 56.

best be carefully monitored by the federal government until they were thoroughly Americanized. Susceptibility to foreign influence and action was too great to risk complete confidence in such people.

Wilson and other progressives cast an increasingly wary eye at native critics. The Socialist party in America in these years was growing, not only in size and influence but in the volume and vehemence of its public positions.[12] The IWW was gaining, both in membership and notoriety, as the spokesman for a large element of down-and-out working-class citizens, ineligible for membership in and generally anathema to the conservative craft unions of the time.[13] The prewar period, as Henry May and others have chronicled,[14] had seen the emergence of a vigorous, inconoclastic, and generally freewheeling movement on the part of young intellectual radicals to achieve new tolerance and permissiveness and to modernize both thought and behavior regarding Victorian/Progressive repressiveness (especially in the literary and artistic world). Their publications, ranging from the *New Republic* in the middle to *Mother Earth* and *The Masses* on the left, seldom lost an opportunity to express dissatisfaction with the failure of progressivism to move far beyond its current reform limits. The membership of such groups was heavily native-born and very much a part of the American tradition of legitimate dissent and protest. Their prewar behavior did not breed serious suspicion that they might engage in activities dangerous to American security.

Wilson found many of these Socialist, Wobbly, and youth-

12. David A. Shannon, *The Socialist Party of America: A History* (New York, 1955), pp. 77–78.

13. Paul F. Brissenden, *The I.W.W.: A Study of American Syndicalism* (New York, 1920), pp. 377–41.

14. Henry F. May, *The End of American Innocence* (New York, 1959); Charles Forcey, *The Crossroads of Liberalism* (New York, 1961); Christopher Lasch, *The New Radicalism in America, 1889–1963* (New York, 1965); and Robert A. Rosenstone, *Romantic Revolutionary: A Biography of John Reed* (New York, 1975). A useful flavor of the period is afforded by Richard Fitzgerald, *Art and Politics: Cartoonists of the Masses and Liberator* (Westport, Conn., 1973).

ful intellectual critics distasteful. His early treatment of such people was cautious and circumspect. To put their behavior beyond the boundaries of protectable civil liberties before America joined the war effort was dangerous, but a wartime crisis might ultimately afford an acceptable public justification. The care with which the administration had moved toward criminalizing dissident expression created a precedent which, once war was declared, could be used to transfer the same stigma borne by aliens to other groups whose support for the war had not been 100 percent from the beginning.

A number of other groups posed far more serious dilemmas for the president. He could expect his Republican opponents to be understandably chary regarding a posture which implied that criticism of his programs was suspect and even potentially disloyal. Dealing with such critics, therefore, posed a different problem, but one which Wilson anticipated and worked on during the prewar and war years. The same was true of the nation's press in general. The fourth estate, itself a big business and a powerful economic unit as well as a molder of public opinion, was naturally going to be suspicious of national efforts to suppress freedom of information and its right to inform the public. Editors were in a position to speak eloquently and with conviction about the dangers both to them and the public of infringing upon a basic right such as freedom of the press. To them the curtailment of such a fundamental civil liberty, even in the name of national security, was a volatile issue, and they seldom lost an opportunity to rally public opinion against further censorship or further curtailment of dissenting views.[15]

Finally, there was the disparate, powerful, and, in many ways, respected body of traditional pacifists and antimilitarists. Such Americans had, from the beginning of the outbreak of war in Europe, rallied to oppose American entry and all preliminary steps toward armament, preparedness, conscription, and the regimentation of opinion behind actions which might draw the nation into that conflict. The prewar activities of this latter group

15. Baker, *Life and Letters*, 7:81–82.

had not been passive but had consisted of aggressive adversarial organizational efforts to draw more and more Americans behind their views and against those of the interventionists. But they had also played upon themes which could hardly have been said to be anti-Wilsonian. Large numbers of prewar pacifists were thorough progressives, committed to expanding domestic reform, encouraging industrial democracy and social justice, and generally upgrading, humanizing, and liberalizing society. Unlike the Socialists or the IWW, such leaders as social worker Jane Addams, reformer and publicist Crystal Eastman, Rabbi Stephen Wise, David Starr Jordan (president of Stanford University), and publisher Oswald Garrison Villard had never been viewed as enemies of the system. They were among its strongest supporters. Through most of their public activism, they had contended that the system was only now beginning to realize its full potential for moral uplift and social regeneration. They feared that American involvement in a foreign war would provide the excuse for scrapping further domestic reform, and even for the return of the immoral business elite to positions of national power, where it would use preparedness as an opening wedge to regain its exploitative license at home and abroad.[16] Further, many of these people were apprehensive that involvement could not fail to have a detrimental effect on civil liberties—that rather than serving to curtail Prussianism, war would actually bring Prussianism to American life.

Wilson's preentry handling of domestic and foreign policy bespoke a clear recognition of the need to deal sensitively with such potential opponents. He was particularly concerned about what he considered the misguided posture of the antimilitarists and antiinterventionists, since many of them were sympathetic

16. The theme of war threatening Progressive gains pervades antipreparedness literature, according to Charles Chatfield, *For Peace and Justice: Pacifism in America, 1914–1941* (Boston, 1971), p. 376. See "Around the Circle against Militarism," *Survey* 36 (April 22, 1916): 95; John Haynes Holmes, "War and the Social Movement," *Survey* 32 (September 26, 1914): 629–30; and Oswald G. Villard, "Shall We Arm for Peace?" *Survey* 35 (December 11, 1915): 299.

liberal supporters who shared many of his domestic views. His manipulation of these people was skillful, if not in the final analysis totally successful in eliminating the civil liberties issue from wartime concerns.

Pacifism had long been a facet of the Progressives' movement for a more rational and humane world order. Prior to the outbreak of European hostilities in 1914, the traditional pacifism of such respectable and conservative bodies as the American Peace Society, the Carnegie Endowment for International Peace, and the Church Peace Union had been accepted as constructive.[17] With the outbreak of the European war, these traditional pacifist groups moved to a wartime stance, promptly taking the position that Prussianism was the enemy of peace and until it was destroyed by military might, hopes for a truly peaceful world were remote, if not nonexistent. Jane Addams liked to characterize this view as "the pathetic belief in the regenerative results of war."[18] The result was, however, that between 1914 and 1917, the old peace societies were largely supplanted by a new and more liberal coalition opposed to American entry and composed now of social workers, publicists, activist peace crusaders, feminists, social-gospel clergymen and church leaders, with a scattering, here and there, of antiwar Socialists. This group included social workers such as Jane Addams, Lillian Wald, and Florence Kelley, editors such as Paul Kellogg of *The Survey* and Oswald Garrison Villard of the *New York Evening Post* and *The Nation,* activist pacifists Louis Lochner and Rosika Schwimmer, clergymen John Haynes Holmes and Rabbi Stephen Wise, and educators David Starr Jordan and Emily G. Balch. They initially attempted to induce Woodrow Wilson to join them in taking firm stands for neutarlity and early peace negotiations.[19] This the president carefully avoided doing, while seem-

17. Chatfield, *Peace and Justice,* pp. 8–11. Such bodies drew heavy sponsorship from the business community.

18. Jane Addams, *Peace and Bread in Time of War* (New York, 1945), p. 62.

19. Donald Johnson, *The Challenge to American Freedoms* (Lexington, Ky., 1963), pp. 5–6.

ing not to deplore such bodies' views. When the American Union Against Militarism, the emergent organization around which the various splinter groups ultimately coalesced, challenged Wilson vigorously on the preparedness issue, circularizing its views widely to civic groups, unions, granges, and key congressmen and senators, the president's response was to urge those people who differed with him to rent halls and take their case to the people. This the AUAM did in a well-attended mass meeting at Carnegie Hall in April 1916, and subsequently in similar meetings in Pittsburgh, Cincinnati, Chicago, Des Moines, Minneapolis, Kansas City, and Detroit. This tolerance, plus the president's apparent friendly support of the body in its 1916 efforts to aid in negotiating a peaceful settlement of trying Mexican problems,[20] led its members generally to support the President in his 1916 bid for re-election[21] despite Wilson's announced propreparedness posture.[22] Following Wilson's narrow victory some AUAM leaders even took the bold public position that pacifist sentiments had been the deciding factor in winning the election for the Democrats.[23] Even as late as February 3, 1917, when Wilson broke diplomatic relations with Germany, AUAM leaders, and leaders of the coordinate Women's Peace Party,[24] still cherished the hope that the president considered their posture of nonintervention a viable alternative to actual participation.

The president's April 2 call for a war declaration seemed a significant act of betrayal to the more doctrinaire pacifists. He had now placed the peace movement in a postion where to support militant pacifism and to oppose American policy would raise strong doubts regarding its loyalty and patriotism in the

20. Marchand, *American Peace Movement,* pp. 243–44.
21. Blanche Wiesen Cook, "Woodrow Wilson and the Anti-Militarists, 1914–1917" (Ph.D. dissertation, Johns Hopkins University, 1970), pp. 166–67.
22. Marchand, *American Peace Movement,* pp. 239–40.
23. Ibid., pp. 248–49.
24. Marie L. Degen, *The History of the Woman's Peace Party* (Baltimore, 1939).

public's mind. But by this time Wilson no longer needed the support of this group, and from here on he was able to ignore it, feeling relatively assured that if its spokesmen became too shrill, a war-mobilized and carefully propagandized patriotic citizenry would apply appropriate social control. With the declaration of war the peace coalition ruptured. A number of outstanding leaders of the various bodies resigned, and the ranks of the movement altered sharply. Some of those who accepted the war effort gave up peace work; others gravitated to the safer old societies. An organization like the AUAM, shaken temporarily by the sudden resignation of Rabbi Wise,[25] turned its attention to opposing conscription, to defending draft opponents and conscientious objectors, to fighting wartime censorship, and to working, through its Civil Liberties Bureau, for the protection of individual freedom under the Constitution in the face of wartime hysteria.

The president, however, had engineered some of this development by another line of prewar tactics which he had pursued. Wilson was anxious to have as large a segment of his liberal constituency as he could hold together support him and American intervention. Therefore, he took pains, when dealing with what he considered America's proper international posture, to tie that posture to an avowed commitment to ongoing liberal domestic reform. This was particularly true in the election of 1916. As the country moved toward that election, the president stepped up his commitment to domestic reform programs, and under his leadership a Democratic Congress enacted sweeping and significant progressive legislation, including workman's compensation, child labor, eight-hour day, and rural credit laws. By the eve of the election, Wilson had seen enacted into law virtually every important domestic plank in the Progressive party platform of 1912. The result was to draw a wide range

25. The ultimate Wise resignation seems to have been instrumental in shaping choices of other members of the body. See Carl H. Voss, *Rabbi and Minister* (Cleveland, 1964), pp. 142–44, and Johnson, *Challenge to American Freedoms,* pp. 8–9.

of formerly skeptical progressives to the president and his party, including such disparate figures as Walter Lippmann, Herbert Croly, Lincoln Steffens, Ida Tarbell, Ray Stannard Baker, John Dewey, Charles A. Beard, George Creel, and Thorstein Veblen. Groups ranging from the Railway Brotherhoods and the American Federation of Labor to the Non-Partisan League and a variety of independent newspapers and periodicals were equally impressed. By posing as a benign alternative to the bombast and military jingoism of Theodore Roosevelt and Charles Evans Hughes, whom many suspected were real interventionists, the president was able to fuse the peace cause with the ideal of progressive democracy. A mark of his success was that some half-million Socialists abandoned their party and voted for him.[26]

Wilson's ideology also figured in this development. Apparently anticipating that a variety of his supporters were anti-interventionists because they feared the domestic repercussions of war, he publicly stated his view that the nation's chosen mission was to enlighten mankind with the principles of its liberal heritage. "America has stood in the years past for that sort of political understanding among men which would let every man feel that his rights were the same as those of another and as good as those of another, and the mission of America in the world is to be the same," he told the Grain Dealer's Association in Baltimore in September 1916.[27] Speaking to a Salesmanship Congress in Detroit, he contended, ". . . let your thoughts and your imaginations run abroad, throughout the whole world, and with the inspiration and the thought that you are Americans and are meant to carry liberty and justice and the principles of humanity wherever you go. . . ."[28] America had the opportunity to use her moral and economic strength to establish a liberal order in the world, and Wilson insisted that the poten-

26. Arno J. Mayer, *Political Origins of the New Diplomacy, 1917–1918* (New Haven, 1959), pp. 346–48.

27. Baker and Dodd, *New Democracy,* 4:323; N. Gordon Levin, Jr., *Woodrow Wilson and World Politics* (New York, 1968), pp. 16–18.

28. Baker and Dodd, *New Democracy,* 4:243.

tial for peace and justice in the kind of international capitalist system which he envisioned would develop progressively once that world was liberated from imperialist irrationality. Surely a leader so committed to spreading American doctrines of liberty and justice abroad could hardly be expected to deal lightly with such doctrines in his domestic policy. The president carefully reiterated such rhetoric once American entry was assured and the time for mobilizing the nation behind the great crusade abroad arrived.

The president had taken great pains to relieve widely held suspicions that the administration was ready to repress civil liberties vigorously. His position had been so persuasive that when federal repression came, a wide range of Americans accepted it, embracing the preliminary rationalizations which Wilson afforded for its justification. Such citizens were apparently persuaded that a temporary suspension of the rights of certain individuals was a necessary wartime cost which posed no serious threat to the future of America's traditional values. This had the effect of leaving the civil liberties issue in the hands of a beleaguered and generally powerless minority which was unable to rally substantial numbers of Americans behind efforts to alleviate the massive wartime depredations on personal rights.

Why did Wilson, his cabinet, and the people who came to support him take the position they did on the civil liberties question? Why were so many Americans in the war years relatively unconcerned about official war-time repression, despite the damage it did to fundamental doctrines such as freedom of speech, freedom of the press, freedom of assembly, and basic due process of law? Examination of a variety of ingredients is necessary in searching for an answer to this dilemma.

On the eve of World War I, the concept or the practice of universal civil liberties received little support from tradition or case law. In a society increasingly controlled by men of property, it continued to be assumed that civil liberties came with the accumulation of property, and not before. By attaining a stake in society, one earned the right to assured civil liberties.

Having gained their rights, most Americans could not visualize themselves being subjected to the kinds of civil liberties deprivations that were the common lot of the propertyless and the more outspoken critics of the beneficent American way. There was no point in simply extending civil liberties for their own sake. In fact, extending them to the wrong people, who might well abuse them, might injure society and damage those rights themselves.

This position, however, did not preclude the view that there should be a national policy on the subject. In fact, it contributed to its development. Such a policy, it was widely felt, should draw more clear-cut lines regarding permissible degrees of civil liberties utilization. Progressivism had, after all, evolved a variety of other national programs articulating limits to particular kinds of human behavior, on subjects as diverse as prostitution, prohibition, censorship, the employment of child labor, and exploitative labor contracts. In these areas national policy had frequently constituted a step toward imposing uniform national standards in the face of disparate state and local practices or, in some instances, in the face of the inability of the states to deal with broad-scale social problems. Civil liberties situations, however, had generally been left to the discretion of local authorities. This had resulted in official and, in some cases, unofficial coercion—vigilantism being a prominent form—with overtones which troubled many progressive moral leaders. Why, then, could not a national policy be developed which drew clear and more scientific lines around excessive individualism in the general national interest of setting forth the permissible limits of dissent? Surely, better prescriptive guidelines could be afforded which would accommodate acceptably unthreatening dissidents and at the same time insure the success and security of the system in the face of external threats. Such a view was central to the thinking of a Progressive like George Creel, a professed anti-individualist, who clearly believed that the federal government would have to take positive action to gain the allegiance of immigrants, hyphenates, and other allegedly gullible and poorly informed individuals. To leave such people to their own devices and patriotism might be ill-advised. Pull them behind the government by persuading them to see the desirability of patriotic conformity, at the same time setting forth a clear national policy on civil liberties, and both they and the government would benefit.

Wilson made it clear that he expected his supporters to embrace such a view as a logical adjunct to his own liberal policies. His goal was the achievement of liberal democracy throughout the world, and his domestic record indicated a sincere commitment to a liberal society at home. A temporary sacrifice of certain rights by those who did not share that vision, and who might indeed impede its achievement, was hardly too much to ask.

Wilson's position implied that the war would be good for civil liberties.[29] If America could extend liberal antiimperialistic progressivism to Europe by destroying the enemies of liberty and justice—Prussianism, autocracy, monarchy—it could solve other people's problems by making their nations more democratic and guaranteeing their human rights. War could be a liberating experience, while at the same time insuring that the liberties of Americans would be safer, in a world made "safe for democracy." Operating on these assumptions—liberty through submission to liberal authority—many people could accept the logic of the temporary suspension of the civil liberties of those whose actions or potential behavior threatened the success of such a noble venture.

Some citizens, however, were distressed by the vehemence of administration officials, from the president down, in expressing their hostility to those who disagreed with their vision and its implementation. As William Allen White wrote a few years later: "I was supporting Wilson and the war, but I came to dislike this man—for his cold, mean, selfish policy, toward those whom he liked to segregate and hate as his enemies."[30]

29. Baker, *Life and Letters,* 7:81.
30. William Allen White, *The Autobiography of William Allen White* (New York, 1946), p. 534.

Another aspect of coercive wartime control added to its palatability. Not only were the new restraints imposed by the people's elected representatives, following the republican principle of majority rule, but by representatives who were steeped in the same kind of progressive paternalism, efficiency, and uplift with which earlier limits had been set on other forms of potentially destructive behavior. These lines were being drawn regarding excessively disruptive activities in an allegedly precise, scientific, and rational way. Ordered liberty meant finding the proper balance between the rights of the individual and the rights of the broader society, so that the individual's use of his liberty did not threaten that society. It was a process which experts could carry out in a more clearly prescribed fashion and, under wartime exigency, had an obligation to refine carefully and responsibly. Implicit in such a position was the view that once public servants had performed that service, subsequent governmental actions to implement the policy should essentially not be debatable, particularly under national emergency conditions. *The New York Times,* for example, in a July 4, 1917, editorial on the National Civil Liberties Bureau,[31] stated explicitly that the civil liberties issue before the country was the line between liberty and license. But to the *Times* it was not an issue at all. In a democratic society the people's leaders will draw that line. Any self-appointed group of radicals who attempt to draw it in the wrong place—that is, too far toward the liberty side for the wrong people—were obviously suspect. The *Times* was not even prepared to speculate how such a distinction between liberty and license might be applied. This was apparently to be done by the leaders of the country, by the right people, by the patriots in power. The question of how much or how little civil liberty should be permitted was to be resolved in upper echelons of government, with popular input considered to be inappropriate in wartime.

The irony of this position was that, based upon a record of past trial and error in the evolution of applicable legal norms

31. *The New York Times,* July 4, 1917, p. 8.

and precedents, it was not and could not be a detached scientific process. The fact was, as we have noted, that there were no operational norms or precedents to turn to, either in statute law or in case law, concerning the permissible limits of free speech, free press, freedom to assemble, the constitutionality of conscription, the legal status of conscientious objectors and other draft opponents, and the precise constitutional rights of foreign-born Americans. Contemporary attitudes toward the permissible limits of extending civil liberties to dissident groups had simply been translated into formal doctrine in federal and state statutes, executive orders, official policies of executive agencies, or in the case law which emerged when the courts were finally called on to interpret the meaning and legitimacy of such action.

The difficulty of suddenly converting such attitudes into formal and enforcible legal doctrine were several. The converters had to overcome the abstract belief of many Americans that the country's ideals committed it to freedom of speech, press, assembly, fair trial, and individualism. There was a point beyond which the government's ability to engage in repressive activities could be carried, depending to a large degree upon whether the public felt that such repression was essential to controlling dangerous groups and individuals, or whether its application might have adverse effects on people who hardly needed or deserved such regimentation.

Another factor involved the appropriate implementation of such policies. The absence, at the outset, of a body of case law setting forth clear-cut guidelines for the implementation of a federal espionage act tended to leave great discretion to federal and state enforcing officials. Some were anxious to utilize this discretion vigorously, in conformity with their own concepts of patriotism. Others were hesitant to utilize it, for fear of being charged with heavyhanded and excessive zeal in repressing basic rights. Such discretionary power was a double-edged sword. Although it frequently circumscribed the actions of some dissidents, it could work to the advantage of others. In the absence of a precise body of law, there was always the danger that if the line was drawn so broadly as to affect a person who was not viewed as a threat to the public security, there might be a sharply negative public reaction. Censuring a congressman who criticized the conduct of the war, for example, or charging an excessively vociferous editor with sedition was not an action taken without considerable trepidation.

However, more often than not the lack of precedent favored the repressionists. Given the progressive mores of the period and its *Gemeinschaft* nature, the actions of federal enforcement officials which went beyond the kind of social control which formal or informal local authorities could successfully exercise were viewed as acceptable and even desirable. The argument was frequently made that reasonable repression would eliminate vigilantism and mob action.[32] However, even here there were problems. While fair and equitable enforcement might be comfortably accepted, the mere fact that broad discretion lay in the hands of enforcing parties caused apprehension as to who might next be placed under criminal sanctions. Such uncertainty contributed to suspicions that the alleged detachment which supposedly marked civil liberties policy was more myth than reality.

Despite attempts by Wilson and other governmental leaders to make civil liberties a nondebatable issue, there were aspects of the situation which impeded such a move. The act of criminalizing a variety of activities previously thought to be beyond the limits of official monitoring put state and national governments into the position of redefining their official relationship to the citizenry. Government took it upon itself to regulate particular forms of dissenting activity, including vigorous verbal and written criticism, public protest, and assembling to plan resistance to formal policy or to form countervailing power groups to alter formal policy. From the outset, certain vocal leaders perceived and deplored the implications of this shift. Prior to war declaration, congressional opponents of various proposals to criminalize various forms of expression voiced

32. Paul L. Murphy, *The Meaning of Freedom of Speech* (Westport, Conn., 1972), pp. 28, 294.

fears about where such a policy might ultimately lead. And as the war advanced, a small but vocal element of noncongressional civil libertarians reiterated the same misgivings. Such criminalization of previously legitimate behavior had not been needed in prior American history. Why was it so essential now? Was it really valid, given the Bill of Rights of both the federal and the state constitutions? These citizens called for public debate regarding the permissible role of the government in the management of people's behavior. With the projection of the government into this role, and this kind of a public-policy function, there was special reason for discussion of the legitimacy of such action. A new process had emerged. Civil liberties had been made an issue by those who had launched this process. It was time to discuss whether this was indeed a suitable role for federal and state governments, or whether it might be more appropriately left to the private sector, where traditional forms of social control could be applied without either the threat of formal criminal penalties or formal government sanctions. Programs associated in the minds of many Americans with the kind of Old World tyranny which they were being called upon to enter a war to destroy dismayed many concerned observers.

Since the earliest days of the nation, government—and particularly central government—had been viewed with suspicion as an enemy of individual rights.[33] While it had increasingly regulated certain other social relationship, it had generally avoided monitoring the use of such rights. Now it was suddenly reversing itself. A deliberately planned program of federal suppression was underway and was about to be expanded, in the form of opinion molding, Americanization, homogenization, the coercing of patriotic support, and the rooting out of disloyalty. Americans were being asked to accept it in the name of the

33. James Madison spoke of the lessons of the Alien and Sedition Act crisis as showing that "if we advert to the nature of Republican Government, we shall find that the censorial power is in the people over the Government, and not in the Government over the people." See James M. Smith, *Freedom's Fetters* (Ithaca, N.Y., 1956), p. i.

creation of a new liberal democratic order at home and abroad. The thrust of these policies was also new. Earlier Americans had been prepared to condone governmental curtailment of the evil behavior of evil men. This action did not produce massive public controversy. But they had also been prepared to tolerate offbeat opinion, as long as there was no serious danger that it would lead people to take actions threatening to the majority. Now the government was moving to repress the individualism and the diversity of opinion of a substantial number of respectable citizens who had no apparent intent to engage in actions damaging to society or to induce others to do likewise. Such a departure could not fail to raise serious questions regarding the propriety, necessity, and utility of such a role.

Thus, civil liberties as a public policy issue emerged as an integral if muted aspect of World War I. The war-time behavior of the governmental and private power bodies, and the condemnation of such behavior by individuals and organizations hostile to and frightened by it, was unique in the American experience. It was furthermore, of considerable concern to those who saw in this new government role the beginning of a type of destructive activity which might extend into postwar America. Progressive paternalism, condonable when it eradicated social evils, was now being used to coerce what many considered to be legitimate activities. Their apprehensions, and the government's need to assuage and silence those apprehensions, grew as the nation was quickly put upon a wartime footing in the weeks and months following April 2, 1917.

4

The Beginnings of the Surveillance State and the Reactions Which Resulted

THE PATTERN OF REPRESSION which unfolded during the nineteen months between America's entry into the European war and the armistice was significant for the history of civil liberties in the United States. With the war declaration the Wilson administration, aided by a number of sympathetic congressmen and senators, pushed through a body of emergency wartime laws calculated to manage domestic opposition to the war in order to prevent that opposition from impeding wartime objectives. When apprehension regarding those laws was expressed in the Congress and throughout the country, administration leaders and defenders quickly turned to patriotic appeals and arguments of constructive intent to rationalize their position. A war had to be won, and the temporary inconvenience of asking people to put aside their criticism so that end could be achieved was certainly not too much of a sacrifice to expect. Only people with highly dubious motives could object to such a reasonable request. Debate on controversial domestic issues might compromise national unity and endanger military victory, and the advocacy of political and social change might aid the enemy. Many argued that if the intention of the speaker or writer was to foment action damaging to the government's cause in war, that speech might reasonably be considered to have criminal intent and be punished.

The most virulent aspect of the pattern of suppression ultimately lay in the actions of those who implemented this legislation and those who set out to carry its spirit into social inter-
relationships at the local level. Unwarranted excesses occurred
in both areas. Federal and state enforcement officials quickly
assumed the role of policymakers in explicit circumstances and
frequently went far beyond the intentions of the framers of the
legislation in their zeal for achieving unquestioning patriotic
compliance with wartime policy. Once the spirit of intolerance
was unleashed, and partially legitimized, containing it was a
difficult, if not impossible, task. National voluntary organizations, anxious to make their own contribution to the war effort,
joined the fray. Local patriots turned to direct action in harrassing unpopular local groups and particularly controversial
local figures. Any spirit of restraint and care embodied in the
program of national suppressive legislation, any careful distinctions between legitimate and illegitimate behavior, quickly
disappeared as numerous local citizens perverted such legislation into an excuse for working off their hostilities against those
whose views, values, positions, purposes, and race or ethnicity
they did not like.

This kind of action was frequently offensive and generally
alarming to members of the Wilson administration. It was not
based on any selfless commitment to successful wartime conduct
but sprang from a spirit of selfish animosity, opportunistically
utilizing the circumstances of a national emergency as a screen
for working off personal hostility toward groups and individuals.
Such a development was particularly distressing, since it lent
support to partisan critics who were charging that the administration's policy of suppressing civil liberties was producing an
unwarranted and massive destruction of those liberties. The Wilson administration also feared that the civil liberties issue could
be manipulated to disrupt the war effort and to deprive the
government of essential support. Radical elements insisted that
if civil liberties deprivations continued and intensified, they
would be compelled to step up their critique of capitalist institutions. Liberals, upon whom Wilson had called for support

in the 1916 election, increasingly made the price of such future support a good-will step toward curtailing further suppression of liberal groups and individuals. The task was to stymie the radicals' threat without losing all support from the liberals. Administration leaders ultimately confronted the potential dangers by charging that those who would manipulate the civil liberties issue for selfish purposes during a wartime crisis were clearly suspect, and in the case of left-wing critics, were themselves just subjects of suppression. Hence, administration leaders found themselves forced to strike various, and at times seemingly ambivalent, postures. On the one hand, they found themselves deploring excessively heavy-handed federal and state implementation, as well as vigilante-type suppression at the local level, as unwarranted excesses. On the other, they found themselves criticizing those Americans who deplored the same actions too aggressively. Since such deprecation was for suspect and destructive purposes, they argued, it was itself out of line and suspect.

Specific aspects of this process are illuminating. When President Wilson asked Congress to recognize a state of war between the United States and Germany, he included the activities of German agents in the United States in his indictment of that nation. "From the outset of the present war," the president contended, "[Germany] has filled our unsuspecting communities and even our offices of government with spies and set criminal intrigues everywhere afoot against our national unity of counsel, our peace within and without, our industries and our commerce." [1] Wilson indicated that he would like to think of German-born Americans as loyal, but he nonetheless warned them that "if there should be disloyalty, it will be dealt with with a firm hand of stern repression; but if it lifts its head at all, it will lift it only here and there without countenance except from a lawless and malignant few." [2] At the conclusion of the message, Representative Edwin Y. Webb and Senator Charles A. Culber-

1. *Congressional Record* LV (65th Cong. Spec. Sess., April 2, 1917): 104.
   2. Ibid.

son introduced bills to provide the president with the instruments of repression which he had requested. Nine weeks later, after lengthy and frequently impassioned debate and considerable revision, the Espionage Act of June 15, 1917, was passed— the basic measure for extending the criminal jurisdiction of the federal government over speech, press, and general dissent during the war period.[3]

Prior to June 15, the administration's program for the suppression of civil liberties had taken more piecemeal form. On April 6, 1917, Wilson had issued a proclamation establishing regulations for the conduct and control of enemy aliens, restricting their movements, forbidding them to publish any attack upon the government, the armed forces, or the policies of the United States, or to engage in any act rendering aid to the enemies of the United States. The proclamation was issued as implementation of the Alien Enemies Act of 1798. It authorized federal officials to make summary arrests if, in their opinion, they were warranted for national security reasons.[4] The following day Wilson imposed a strict loyalty-security program, issuing a secret executive order authorizing heads of federal departments to remove any employee deemed a loyalty risk, "by reason of his conduct, sympathies, or utterances, or because of other reasons growing out of the war." [5] One week later the president, under his emergency powers, created the Committee on Public Information and assigned funds for its operation from his emergency reserve. In the first wave of repressive actions, its censorship function was a particular concern. Sup-

3. 40 *Stat.* 217 (1917).
4. *Report of the Attorney General, 1917* (Washington, 1918), pp. 57–59. On the basis of the proclamation and an enforcing executive order, the Justice Department registered enemy aliens, arresting 6,300, of whom 2,300 were interned by the military as dangerous to the national security. *Report of the Attorney General, 1918* (Washington, 1919), p. 26.
5. Text is in Paul P. Van Riper, *History of the United States Civil Service* (Evanston, Ill., 1958), p. 266. Under the order 135 loyalty investigations were conducted in 1917, and 2,537 more in 1918. In the latter year, 660 applicants were debarred from federal employment for questionable loyalty. Harold M. Hyman, *To Try Men's Souls* (Berkeley, 1959), pp. 268–69.

porters of the creation of the agency, particularly Secretary of War Newton D. Baker, Secretary of the Navy Josephus Daniels, and Secretary of State Robert Lansing,[6] argued, in pushing for the measure, that "censorship and publicity can be joined in honesty, and with profit." [7] Before the passage of the Espionage Act, the agency's head, Progressive journalist George Creel, organized a program for the voluntary self-censorship of the press, which the press somewhat gingerly and tentatively accepted. With the passage of the Espionage Act, the censorship functions of the CPI became far less significant.[8]

Wilson, nonetheless, was chronically concerned about censorship. In the Mexican troubles of 1916, informal censorship had been put into effect, based on a gentlemen's agreement with the press on what to publish with respect to naval and military movements. The arrangement appeared to work with a minimum of friction and bad faith.[9] Nevertheless, Wilson distrusted the fourth estate and feared the possibility of irresponsible reporting. He felt that legislation carrying stiff legal penalties was in order to keep the profession in line during the European war. His executive order of April 28, 1917, involving cable and land telegraph lines broadened the censorship authority of the Navy Department and gave the War Department authority to censor messages sent out of the country. Since this included use of all essential cables, it covered virtually all American news sent to foreign newspapers.[10] All such steps plugged the gap until Congress could be persuaded to pass a broad espionage act affording legislative sanctions for the type of legal strictures that the White House desired.

A number of congressmen and senators viewed this action

6. Lansing, while temporarily acquiescing, actually wanted far stricter censorship, to the point of almost total suppression. Josephus Daniels, *The Wilson Era* (Chapel Hill, N.C., 1946), p. 222.

7. Ray Stannard Baker, *Woodrow Wilson: Life and Letters* (New York, 1939), 7:20.

8. There is extensive information on the Censorship Board's role in the Committee on Public Information 1, series, *National Archives*. Washington, D.C.

9. James R. Mock, *Censorship, 1917* (Princeton, 1941), pp. 21, 40.

10. Ibid., pp. 79, 81, 93.

with considerable apprehension. When, on February 8, 1917, the attorney general recommended legislation concerning "publication of information which might be useful to an enemy of the United States," congressional concern intensified.[11] But there were always overzealous patriots out of tune both with congressional moderates and the executive. After the declaration of war, Senator George E. Chamberlain of Oregon introduced a bill classifying as a "spy" every person who published anything "endangering the success of the military forces" and would have gone so far as to make such a person subject to the death sentence by court martial.[12] Wilson quickly made it clear that he would not endorse such a measure.

The Espionage Act, which was introduced on April 2, was an amalgamation of seventeen bills prepared in the attorney general's office, and was cast as a measure intended to outlaw spies and subversive activities by foreign enemies. Congressmen quickly realized that several of its provisions could easily be used to harrass opponents of the war. On April 18, 1917, Senator Henry Cabot Lodge of Massachusetts complained that Chapter II, Section 2, of the measure was much too restrictive. "To attempt to deny to the press all legitimate criticism either of Congress or the Executive is going very dangerously too far," Lodge argued.[13] And Senator William E. Borah of Idaho quickly agreed, pointing out the under the American theory of freedom of the press, the Blackstone concept of "no prior restraint" was the rule. Only subsequent punishment for such actions as libel could be warranted under the First Amendment's freedom of the press guarantee.[14]

Borah's lengthy profession of concern, however, contained more subtle overtones. He was aware that in the absence of any

11. Thomas F. Carroll, "Freedom of Speech and of the Press in Wartime: The Espionage Act," *Michigan Law Review* 17 (June 1919): 622.

12. Ernest S. Bates, *This Land of Liberty* (New York, 1930), p. 97.

13. *Congressional Record* LV (65th Cong. 1st Sess., April 18, 1917): 779.

14. Ibid., 779–80.

substantial body of case law, the principles of freedom of speech and of the press were not sharply defined. As such, they were vulnerable to those who would call for their modification in a national crisis. Borah also realized that the enactment of legislation was going to set new and formal limits on permissible expression and create a precedent for justifiable repression which could well carry into the postwar period. Thus, he saw the issue in the light of its potentially dangerous and possibly permanent effect on large segments of American society. He felt that these Americans should be aware of the implications of this act and should participate in the decisionmaking process. Conversely, most of the senators who opposed him saw the issue as simply one of temporary curtailment of certain freedoms justified by the exigencies of war.

From late April until early June, various provisions of the espionage measure were debated. Frequent misgivings were voiced by the senators regarding the president's being given broad censorship discretion. After the extension of certain censorship functions to the Committee on Public Information, even stronger concern was expressed. Senator Oscar Underwood of Alabama stated:

I thoroughly believe the Congress of the United States owes it to the Nation to sustain the President in his effort to conduct the war in every respect that it is possible to do so, but I do not believe the time has come when it is necessary for the Congress to betray the fundamental principles of the government in order to carry on the war at this time. . . . Is . . . a newspaper to be condemned for the news it prints? [15]

Underwood was calling for the development of sharper and more precise criteria to distinguish between permissible publication regarding the war generally and dangerous revelations about matters of military security.

But if members of Congress were concerned about the wisdom of restricting the dissemination of public information, lead-

15. *Congressional Record* LV (65th Cong. 1st Sess., May 11, 1917): 2114.

ers of the press were genuinely distraught. Newspapers throughout the country objected to the section of the bill giving the president the right to censor the press.[16] On April 26, the American Newspaper Publishers petitioned Congress to delete the applicable section.[17] The move drew Senate support, with Hiram Johnson of California, Borah of Idaho, and Frank Brandegee of Connecticut speaking strongly against the measure.[18] Such action alarmed the president: On May 23, in a letter to Congressman Webb, which was printed in *The New York Times,* Wilson stated that the administration must have authority to censor the press, since this was "absolutely necessary to the public safety." [19] The president's firm stand—particularly his contention that he had to have authority to deal with persons who could not be trusted to show patriotic reticence in publishing war news—not only further inflamed the press but angered House Republicans, who felt that was a gratuitous slap at them. When Attorney General Gregory circulated to House conferees a Department of Justice memorandum revealing the extent of enemy influence in journalistic quarters, press leaders cried foul, arguing that their unwavering support of the administration as the country moved into war hardly warranted their being bracketed with foreign-language publications or Socialist and other radical journals now agitating for an immediate end to hostilities.[20] More generally, they feared, as Borah had earlier, that the precedent which was here being urged by the White House was dangerous, not only immediately but in the long run. The issue was not simply one of wartime restraint, but the broader one of whether a basic civil liberty such as press freedom could be made expendable at the discretion either of members of Congress or the executive

16. *Literary Digest,* May 5, 1917, p. 1318; Mock, *Censorship,* pp. 45–49; Carroll, "Freedom of Speech," pp. 624–25.

17. *Congressional Record* LV (65th Cong. 1st Sess., April 26, 1917): 1167.

18. Ibid, 777–87.

19. *The New York Times,* May 23, 1917, p. 1.

20. Seward W. Livermore, *Politics Is Adjourned* (Middletown, Conn., 1966), p. 36.

branch. Such arguments, supported by hostile Republicans, led to the defeat of the proposed censorship provisions on May 31 in the House, by a vote of 184 to 144. The Senate, apparently acquiescing in the result, did not bring the measure to a vote. This congressional action had the effect of silencing further press criticism of the measure.[21]

Wilson was not to be deterred so easily. He made no secret of his feeling that the final Espionage Act should be a measure which could be used against the domestic enemies of the war. His Flag Day address of June 14 clearly revealed this posture. While assailing the "masters of Germany" for using Socialists, pacifists, the leaders of labor, and other liberals as stalking horses, he went on to suggest that Americans so duped were not engaging in discussion when they articulated their positions, but in sedition. He implied that all dissent was disloyalty. It was not possible that the disenter could be mistaken or misinformed, could oppose war on principles in good faith, or could honestly disagree with the president. So, Wilson warned, "Woe be to the man or group of men who seeks to stand in our way in this day of high resolution when every principle we hold dearest is to be vindicated and made secure for the salvation of the nation."[22]

The Espionage Act of 1917 was not, on its face, an overt assault upon First Amendment freedoms. Two of its provisions, however, were so worded that they could be used by federal officials to punish not only general assaults upon the government and its war policies but even "individual casual or impulsive disloyal utterance."[23] Section 3 of Title I established three new offenses punishing:

21. A typical statement prior to this time was a *New York Times* editorial of May 4, 1917, which exhorted, "Let the attempt to suppress freedom of speech, in whatever guise it appears, be defeated unanimously. While we are warring to make democracy safe in the world, let us keep it safe in the United States." Baker, *Life and Letters*, 7:51.

22. Ray Stannard Baker and William E. Dodd, *The New Democracy: Public Papers of Woodrow Wilson* (New York, 1926), 5:66–67.

23. Attorney General Gregory, however, was unhappy with it, since he felt that it failed to do just this. Zechariah Chafee, Jr., *Free Speech in the United States* (Cambridge, Mass., 1941), pp. 39–40.

(1) Whoever, when the United States is at war, shall willfully make or convey false reports or false statements with intent to interfere with the operation or success of the military or naval forces of the United States or to promote the success of its enemies; (2) and whoever, when the United States is at war, shall willfully cause or attempt to cause insubordination, disloyalty, mutiny, or refusal of duty, in the military or naval forces of the United States; (3) or shall willfully obstruct the recruiting or enlistment service of the United States, to the injury of the service or of the United States.

Punishment constituted a $10,000 fine, imprisonment for up to twenty years, or both.[24] It was under this section, and later amendments to it, that the Department of Justice prosecuted more than two thousand alleged violations of the measure, securing well over a thousand convictions of persons ranging from leaders of the radical IWW, to one senatorial nominee (J. A. Peterson, Republican of Minnesota), and to Eugene V. Debs, a national Socialist party leader and the party's frequent candidate for the presidency.

Under Title XII of the Espionage Act, the postmaster general was given the authority to ban from the mails any matter "advocating or urging treason, insurrection, or forcible resistance to any law of the United States." Carrying a maximum penalty of five years in prison or a $5,000 fine, the measure gave virtual dictatorial control to post officials over the effective circulation of "the subsidiary press" of the nation.[25] Enforcement turned out to be rigorous, frequently capricious, and subjectively punitive.

As the war progressed, further refinements were added by statute and executive order. On October 6, 1917, Congress enacted a Trading-with-the-Enemy Act.[26] Through it the president gained the power to control and censor international communications, but more significantly the postmaster general re-

---

24. *Stat.* 217 (1917).
25. The term referred to small, often foreign-language, journals or irregularly issued pamphlet type material.
26. Harry N. Scheiber, *The Wilson Administration and Civil Liberties* (Ithaca, N.Y., 1960), p. 21.

ceived almost absolute censorship powers over the American foreign-language press. Foreign-language newspapers were required to submit for the Post Office Department's approval literal translations of all news and editorial articles which contained material on the government, the policies of the belligerent powers, or the conduct of the war. If the president determined that a particular newspaper was trustworthy, he might issue a permit which would allow publication without the filing of such translation. Wilson largely turned this discretion over again to Postmaster General Burleson. Burleson used it to insure that German-language newspapers, especially, were forced into a position of publishing virtually nothing except uncritical praise of the government's position. The measure also authorized the president to "censor . . . communications by mail, cable, radio, or other means of transmission passing between the United States and any foreign country." A few days after its enactment, Wilson created a board of censorship—again by executive order—to handle such matters.[27] The board, although composed of representatives of the War and Navy Departments, the Post Office Department, the War Trade Board, and the chairman of the Committee on Public Information, quickly fell under the authority of Burleson, who turned it into an agency for examining private letters of many antiinterventionist progressives. It was also used to gather information regarding radical groups which was subsequently used in preparing the government's case against them.

The last two major enactments to take place during the war, the Sedition and Alien Acts, capped the process of creating an airtight national repression network. The Sedition Act of May 16, 1918,[28] made explicit much of what had simply been implicit in the earlier Espionage Act, to which it was a formal amendment. Advocates of the measure made a number of appeals for its passage. The war period had seen an alarming outbreak of mob violence as local citizens worked off allegedly patriotic

27. Mock, *Censorship,* p. 53.
28. 40 *Stat.* 553 (1918).

hostilities on German-Americans, opponents of the draft, critics of the war, and radicals generally. Many people alarmed by such vigilantism argued that the weakness of existing disloyalty legislation forced citizens to take the law into their own hands. If firmer federal policies existed, such distasteful forms of repression might be averted. Attorney General Gregory, although harboring mixed feelings about enforcement of the Espionage Act, did feel strongly that the measure itself was defective, contending that it was useful only against conspiracies, leaving the government powerless to act against disloyal individuals.[29] He also maintained that Congress should make attempts to obstruct the recruiting service and to interfere with the sale of war bonds explicitly punishable.

However, there were still some distressed voices, especially in the Senate. Charles Thomas of Colorado, Thomas Gore of Oklahoma, Henry Cabot Lodge of Massachusetts, and particularly Joseph France of Maryland were alarmed by the callousness with which the measure virtually terminated freedom of expression. France, in an attempt to salvage the principle that legitimate criticism was still possible, introduced an amendment to the effect that "nothing in this act shall be construed as limiting the liberty or impairing the right of any individual to publish or speak what is true, with good motives, and for justifiable ends."[30] He was subsequently strongly supported by Hiram Johnson of California. Johnson was appalled by the measure which categorically rejected, by legislature enactment, freedom of expression for the first time in American history. He believed that France's amendment drew distinctions that were essential if the legislation was to be in conformity with the American tradition of free speech.[31] Debate over this amend-

29. 4 *American Bar Association Journal*, 306.
30. *Congressional Record* LVI (65th Cong. 2nd Sess., April 9, 1918): 4826.
31. *Congressional Record* LVI (65th Cong. 2nd Sess., April 24, 1918): 5542.

ment was sharp. Attorney General Gregory sent a message to Congress arguing that "some of the most dangerous types of propaganda were either made from good motives, or else their traitorous motives were not provable" and contending that such an amendment would destroy the value of the act as a weapon against propaganda.[32] But the vehement supporters of the act were not content to stop there. Senator Lee Overman of North Carolina argued loudly on the Senate floor that "every Senator who votes against this conference report can have the satisfaction of knowing that he has voted for an amendment that will throw a cloak of protection around every spy in this country and every traitor and every Bolshevik and every I.W.W. that is denied to a loyal American citizen." [33] The amendment was voted down, but not before Senator France, one of the courageous opponents of the postwar Red Scare, asserted that the Western world had seen "no such repressive a criminal statute since the dark ages." [34]

In drafting the Sedition Act amendment, the Senate Judiciary Committee defined eight new offenses, closely following Gregory's recommendations. These included:

uttering, printing, writing, or publishing any disloyal, profane, scurrilous, or abusive language intended to cause contempt, scorn, contumely or disrepute as regards the form of government of the United States, or the Constitution, or the flag, or the uniform of the Army or Navy, or any language intended to incite resistance to the United States or to promote the cause of its enemies; urging any curtailment of production of any thing necessary to the prosecution of the war with intent to hinder its prosecution; advocating, teaching, defending, or suggesting the doing of any of these acts; and words or acts supporting or favoring the cause of any country at war with the United States, or opposing the cause of the United States therein.

32. Committee on Public Information, *Official Bulletin,* April 16, 1918.

33. *Congressional Record* LVI (65th Cong. 2nd Sess., May 4, 1918): 6050.

34. Ibid., 6050–51.

The measure's criminal penalties included $10,000 fine, or not more than twenty years' imprisonment, or both.[35]

The measure enlarged the already well-established censorship functions of the postmaster general. Attorney General Gregory was not enthusistic about this facet of the bill, fearing that it left too much discretion, to "inhibit the right of free public discussion" [36] in the hands of an administrative officer whose previous behavior in using censorship power had shown little, if any, discretion or discernment. The measure passed the House and Senate with strong Democratic support, and Wilson signed it into law. Republican critics remained largely silent or did not vote. They did, however, appreciate the potentially partisan overtones of the situation. Theodore Roosevelt had carried on a running battle with both George Creel, head of the Committee on Public Information, and Burleson regarding the permissible limits of censorship. Roosevelt had called for closing down the Hearst newspapers, and in response Burleson had charged that he had received more complaints from the public alleging that Mr. Roosevelt's articles were in violation of the Espionage Act than he had had against the Hearst press.[37] Roosevelt, most of whose articles had been on the values of free speech in a democracy, had condemned aspects of the proposed Sedition Act from its inception. After its enactment he personalized his opposition, arguing that despite the measure, public expression should be used to criticize the president, particularly when the president was using his authority to curtail its legitimate use and doing so in such a way as to suggest

35. John Lord O'Brian contended at the time that the law was so broad and vague in its language that it "covered in all degrees of conduct and speech, serious and trifling alike, and in the popular mind, gave the dignity of treason to what were often neighborhood quarrels or barroom brawls." "Civil Liberty in War Time" (65th Cong. 3d Sess.), Senate Doc. 434 (Washington, D.C., 1919): 18.

36. Thomas W. Gregory to Woodrow Wilson, May 14, 1918 (Wilson Papers, LC).

37. Baker, *Life and Letters*, 8:150.

that his position should be above criticism.[38] "Our governmental officers, from the President down," Roosevelt wrote to Senator Miles Poindexter, "are of right the servants of the people. This is the fundamenal difference between an autocracy and a democracy." And Roosevelt, who loathed Wilson, went on, "The higher the public servant and the more important his task, the more necessary it is that we tell the full truth about him." Other Republicans came to express the same view, especially as the president sought, in the 1918 congressional election campaigns, to suggest that partisan criticism of how the war was being conducted should be curtailed so that it would not unpatriotically hamper the war effort.[39]

The Alien Act was enacted less than a month before the armistice. It augmented an earlier body of law dating from 1903 and extended in February of 1917 that was aimed specifically at anarchists seeking to enter the country. Passed with the intent of stifling anarchist views and propaganda, the measure of October 16, 1918, empowered the government to deport, upon the warrant of the Secretary of Labor, "any alien who, at any time after entering the United States, is found to have been at the time of entry, or to have become thereafter" a member of any anarchist organization.[40] The measure operated on the principle of guilt by association and the assumption that anarchist expression of any kind was a menace, not only to the war effort but to the nation at large, and should be criminalized so as to be quickly eradicated.

Enforcement of these measures will be discussed shortly. Suffice it to say that their effect was not only to put the federal government into the business of suppressing civil liberties formally and officially but to create a climate which encouraged other state, local, and informal agencies to join in the process.

38. Elting E. Morison, *The Letters of Theodore Roosevelt* (Cambridge, Mass., 1954), 8:1320.
39. Livermore, *Politics Is Adjourned*, pp. 220 ff.
40. 40 *Stat.* 1012 (1918).

As the war progressed, unquestioned acquiescence to the principles advocated by these laws was stressed so forcefully and effectively that congressmen and senators who had openly expressed misgivings about censorship and the general overtones of the Espionage Act now either desisted from such criticism or carefully avoided putting themselves on public record by voting against them when the measures came up for approval.

Participation of the states in the process of the suppression of civil liberties, while frequently growing out of different sources and slightly different motivations, took similar forms in their formal structure. State and local officials had traditionally been the agents who had held the lid on dissident behavior and expression [41] through the "creative" interpretation of a variety of laws and ordinances. Now, however, they moved in a more formal and rigorous way to criminalize a variety of allegedly disloyal actions. Aware of the value of public identification with patriotism and loyalty in a period of national hysteria, many legislatures and state officials rushed to take such action to project a public image of coping quickly and squarely with the menace of wartime disloyalty. The form of this legislation varied. Eleven states passed sedition statutes providing, in one way or another, for punishment of overt expression.[42] Four states—Idaho, Minnesota, Montana, and South Dakota—where hysteria about the radical IWW was particularly rampant,

41. For a discussion of this process, see John P. Roche, "American Liberty: An Examination of the 'Tradition' of Freedom," in Milton Konvitz, ed., *Aspects of Liberty* (Ithaca, N.Y., 1958), p. 138. See also Justice Douglas's dissent, in Adderly v. Florida, 385 U.S. 39 (1966), at 54–56.

42. Such sedition measures did not follow a single model as did the Criminal Syndicalism and Criminal Anarchy acts. Connecticut punished public advocacy of "any measure, doctrine, proposal or propaganda intended to injuriously affect the government;" New Jersey punished inciting to insurrection or sedition or attempts to do so and also any book encouraging hostility to the government of the United States or the state; and Rhode Island punished language intended to incite "a . . . disregard of the Constitution or laws." Zechariah Chafee, Jr., "Sedition," *Encyclopedia of the Social Sciences* (New York, 1935), 13:638.

passed Criminal Syndicalism laws.[43] In addition to these laws, which make it a crime to use language opposing various aspects of the war effect, a vast hodgepodge of local ordinances were passed to criminalize actions or speech calculated to interfere with the war effort. Such ordinances normally left considerable discretion to the district attorney or prosecuting attorney to bring action in cases which seemed to fall within the prohibitions of the law.

Formal statutory authorization for the anti-civil liberties actions of private or quasi-official bodies was more tenuous. A great many such groups emerged, ranging from the superpatriotic American Defense Society and National Security League to the spy-chasing American Protective League and the Committee for Immigrants in America, with its crash programs for coerced Americanization. There were numerous local organizations, including the Home Defense League, the Liberty League, the Knights of Liberty, the American Rights League, the Boy Spies of America, the Sedition Slammers, and the Terrible Threateners.[44] These groups, while anxious to project themselves as patriotic implementers of official national and local policy, frequently took the law into their own hands, thereby assuming the responsibility for distinguishing between permissible and proscribable expression. When citizens of a Nevada community, for example, led by the local sheriff, tarred and feathered an unpopular local figure, who was found guilty in an improvised trial of "lukewarmness toward the cause of the United States and their allies," the governor—while apprehensive that "some of the boys were pulling a little rough stuff"—condoned the action because "it all helped the cause." [45] Hun-

43. See Eldridge F. Dowell, *A History of Criminal Syndicalism Legislation in the United States* (Baltimore, 1939). See also Brandenburg *v.* Ohio, 395 U.S. 444 (1969).

44. H. C. Peterson and Gilbert C. Fite, *Opponents of War* (Madison, Wis., 1957), p. 18; Frederick C. Luebke, *Bonds of Loyalty* (DeKalb, Ill., 1974), pp. 215–18.

45. O. A. Hilton, "Public Opinion and Civil Liberties in Wartime, 1917–1919," *Southwestern Social Science Quarterly* 28 (December 1947): 208.

dreds of comparable examples could be mentioned. While such behavior was often immediately popular with militant local majorities, it disturbed national and state officials, especially when its virulence tended to raise broader questions regarding the total impact of wartime suppression of civil liberties. Creel, for example, anxious to project the government's role in mobilizing public opinion as positive and constructive, spoke out frequently against extralegal actions. Looking back some years later at the callous abuses perpetrated by groups such as the National Security League, he admitted that they constituted an extreme and unwarranted form of "savage intolerance." [46]

Contemporary condemnations had the effect of sending such bodies scurrying for the shelter of the Council of National Defense. That agency was created by an act of Congress on August 29, 1916, "to coordinate industries and resources for the national security and welfare" and manage the "creation of relations" for the concentration and utilization of the nation's resources in wartime. It became responsible, through its advisory commission, for planning preparedness in fields including transportation, munitions and manufacturing, labor, raw materials, supplies, engineering and education, and medicine and surgery. It thus served as the activating instrument for mobilization of civilian forces and leaders, ultimately claiming a nationwide network of about 184,000 state and local organizations and committees through which the policies, programs, and propaganda of the federal government flowed.[47] State councils of defense were created, with county and local councils below them, and were authorized (usually by state law) to unite people behind the war effort at the local level. While the national pattern of such councils was spotty—some, such as the powerful Minnesota Commission of Public Safety, virtually running the state

46. George Creel, *Rebel at Large* (New York, 1947), p. 196.
47. The council as established was wholly an organ of the administrative branch of the government, and its function was exclusively that of acting as an aid to the Executive in taking steps for the protection of the public interest. William F. Willoughby, *Government Organization in War Time and After* (New York, 1919), p. 12.

during the war, and others participating feebly, if at all—the picture which emerges is one which clearly included supervision of disloyalty and seditious utterances and generally strong action against excessively militant opponents of the war effort.[48] Typical of the situation in states with strong councils was South Dakota. Although the council there lacked specific legal authority, for example, to "deal with people who refused to subscribe to their quota of Liberty Bonds," its leaders nonetheless condoned the practice of "classifying such citizens as slackers," explaining to county councils that "there is no law upon our statute books governing such cases, but in these times there is a recognition of authority that has the right and power to inquire into the general conditions and reasons. . . ."[49] The county councils were advised to subpoena the delinquents and interrogate them about their ability to buy bonds. An ad hoc common law thus evolved which, since few had the temerity to challenge it, functioned to validate local suppression during the war period.[50]

The American Protective League was another special case. The league was a private, voluntary organization established in 1917 by a Chicago advertising executive, Albert M. Briggs, to aid the understaffed Bureau of Investigation (the forerunner of the Federal Bureau of Investigation—the FBI.) The head of the bureau from 1912 to 1919, A. Bruce Bielaski, convinced Attorney General Gregory that such a body as the league would be of assistance to him. Furthermore, Gregory authorized the organization, in its campaign to recruit voluntary members, to state on its letterhead: "Organized with the Approval, and Op-

48. See Frederick Lewis Allen, "The 48 Defenders," *Century* 95 (December 1917): 261–66; Leubke, *Bonds of Loyalty,* pp. 222–23.

49. Hilton, "Public Opinion and Civil Liberties," p. 202.

50. David B. Danbom of North Dakota State University has explored local aspects of coerced conformity in an unpublished paper, "The County Agents and the First World War," demonstrating the role of such agricultural experts as prime movers in wartime social mobilization and "battling Socialists, Wobblies, Non-Partisan Leaguers, and other local forces of the left."

erating under the Direction of the United States Department of Justice, Bureau of Investigation." By the middle of June 1917, the league had branches in almost 600 cities and towns and a membership of nearly 100,000. At its height the membership reached 250,000. Members paid $1.00 to get a badge which first said "Secret Service Division" and later (after the Treasury Department protested about possible confusion with *its* Secret Service), "Auxiliary to the U.S. Department of Justice." [51] From its Washington, D.C., headquarters, the American Protector League used Justice Department stationery and operated as if its members were formal deputies of that body. The result was appalling to many. Having no formal statutory authority to make arrests, operatives of the league engaged in a variety of investigations probing the loyalty of citizens, the actions of the draft exemption board, the actual status of conscientious objectors, and the monitoring, in thousands of cases, of suspicious activities reported by people throughout the country in response to appeals for vigilance in detecting spies and persons guilty of sabotage. So vigorous did its members become in their crusade against disloyalty that the Justice Department eventually sought to restrain league agents. This was particularly true following the passage of the Sedition Act. John Lord O'Brian, head of the War Emergency Division of the Department of Justice, feared that under the aegis of that statute, league operatives would move even more vigorously into the role of surveillance of unpopular expression. In a circular to all federal attorneys, the attorney general, seeking to forestall that fear, insisted that the Sedition Act

should not become the medium whereby efforts are made to suppress honest, legitimate criticism of the administration or discussion of

51. Secretary of State William Gibbs McAdoo strongly questioned the legal basis of the APL. Homer Cummings and Carl McFarland, *Federal Justice* (New York, 1937), p. 422. McAdoo preferred a bureau of intelligence in the Department of State to coordinate the war work of the Secret Service, the Bureau of Investigation of the Department of Justice, and the Postal Inspection Service, and used the APL situation to argue for it.

government policies; nor should it be permitted to become a medium for personal feuds or persecution. . . . Protection of loyal persons from unjust suspicion and prosecution is quite as important as the suppression of actual disloyalty.[52]

Nonetheless, given the vagueness of the guidelines afforded the body, the patriotic zeal of many of its members and the reluctance of federal officials to blow the whistle on its excess (to say nothing of the attorney general's actual willingness to condone many of the body's actions), it intimidated a large number of citizens into silent submission.

Wartime doctrine toward civil liberties incorporated a range of explicit premises regarding the permissible limits of personal freedom and the proper relationship between government authority and the individual. The test of this legislation lay both in the attitude toward its use and the behavior that this attitude produced. Many Americans were prepared to embrace the doctrine embodied in these new laws and orders fully—but carefully. Many officials charged with implementing it were prepared to do so in a spirit of restraint, confining its restrictions to circumstances for which it was specifically developed. Others, however, were prepared to use that doctrine as a point of departure, for legitimization of the harrassment and persecution of opponents of the war and critics of the government. A minority of Americans, however, saw no need for wartime criminalization of previously permissible behavior. They were troubled by the precedents being established for massive governmental intervention into the private lives of citizens. As the excesses of the implementers produced increasingly gross violations of personal freedom, these citizens reacted sharply to the limitation of certain basic rights in the name of national security. These responses were further refined in reaction to the behavior of federal and state officials and the members of local and voluntary bodies. It is useful to explore the sensitivity which emerged in each of these circumstances to the new government-to-citizen relationship, particularly now that they were more

52. *Annual Report of the Attorney General, 1918*, p. 674.

clearly defined by law. This is made more intriguing when one attempts to determine the impact of the fact that new and important public policy questions regarding people's basic freedoms were centrally involved.

At the federal level a divergent pattern of behavior occurred. The key to it lay in the agencies assigned to carry out restrictive policy, and in the styles, ambitions, and goals of the men who headed and staffed those agencies. Here a lack of legal precedent for implementing such policy played a factor. Prior to the mid-teens, the principal agency for investigating threats to the government and its officials had been the Secret Service division of the Treasury Department. The agency had engaged in such activities as tracking down counterfeiters, investigating land frauds, and other actions which had at least a peripheral relationship toward the government's financial business. But its role in pure espionage work had been limited. In 1909, a Bureau of Investigation was set up within the Justice Department,[53] initially designed to assist the attorney general in investigating violations of federal law which his agency was expected to enforce. The bureau's authority and activities expanded, until its agents numbered over one hundred by 1914; this, despite a growing annoyance on the part of politically ambitious Secretary of the Treasury William Gibbs McAdoo, who suspected that the agency was invading his department's territory.[54] By mid-1916 Congress came to agree that the Justice Department was the principal law enforcement agency of the federal government and that it needed more help to carry out its principal functions. Congress expanded the bureau still further, and by the end of the year, Gregory was

53. The bureau was largely the brainchild of Charles J. Bonaparte, grandson of the French emperor's brother and attorney general under Theodore Roosevelt. Bonaparte in 1907 had called for "a small carefully selected and experienced force under the immediate orders of the Justice Department." Sanford J. Unger, *F.B.I.: An Uncensored Look Behind the Walls* (New York, 1976), pp. 39–40.

54. McAdoo was impatient at the bureau's restraint, arguing at one point that "misguided people who talk inopportunely of peace . . . should be silenced . . . since every pacifist speech . . . is in effect traitorous." Peterson and Fite, *Opponents of War,* p. 149.

using an enlarged force of more than three hundred agents to police the war-related activities of aliens and citizens. By the time the war came, the bureau was the principle agency for hunting down wartime disloyalty.

Gregory was the first of the key federal officials whose actions shaped civil liberties during the war period. Although as attorney general he welcomed the new role of the Bureau of Investigation, he was still apprehensive about the lack of formal statutory authority for governmental "counter-espionage" work. He therefore called for espionage legislation, antispy laws, and ultimately pushed Wilson toward endorsing the enactment of formal authorization for actions to deal with domestic opponents of the war. Gregory showed considerable awareness of the backlash which an excessive repression of civil liberties might bring upon him and his department. Responding to criticism that the Espionage Act was really directed against disloyal utterances, he denied the charge and claimed that the sole aim of the act was to protect the process of raising and maintaining our armed forces from the dangers of disloyal propaganda.[55] When accusations flooded his office that overzealous patriots were implementing the law so restrictively as to damage individual freedom, he appealed to various governors and state officials, urging absolute compliance with the letter of the law. In one letter to a Georgia official, he insisted that:

the Department deprecates unjust and unfounded criticism or suspicion of citizens or aliens who are law abiding and loyal. . . . Certainly it should not come about that by unwarranted suspicion such persons should be caused loss of business, loss of employment, or other loss. . . . No possible good will come from any unnecessary hardships or discrimination inflicted by private citizens upon those alien enemies who remain law-abiding and loyal, or from any such hardships and criminations unjustly inflicted upon local citizens of the United States.[56]

When various beleagured members of left-wing bodies, in-

55. O'Brian, "Civil Liberties in War Time," p. 20.
56. Ibid., p. 17.

cluding the Non-Partisan League, the IWW, and the Socialist party, protested that they were being harrassed on the dubious grounds of guilt by association, rather than for disloyal actions, the attorney general insisted that "the Federal Law Department adhered to the fundamental doctrine that guilt was personal, and would not lend itself to proscribing any class of individuals as a class." [57] When the Sedition Act amendment was added to the original Espionage Act, Gregory instructed all United States attorneys that:

The prompt and aggressive enforcement of this act is of the highest importance in suppressing disloyal utterances and preventing breaches of peace. It is also of great importance that this statute be administered with discretion. It should not be permitted to become the medium whereby efforts are made to suppress honest, legitimate criticism of the administration or discussion of Government policies; nor should it be permitted to become a medium for personal feuds or persecution. The wide scope of the act and powers conferred increase the importance of discretion in administering it. Protection of loyal persons from unjust suspicion and prosecution is quite as important as the suppression of actual disloyalty.[58]

But Gregory's reaction reflected neither his personal attitude nor the type of behavior which he really expected from the agents of his department. For along with such public posturing, Gregory made statements and took actions which encouraged the very behavior that he was deploring. When American entry occurred the attorney general ordered federal attorneys across the country to maintain "constant vigilance" and requested municipal police chiefs to keep known pacifists and German sympathizers under surveillance. Then, in the first month of the war, before the Bureau of Investigation could be expanded and additional agents sent into the field, he asked every loyal American to act as a "voluntary detective," suggesting that "citizens should feel free to bring their suspicions and information to

57. Ibid., p. 13.
58. Thomas W. Gregory to all U.S. attorneys, May 23, 1918 (Justice Department Archives).

the . . . Department of Justice." [59] The results were so staggering that Gregory was taken aback, as thousands of accusations of disloyalty flooded into the offices of Justice Department officials each day. And although he insisted that all such information would remain confidential in the custody of the department, this did not turn out to be the case.

Gregory's statements betrayed a lack of careful definition regarding what constituted permissible speech. In early June 1917, a Unitarian minister in Long Beach, California, was accused of disloyalty because he objected to a remark by the attorney general that "people should keep their mouths shut and obey the law." [60] In November of the same year, the attorney general was quoted publicly as stating that as for dissenters, "May God have mercy on them, for they need expect none from an outraged people and an avenging government." [61] His emphasis on the importance of individual guilt was belied by his active role in the Justice Department's frenetic prosecution of the IWW. In responding to mounting local hysteria regarding Wobblies, Gregory condoned the mass prosecution of the leaders of the organization. Local IWW headquarters were raided, frequently without search warrants, and fishing expeditions were conducted by Bureau of Investigation agents into its books, accounts, letters, and papers. Gregory seldom sought to discriminate between people who subscribed to the IWW's theories and ideology and members who had committed crimes punishable under federal law.[62]

Despite statements calling for care in prosecuting citizens under the new Sedition Act, the attorney general asked for its

59. Cummings and McFarland, *Federal Justice*, p. 420.
60. Peterson and Fite, *Opponents of War*, p. 115.
61. *The New York Times,* November 21, 1917, p. 3.
62. Justice Department officials also warned individuals who might be inclined to support the IWW or call for fair trial against contributing to "so-called 'civil liberties' . . . 'popular council,' 'legal advice,' or anti-war organizations," hinting that these groups were federated in a disloyal conspiracy to impede the prosecution of the war." *New York World,* January 28, 1918, pp. 1–2; *New York Times,* June 18, 1919, p. 8.

"liberal construction." He promptly condoned a variety of convictions obtained under it, including such famous examples as
those of Socialist leader Eugene V. Debs for a speech in Canton,
Ohio, that expressed antagonism toward war [63] and of Rose
Pastor Stokes, who had written to a St. Louis newspaper that
the government should not have unqualified support in the war.
"I am for the people," Mrs. Stokes declared, "and the government is for the profiteers." [64] In the latter instance Gregory supported the conviction and Stokes's ten-year prison sentence,
contending that her remarks were "capable of the meaning that
the war was a war for the so-called capitalist class, and not for
democracy or the benefit of all the people of this country." [65]
He retreated, however, when such actions drew criticism from
the general public and from civil liberties–conscious officials
within his own department—particularly, the men in charge of
prosecutions under the Espionage statutes, John Lord O'Brian
and Alfred Bettman. Toward the end of his term of office, he
instituted the practice of reviewing the cases of all those convicted under the wartime Espionage legislation and recommend-
ing clemency where the verdict seemed unjust or the sentence
unnecessarily severe. Thus, the Justice Department, which Gregory headed until March 1919—when he was replaced by wartime Alien Property Custodian A. Mitchell Palmer, played the
game both ways. Claims that the department performed its
wartime job with sensitivity and restraint notwithstanding, it was
ready at any time to do whatever seemed necessary to keep
opponents of the war in line.

Wartime behavior of two other key cabinet officials, whose
positions forced them into civil liberties situations, offers an
interesting view of the ambivalence which operated at the highest level of Wilson's administration. Albert S. Burleson served

63. On the Debs situation see Ray Ginger, *The Bending Cross* (New
Brunswick, N.J., 1949), pp. 356–59.
64. Peterson and Fite, *Opponents of War,* pp. 185–86.
65. Thomas W. Gregory to William Redfield, February 20, 1919
(Justice Department Archives).

as postmaster general from the beginning of Wilson's first term. Proud, pompous, and myopic, Burleson, "the scion of Texas heroes," was from small-town America and had served as an agrarian-oriented congressman from 1899 to 1913. Immediately upon taking over the Post Office Department, he instituted a policy of racial segregation within it, downgrading and dismissing black employees in the South in order to open up positions for loyal white Democrats.[66] Not one to minimize the power of his office, he never failed to take advantage of opportunities which he felt would contribute to its prestige. Standing at his side and reassuring him was the department's solicitor, William H. Lamar. Lamar sought to identify and distinguish between loyal and disloyal public figures in the public mind. At one point, for example, he said of Samuel Gompers, who was then co-operating fully with government repression, "while this war is on, we are not going to allow any newspaper in this country to attack him." [67] As the government moved into the censorship area, Burleson became a key figure. In contrast with Gregory he seemed generally oblivious to the importance of projecting any image of sensitivity to civil liberties considerations. After the war O'Brian claimed that "the powers granted the Postmaster General were exercised by him alone; the Department of Justice had no share or part in administering them . . . in fact post office officials worked at cross purposes with Justice, on most occasions." [68]

From the enactment of the Espionage Act in June 1917 to the end of the war period, Burleson exercised complete discretion regarding the circulation through the mails of material published in this country. The test of his sensitivity to limits on freedom of the press and on the public's right to know and to the political overtones of his anti–civil liberties behavior lay in

66. John Morton Blum, "Albert Sidney Burleson," *Dictionary of American Biography,* Supplement Two (New York, 1958), pp. 74–75.
67. Oswald Garrison Villard, *Fighting Years: Memoirs of a Liberal Editor* (New York, 1939), p. 355.
68. John Lord O'Brian, "New Encroachments on Individual Freedom," *Harvard Law Review,* 66 (1952): 14.

the way that he used that discretion. An awareness of Burleson's arbitrariness emerged shortly after the beginning of the war. Theodore Roosevelt, on the right, charged that Burleson's policies virtually prevented the truth from being expressed regarding governmental authorities in Washington. Upton Sinclair, on the left, echoed the same sentiments, with the *New York World,* somewhere in the middle, summarizing a fairly widely held liberal view that "the bureaucrats of the Post Office Department . . . seemed determined to set up an intellectual reign of terror in the United States." [69]

The Espionage Act itself provided harsh penalties for any person who willfully attempted to obstruct the war effort or who induced others to do so. Under a highly controversial provision of the law, the postmaster general was empowered to use his own judgment in determining whether mailing of certain kinds of matter constituted willful obstruction to the progress of the war. Material so designated could be excluded from the mails without a court order; the burden of proof in any resulting legal action would be on the person who mailed the allegedly subversive matter. Thus, although Woodrow Wilson argued publicly that such broad censorship would not be used to suppress civil liberties,[70] Burleson did just that. On June 16, 1917, Burleson secretly directed local postmasters:

keep a close watch on unsealed matters, newspapers, etc., containing matter which is calculated to interfere with the success of any Federal loan . . . or to cause insubordination, disloyalty, mutiny, or refusal of duty in the military or naval service, or to obstruct the recruiting, draft or enlistment services . . . or otherwise to embarrass or hamper the Government in conducting the war.[71]

Local postmasters were to forward any suspicious material to Washington. Although the act said nothing of embarrassing ma-

69. Scheiber, *Wilson Administration and Civil Liberties,* p. 30.

70. Woodrow Wilson to Arthur Brisbane, April 25, 1917 (Wilson Papers, LC).

71. Albert S. Burleson to postmasters of the first, second, and third classes, June 16, 1917, Post Office Department Files (National Archives).

terial, the implications of the order clearly suggested that he was ready to move against any citizen whose views he found anathema and thus to exceed his authority.

Postmasters quickly moved to comply, and the national office was promptly flooded with newspapers, periodicals, and pamphlets which seemed to fit his proscriptions. Within a month fifteen publications had been excluded from the mails, including *The Masses,* the *International Socialist Review,* the *Appeal to Reason,* the *American Socialist,* and the *Milwaukee Leader.* The suppression of *The Masses* and the *Milwaukee Leader*— and the attempted suppression of *The Nation*—became a national *cause célèbre* and are revealing case studies of Burleson's behavior.

The Masses, a liberal-left publication edited by Max Eastman and aimed principally at a young, liberal, intellectual audience, took a strong stand against the war and commended many of its most controversial domestic opponents. Clearly, its cartoons and articles could be called unpatriotic. But whether they constituted a willful attempt to obstruct the war was a judgment which required considerable sensitivity to the relationship between the printed word and punishable action.[72] If Burleson understood this distinction, there was nothing in his behavior which gave any indication that he intended to act upon it. While excluding the controversial issue of June 1917 which contained antiwar cartoons and articles, he also withdrew the magazine's second-class mailing privileges. When critics of this ruling went to Washington to challenge it, Burleson proclaimed their criticism and that of a number of congressmen and senators "impertinent" and defended the action as essential.[73] Eastman protested directly to President Wilson, who in turn advised Burleson of the general discontent with his behavior. Burleson

72. On *The Masses* cartoons see Richard Fitzgerald, *Art and Politics* (Westport Conn., 1973). On the episode see Max Eastman, *Love and Revolution: My Journey Through an Epoch* (New York, 1964), pp. 58–63.

73. Donald Johnson, "Wilson, Burleson, and Censorship in the First World War," *Journal of Southern History* 28 (February 1962): 50.

denied that he had suppressed *The Masses* or anything else, contending that since the magazine had printed matter calculated to obstruct the war effort, he was simply carrying out his duty in enforcing federal law against criminal behavior. Wilson agreed with his judgment and wrote to Eastman "that a line must be drawn and that we are trying, it may be clumsily but genuinely, to draw it without fear or favor or prejudice." [74] Fortified by such presidential sanction, Burleson went on using censorship as an effective device to destroy the left-wing press, denying second-class mailing privileges to some twenty-two Socialist newspapers and attacking a wide range of pamphlets, including one by the National Civil Liberties Bureau which deplored mob violence. [75]

Burleson similarly utilized the authority he had been given by the Trading with the Enemy Act against the foreign-language press. Asked by reporters how he planned to use the discretion which the act afforded him, he indicated that

no publication could say that this Government got in the war wrong, that it is in it for wrong purposes, or anything that will impugn the motives of the Government for going into the war. They cannot say that the Government is the tool of Wall Street or the munitions-makers. That kind of thing makes for insubordination in the Army and Navy and breeds a spirit of disloyalty through the country. It is a false statement, a lie, and it will not be permitted.

The postmaster general denied that he was out to suppress legitimate criticism of the government but went on, "Nothing can be said inciting people to resist the laws. There can be no campaign against conscription and the Draft Law, nothing that will interfere with enlistments or the raising of an army. There can be nothing said to hamper and obstruct the Government in the prosecution of the war." [76]

Again, loud complaints were heard from the media. Herbert Croly of the *New Republic* protested to Woodrow Wilson that

---

74. Eastman, *Love and Revolution,* pp. 62–63.
75. Scheiber, *Wilson Administration and Civil Liberties,* p. 32.
76. Quoted in *Literary Digest* 55 (October 4, 1917): 12.

such suppression would quickly become counterproductive.[77] Wilson promptly replied publicly that he had complete confidence in Burleson's discretion.[78] But he was clearly troubled privately. Again, hoping to avoid having the civil liberties issue become a bone of contention, he urged Burleson to "act with the utmost caution and liberality in all our censorship." [79] Burleson testily replied that that was exactly what was being done.[80] About the same time Solicitor William Lamar justified the department's censorship policy in an article, "The Government's Attitude Toward the Press," in which he contended that a "misapplied reverence for legal axioms . . . would be criminal not only to our soldiers, and ourselves, but to posterity." [81]

Although by this time the Justice Department was beginning to refuse to defend cases arising out of the official acts of Burleson and Lamar, the latter were attempting to assist the Justice Department in its assault upon the IWW. Postmasters in areas where Wobblies were active, particularly in Chicago, refused to deliver IWW mail, and when disturbed liberals such as John Dewey, Helen Keller, Thorstein Veblen, and Walter Weyl sought to raise funds for the IWW's defense, *The New Republic* refused to carry an advertisement to this effect, for fear that the Post Office Department would deny its second-class mailing privileges also.[82] If Wilson failed to comprehend the implications for *The New Republic,* others did not. Oswald Garrison Villard of *The Nation* especially pointed out the

77. Herbert Croly to Woodrow Wilson, October 19, 1917 (Wilson Papers, LC).

78. Woodrow Wilson to Herbert Croly, October 22, 1917 (Wilson Papers, LC).

79. Woodrow Wilson to Albert Burleson, October 11, 1917 (Wilson Papers, LC).

80. Albert S. Burleson to Woodrow Wilson, October 16, 1917 (Burleson Papers).

81. William H. Lamar, "The Government's Attitude Toward the Press," *Forum* 59 (February 1918): 132.

82. Johnson, *Challenge to American Freedoms,* p. 96. On *The New Republic's* ambivalence on Wilson, see Michael Wreszin, *Oswald Garrison Villard: Pacifist at War* (Bloomington, Ind., 1965), pp. 94–95.

ominous threat to civil liberties of the Wilson position. Others wondered aloud whether Wilson fully realized the political over-tones of supporting conservative repressionists in office, while threatening liberal supporters outside with criminal sanctions.[83]

This position and similar ones taken by the liberal opinion journals did trouble the president. On two occasions Wilson intervened in a Burleson-designated action. When Solicitor Lamar withheld the September 14, 1918, issue of *The Nation* because it contained an article ("Civil Liberty Dead") attacking various suppressions of civil liberties, Wilson directed Burleson to release the issue immediately, and the following day the Post Office Department lifted its ban.[84] Wilson intervened again when Lamar suppressed an issue of Norman Thomas's *World Tomorrow,* a periodical published by the pacifist Fellowship of Reconciliation. On the appeal of John Nevin Sayre, brother of the President's son-in-law, the president urged Burleson to re-move the "non-mailable" designation from the journal. Burleson promptly obeyed his superior, and the publication was not bothered again during the war period.[85] However, Burleson was determined to take his revocation of the second-class privileges of Victor Berger's Socialist *Milwaukee Leader* to the courts for vindication, and he did so after the war. Wilson initially de-plored the action, stating in a letter to Burleson in October 1918 that "some of the things quoted probably cross the line and I have very little doubt that they were all intended to have sinister results." Nonetheless, he argued that "I think doubt ought al-

83. Wreszin, *Villard,* pp. 79–80, 93–94, 97–98, 101. Congressional opposition to Post Office Department arbitrariness was also vigorous during this period, particularly when proposals came forward for further strengthening censorship authority through amending the Espionage Act. For details see Dorothy G. Fowler, *Unmailable* (Athens, Ga., 1977), pp. 119–20.

84. Baker, *Life and Letters,* 7:273.

85. Harry Fleischman, *Norman Thomas* (New York, 1964), pp. 21, 29; W. A. Swanberg, *Norman Thomas: The Last Idealist* (New York, 1976), pp. 63–64.

ways be resolved in favor of the utmost freedom of speech." [86]
Getting little response, he reiterated four months later his strong
feeling that "it would not be wise to do any more suppressing.
We must meet these poisons in some other way." [87] But Burleson, resolute to the end, pushed the case, and in 1921 the Supreme Court not only sustained him but sanctioned his general
censorship policies. [88]

To Burleson this was ultimate vindication. In an address
in October 1919, he articulated his perception of his role. It
had been an unwelcome one, he argued, but he had performed
it. He denied the charges that he had chronically suppressed
freedom of speech. Instead, he contended that he had "performed the service with moderation, exercising no arbitrary
power whatever, but enforcing the law as it was written." [89] The
fact remained that the nation's press never shared this vision
and acted quickly in the immediate postwar period to reassert
publicly and loudly the necessity for a quick end to censorship
policies and a quick restoration of freedom of information to
the American public. [90]

The behavior of Secretary of Labor William B. Wilson in
the war years makes an illuminating contrast to Burleson. Wilson's pre-cabinet career was intimately tied up with the stormy
history of the labor movement. Of humble background, with
little schooling, he had begun work in the mines at the age of
nine and had suffered company tyranny in the form of eviction,
injunction, and blacklist—all of which made him sympathetic

86. O. A. Hilton, "Freedom of the Press in Wartime, 1917–1918,"
Southwestern Social Science Quarterly 28 (March 1948): 351, 358–59.
Baker, *Life and Letters,* 7:313.

87. Woodrow Wilson to Albert S. Burleson, February 28, 1919
(Burleson Papers).

88. Milwaukee Publishing Co. *v.* Burleson, 255 U.S. 407 (1921).

89. Address of Hon. A. S. Burleson to the Annual Convention of
the National Hardware Association, October 15, 1919 (Burleson Papers).

90. On the role of the press in blowing the whistle on A. Mitchell
Palmer and the Red Scare of 1920, see Paul L. Murphy, *The Meaning
of Freedom of Speech* (Westport Ct., 1972), pp. 93–94.

to the workers' fight to get their rights through unionization and to the struggle for a better bargaining position. As a member of the national executive board of the United Mine Workers, he was involved in the coal strikes of 1899 and 1902, and as a congressman from Pennsylvania from 1907 to 1913, he worked for legislation to provide for mine safety, an eight-hour day for public employees, antiinjunction laws, and child labor restriction. He became the nation's first secretary of labor as a result of his fitting in with Woodrow Wilson's professed concern for working-class people. During his tenure as Secretary of Labor, he was concerned with developing better federal mediation machinery, encouraging collective bargaining, and reorganizing the Bureau of Immigration and Naturalization, which was housed in the Labor Department.[91]

Secretary Wilson's attitudes toward wartime suppression surfaced most clearly in connection with the government's harrassment of the IWW. After Attorney General Gregory had decided that the organization was "a grave menace to the nation" and that it was financed by "some hostile organization," [92] the government, with the urging of eight Western governors, set out to prosecute the IWW under the Espionage Act. William Wilson, along with Secretary of War Newton D. Baker, George Creel, Supreme Court Justice Louis D. Brandeis, and presidential advisors Colonel Edward House and Joseph Tumulty, deplored the action.[93] As head of the president's Labor Mediation Commission, which was investigating an Arizona copper strike, Wilson concluded that the problem was not subversion, but the insistence by the men involved that "the right and power to obtain just treatment were in themselves basic conditions of employment." [94] The president, however, remained unconvinced, believing that his policy of prosecuting under the Espionage Act

91. Witt Bowden, "William Banchop Wilson," *Dictionary of American Biography* (New York, 1936), 20:348–49.

92. Thomas W. Gregory to Charles Warren, July 11, 1917 (Justice Department Archives).

93. Johnson, *Challenge to American Freedoms,* p. 93.

94. Ibid.

was far milder than arresting all IWW agitators and deporting those with alien backgrounds—moves that Western governors were urging at the time. The governors argued that such action would be enough to frighten the native labor force into acquiescence and would not remove sufficient members of that force to create wartime labor shortages for industry.

Secretary Wilson was hostile to this approach. Deportation would have to proceed through his department, and even if he could not impose reasonable standards on the Justice Department in applying the Espionage Act, he could attempt to do so with his own personnel. Thus, before developing plans to implement the deportation sections of the 1917 Immigration Act, he ordered a thorough investigation of the IWW constitution, preamble, and literature, asking Labor Department officials to determine whether the organization actually advocated and taught the unlawful destruction of property. He further demanded clarification of whether mere membership made individuals punishable by penalties imposed against the organization. Upon careful examination the Labor Department's Immigration Bureau determined that although IWW writings hinted at resistance to organized government and its representatives, they contained nothing in the way of direct advocacy of anarchism, active opposition to organized government, or the destruction of public or private property.[95] Secretary Wilson then ordered department officials to adhere to an extremely limited application of the 1917 law. More precisely, he insisted that inspectors thoroughly substantiate personal guilt before requesting a warrant of arrest. Warrants would be issued only after an exhaustive inquiry into alien's beliefs, teachings, and actions.[96] This interpretation of the law stunned the local offices of the immigration bureau, for it created a standard of guilt as exacting—if not more so—as that exercised in current judicial proceedings. In

95. William Preston, *Aliens and Dissenters* (Cambridge, Mass., 1963), pp. 102, 164; Zechariah Chafee, Jr., *Free Speech in the United States* (Cambridge, Mass., 1941), p. 226.
96. Preston, *Aliens and Dissenters,* p. 102.

practice Wilson's policy demanded an investigation of migratory agitators so thorough as to be beyond the capacity of the modest number of agency officials. He thus raised the civil liberties issue in a direct way, placing the burden on the public and the Congress to support and implement more rigorous suppression than he felt was justified.

Response was generally hostile and disappointing. Secretary Wilson's strict criterion of individual guilt could not prevail in the face of wartime intolerance and hysteria. Under local pressure for deportation, immigration department inspectors repeatedly violated the standards that he had established. Furthermore, in 1918 Congress passed a new immigration law which established guilt by association, superceding Wilson's narrow definition of criminality. Under its provisions any alien who advocated anarchism, syndicalism, or violent revolution—or who belonged to an organization that advocated any of these things— could be deported.[97]

Justice and Immigration Department officials concluded that membership in the IWW was a deportable offense and that in many instances deportation was preferable to expensive prosecutions under the Espionage Act. Subsequently a number of alien IWW members who had been arrested earlier in the war were convicted of violating the new deportation statute and were sent to Ellis Island for deportation. None was afforded counsel in this process, for the new law did not require any normal legal proceedings in such cases. Secretary Wilson initially approved this action, although with grave misgivings. But under the pressure of attorneys who rushed to the defense of the IWW and of various reformers, including the redoubtable commissioner of immigration, Frederic C. Howe, he agreed to reopen the cases.[98] At this point Wilson learned that most charges levied by the immigration inspector against the individuals had been spurious

97. Charles Recht, *American Deportation and Exclusion Laws* (New York, 1919), p. 13.
98. Frederic C. Howe, *The Confessions of a Reformer* (New York, 1925), pp. 274–75.

and that information conveyed to him regarding their criminal and revolutionary activities had been deceitful. The result was that in the months that followed the war, the Labor Department and the courts cancelled almost all of the deportation warrants, thus heading off a further miscarriage of justice under the department's auspices.[99]

William B. Wilson thus is revealed as a man of good will determined to stand against the excesses of wartime produced hysteria. Compelled to contradict the attorney general, the postmaster general, and even the president on frequent occasions, he also confronted insubordination in his own department by officers who were susceptible to the anti-civil liberties hysteria of the war period. That he persisted and prevailed attests to the seriousness of his own concerns for the rights of working-class people. That this action was widely unpopular and ultimately terminated his public career speaks poignantly to the risks inherent in striking such a public posture at that time.

George Creel occupies a unique position in the history of civil liberties in the war years. His Committee on Public Information, the agency set up by emergency presidential order to "sell the war" to the American people, engaged in actions with subtle and not-so-subtle civil liberties overtones. But, by and large, Creel saw himself in an educator's, rather than a repressor's, role. Charged with generating a constructive war spirit to aid in the ultimate achievement of liberal democracy at home and abroad, he contended that his major concern was "expression not repression." Even when his office was briefly charged with carrying out censorship functions he worked hard to establish a positive image of his agency. Those who sponsored the agency hoped that a positive publicity program designed to disseminate as much safe war information as possible and to stimulate enthusiasm for vigorous prosecution of the war would avoid the worst excesses of censorship. Creel presented his mission to the public as one of "driving home to

99. Johnson, *Challenge,* pp. 124–25.

the people the causes behind the war, the great fundamental necessities that compelled a peace loving nation to take up arms to protect free institutions and preserve our liberties." [100]

Creel was a former newspaper man, active in reform politics, who had displayed considerable sympathy with socialism. By 1912, however, he had become an ardent Wilson Democrat, committed to Wilsonian reform at home and abroad. His progressive mentality allowed him to believe that salesmanship was an entirely appropriate method of attracting support for ideals. Thus, he took over the CPI with a commitment to sell the American people a proper view of their role and responsibilities in the war, of aliens and hyphenated Americans, and of the limits and nature of civil liberties. Under his leadership, the rather loosely knit and volatile agency swiftly improvised a program of pamphlets, handouts, managed news, celebrity tours, stunts, public-speaking programs, and other devices of publicity, ballyhoo, persuasion, engineering, and saturation. The agency prepared articles, editorials, and cartoons for the use of newspapers and published the *Official Bulletin,* by which public documents and digests of information were circulated among the offices of the government, displayed in post offices, and sent to subscribers. The committee provided advertisments and posters for Liberty Loan drives and other propaganda ventures, sent out "four-minute men" and celebrities to address public assemblies, and even supplied appropriate scripts to motion pictures.[101]

100. George Creel, "Public Opinion in War Time," *Annals of the American Academy of Political & Social Science* 78 (1918):185–86. Creel's appointment had come in an atmosphere in which Walter Lippmann had called for a federal censorship program. David Lawrence had done the same. And Arthur Bullard, whose brainchild the CPI really was, had expressed outrage at demands of Douglas MacArthur, censor for the War Department, for the military to take over and exercise this function vigorously in the civilian area. Stephen Vaughn, "Holding Fast the Inner Lines: Democracy, Nationalism, and the Committee on Public Information" (Ph.D. dissertation, Indiana University, 1977), pp. 3–8.

101. For Creel's version of the work of the committee, see George Creel, *How We Advertised America* (New York, 1920).

Several aspects of this operation bear scrutiny. Although the committee's initial censorship functions became insignificant with the enactment of the Espionage Act, it retained considerable discretionary authority through the reliance of the Wilson administration on its judgment regarding the dissemination of information. In addition, Creel became a member of the censorship board established under the Trading-with-the-Enemy Act to deal with foreign communications, and in this capacity he gained further discretionary authority over the dispersal of transatlantic news. Creel also maintained close contact with the postmaster general. This enabled him to utilize that officer as an instrument for restricting publication and circulation of news and propaganda which did not have his committee approval. And if such support did not look as if it would do the job, Creel was prepared to push law enforcement bodies to use Title I, Section 3, of the Espionage Act to force compliance with the committee's wishes.

The committee's own widely distributed propaganda also contributed to the suppression process. Its *Red, White, and Blue Series*—small pamphlets issued through the war years by the thousands and used by schools and colleges to explain why America was at war—was often highly incendiary in content. These booklets included "proof" of extensive disloyalty in the United States and "proof" that Germans regularly committed unspeakable atrocities. They explained that the government's restrictions on expression were proper and constitutional in wartime, reflecting Creel's belief that there were clear limits to freedom of expression and that federal legislation curtailing civil liberties represented the views of a democratic Congress and should be respected and enforced. Other pamphlets were deliberately anti-German, frequently filled with exaggerated charges about the decadence of German culture, German values, and German behavior. Allegedly, German agents were behind most strikes in the United States, German money was used to finance pacifist newspapers, and German agents were out to impose the worst attributes of Prussianism upon the American people. These documents fed the notion that German-Americans were disloyal and that pacifists were pro-German, and by so impugning their loyalty, they opened both up to hostility and harrassment from a variety of individuals and groups.[102]

The committee's *War Cyclopedia,* edited by distinguished academics Edward S. Corwin, Samuel B. Harding, and Frederick L. Paxson, was particularly revealing. This work, a compilation of brief articles by dozens of scholars, afforded "proper" wartime definitions of such terms as free speech, freedom of the press (which contained strong justification of government censorship), espionage, the Trading-with-the-Enemy Act, and sedition. Clearly propagandistic, it conveyed the general idea that restrictions on civil liberties were legal and sensible and that no valid constitutional issues were raised by such measures as the Espionage Act and its amendment, the Sedition Act. The tone of the volume projected a clear impression that those who disagreed with such interpretations, those who might wish to raise questions about whether government policies and measures reflected the proper governmental attitude toward the rights of citizens, were either unreasonable or disloyal.[103]

An interesting aspect of the work of the committee involved such recruitment of leading scholars across the country to join in its activities. Many professors were anxious to serve the government as a way of displaying their loyalty and commitment to the war. This, they hoped, would afford them some public credibility and acknowledgment at a time when the academic world was the object of suspicion and hostility, particularly from

102. James R. Mock and Cedric Larson, *Words that Won the War* (Princeton, 1939), pp. 162ff.
103. United States Committee on Public Information, *The Red, White, and Blue Series,* VII, *War Cyclopedia* (Washington, 1918). Corwin was strongly of the belief that the First Amendment did not release the press or the individual from the restraints imposed by the common-law doctrine of seditious libel. This view continued into the postwar period, when he disagreed with both Oliver Wendell Holmes and Zechariah Chafee regarding Holmes's Chafee-inspired dissent in *Abrams* vs. *U.S.* Edward S. Corwin, "Freedom of Speech and Press under the First Amendment: A Resume," *Yale Law Journal* 30 (November 1920): 48

superpatriotic boards of trustees and regents and academic administrations.[104] Despite the fact that many of the nation's leading academics were trained in Germany and had a high regard for the impeccable standards of German higher education, many academics were repelled by German autocracy and militarism, and they desired to combat it. The result was the willingness of a number of leading academic figures, mustered by Dean Guy Stanton Ford of the University of Minnesota—director of the committee's Division of Civic and Educational Cooperation—to embrace "mind mobilization" as their contribution to the cause and to work enthusiastically with Creel's committee in teaching the American people the right and wrong about the war.[105]

Had such scholars been prepared to acknowledge that their role was one of deliberate propaganda, tensions might have been avoided. But overt efforts were made to wrap a large number of the pamphlets and publications produced by respectable scholars in a mantle of total objectivity, even when—as in one extreme and widely criticized case—the work "proved" that Bolshevik leaders in the Russian Revolution had been paid agents of the German general staff and that Germany had materially assisted the Bolsheviks in coming to power in Russia.[106] Similarly, a number of scholars might also have been less vulnerable to charges of violating academic tenets had they not been willing to implement the Espionage Act against the foreign-language press by translating "seditious" newspapers in order to open them up to censorship.[107] In any event, the actions of such "loyal" members of the academic community, and the com-

104. Carol S. Gruber, *Mars and Minerva: World War I and the Uses of the Higher Learning in America* (Baton Rouge, La., 1975), pp. 163 ff.
105. Ibid. pp. 144–46, 157. See also George T. Blakey, *Historians on the Homefront* (Lexington, Ky., 1970); and Harold Josephson, "History for Victory: The National Board for Historical Service," *Mid-America* 52 (July 1970): 205–24.
106. Gruber, *Mars and Minerva*, pp. 151–52.
107. Ibid., pp. 157–58.

mendation they drew, placed an intolerable burden upon those professors who were unwilling to surrender to the tantalizing rewards of wartime conformity. In some cases such scholars were left open to charges that their commitment to academic freedom and the right to pursue impartial truth on the campus constituted a form of unpatriotic neutrality which contributed adversely to the nation at arms. A number of professors were dismissed because of suspected or acknowledged lack of enthusiasm for the American cause.[108]

George Creel was not an ultraconservative champion of the status quo or of the powerful American business establishment. On the contrary, he took seriously the Wilsonian view that participation in the war was ultimately to serve a liberal and liberalizing purpose. An integral part of the function of the CPI, was to "convince the great mass of workers that our interest in democracy and justice begins at home."[109] The committee material called upon both employers and employees to make equal sacrifices in the name of ultimate victory. Furthermore, Creel was hesitant to jump upon the bandwagon of criticism of such groups as the IWW, the Socialists, and the radical agrarian Non-Partisan League, feeling that as long as such groups were not overtly interfering with the nation's war effort, the reform spirit for which they stood should be kept alive as an adjunct to, and in support of, general Wilsonian idealism. In spite of the rhetoric of CPI publications, Creel believed that unpopular ethnics, particularly German-Americans, should be used as agents for patriotic propaganda rather than attacked as subversive and un-American.[110]

Such a posture produced two rather distinct responses. His frequent support of unpopular groups and individuals, to say nothing of his clear ambition and expansiveness, made Creel a chronic target of conservative congressmen and senators, to such a degree that "jumping on George," as it was called, be-

108. Ibid., pp. 166–212.
109 Mock and Larson, *Words that Won the War,* p. 211.
110. Leubke, *Bonds of Loyalty,* p. 213.

came a regular congressional pastime. Attacking Creel was a safe and convenient way of attacking the national administration without the political dangers incurred by direct criticism of Wilson. It also enabled certain congressmen to strike a pose against the activities of the CPI, without having to accept the responsibility of posing positive alternatives which inevitably would have been more repressive. This confrontation reached its bitterest point in June 1918, when Congress halved his appropriation requests—and in the process advised Creel to tone down the liberal bias of his organization's posture.[111]

His second set of detractors constituted state leaders, particularly the heads of state councils of defense and public safety commissions, whose excessive exuberance for repression he frequently deplored and whose highly partisan conservatism he saw as a threat to liberal wartime aims. His conflict with the Minnesota Public Safety Commission, the most powerful state council in the nation, over its persecution of the Non-Partisan League is a revealing example of the tensions which existed between powerful local authorities and the committee,[112] and of the partisan use of wartime repression. By the eve of the war the Non-Partisan League was a powerful agrarian radical group whose political successes in North Dakota—where it controlled the state—and, increasingly, in Minnesota were proving alarming, especially to the Republican leaders of the latter state. The White House, however, welcomed the league's success as herald-

111. A typical example of anti-Creel hyperbole was a statement on the Senate floor by Boies Penrose qf Pennsylvania: "I do not see why we should permit men like Mr. Creel . . . whose scurrilous and defamatory utterances . . . were read in this body . . . to be holding an office and publishing a publicity chronicle when he is smeared all over with treason." *Congressional Record* LVI (65th Cong. 2nd Sess., April 9, 1918): 4827.

112. On the Commission see O. A. Hilton, "The Minnesota Commission of Public Safety in World War I, 1917–1919," *Bulletin of the Oklahoma Agricultural and Mechanical College* 68 (May 15, 1951); and Charles S. Ward, "The Minnesota Commission of Public Safety: Its Formation and Activities" (M.A. thesis, University of Minnesota, 1965).

ing the end of Republican domination in rural areas where the Democratic party had long strived, with indifferent results, to establish a foothold.[113] Moreover, the harsh, repressive measures taken by the Republican dominated State Defense Councils disturbed Wilson's liberal advisors, who felt that the Republicans should not be allowed to use the war to crush all opposition to their local regimes. Creel was the strongest of all administration supporters of the league. He had formerly been an associate of A. C. Townley, the leagues' volatile and outspoken leader in the early days of the nonpartisan movement. In November 1917 Creel brought Townley to the White House to plead the cause of the Western farmers and to defend their loyalty.[114] In return for some general support and positive acknowledgement, Townley indicated that he was willing to put his organization at Wilson's service, particularly to assist in reaching the farm vote. Wilson, determined that the congressional elections of 1918 should vindicate his policies, was impressed. When the league held a meeting in St. Paul, Minnesota, on March 18, 1918, he sent his tariff commissioner, William Kent, to speak to the group of the desirability of supporting administration policies.[115]

The reaction from local Republican leaders was hostile. Minnesota's conservative Republican governor, Joseph A. A. Burnquist had already expressed outrage regarding the league's activities. Following an impassioned antiwar speech by Wisconsin Senator Robert LaFollette to a league meeting the previous September,[116] Burnquist had deplored both the senator and his sponsors and indicated that he would be arrested if his statements proved to be seditious.[117] In reply to an invitation from the league to address its March 18 meeting, Burnquist denounced the organization for fostering the spirit of factionalism and charged that it had made an "eleventh hour claim to pure

113. Livermore, *Politics Is Adjourned,* pp. 153–54.

114. Ibid., p. 154.

115. *The Non-Partisan Leaguer,* April 8, 1918, reprinted the speech.

116. Robert L. Morlan, *Political Prairie Fire* (Minneapolis, 1955), pp. 143–44.

117. *The New York Times,* September 22, 1917, p. 11.

loyalty" after seeing that its earlier course would bring disaster. He further charged that the league had embraced the pro-Germans, IWW's, "Red Socialists," pacifists, and others "whose doctrines are of benefit to Germany." [118] The appearance of a prominent administration official on the same platform with league leaders therefore created major tensions, in no way diminished by the fact that the St. Paul convention ultimately qualified its pledge of support to Wilson by denouncing his administration for failing to protect the farmer against war-profiteers. Nonetheless, during the subsequent political campaign, Creel's committee sent "Loyalty Speakers" into the state to deliver a series of patriotic addresses under league sponsorship, particularly in areas in which it believed that support of the war might be lukewarm. Local Minnesota officials, with the support of the Public Safety Commission, refused to permit them to speak under such auspices. A number, however, requested to use the speakers themselves.[119] Clearly, as Creel later wrote to a League partisan, ". . . there was fear of the political power of the Non-Partisan League, and its opponents did not want it to be given any reputation for loyalty. In plain words, Minnesota Republican leaders preferred that the Non-Partisan League should be disloyal rather than loyal, in order that they might be provided with a campaign weapon." [120]

Despite strong words of anxious caution from Woodrow Wilson, Creel did not back off completely. He continued to maintain that the league was "absolutely loyal" and that the Public Safety Commission was trying to drive it into disloyalty to further its own reactionary political ends. Nevertheless, he was forced to agree with the president that breaking openly with state authorities over the issue would be counterproductive.[121] The result was that while not condoning the local tyranny of

118. Hilton, "Minnesota Commission of Public Safety," 27–28.

119. Livermore, *Politics Is Adjourned,* p. 156.

120. Morlan, *Political Prairie Fire,* p. 164. For further insights into Creel and the NPL. see Carl H. Chrislock, *The Progressive Era in Minnesota, 1899–1918* (St. Paul, Minn., 1971), p. 155.

121. Hilton, "Minnesota Commission of Public Safety," 35.

the Public Safety Commission and its local officers—who were prepared to suspend civil liberties by fiat—Creel became more cautious in deploring it openly.[122] When Townley was subsequently indicted by Minnesota authorities for sedition, Creel's public response was, "Mr. Townley is under indictment in Minnesota, and there is a very bitter fight being made on the League in that state by certain groups. With this, the [national] government has nothing to do, refusing absolutely to take part in these local differences." [123] The statement was indicative of the federal government's reluctance to interfere with the states' efforts to implement and enforce their own loyalty legislation, using local standards.[124]

The vigor of state enforcement was highly divergent. As at the national level, enforcement depended heavily upon the attitudes and values of the officers charged with carrying out policy. A variety of local conditions came into play, including the enthnicity of the local population, the local antiwar activities, the size and effectiveness of those local organizations against which the local militants for conformity demanded action, and a wide range of animosities growing out of tensions in the community which had been festering over time. The formal powers extended to local officers differed from state to state. In some states the governor simply appointed a panel of prominent citizens to administer the state Council of Defense and afforded them little formal or statutory authority commensurate with their assignment. In others, where the legislature had rushed "loyalty" legislation onto the books and afforded enforcement officers sweeping legal powers, this authority was frequently exercized vigorously, in the form of warrantless searches, subpoenas, and contempt citations. On the whole, however, any distinction between the statutory and non-statutory authority was artificial. The absence of legal authority seldom seemed a great handicap to an official who understood the potentialities inherent in the war psychosis.

122. Peterson and Fite, *Opponents of War,* pp. 192–93.
123. Morlan, *Political Prairie Fire,* p. 167.
124. O'Brian, "Civil Liberty in Wartime," 13–14.

In spite of different local conditions, a pattern of enforcement can be discussed. Generally, the activities of the state committees and councils of defense mirrored the national disregard for civil liberties and the national sentiment against foreigners. Most state bodies saw their mandate as promoting war spirit, organizing the production of war goods, limiting consumption of strategic commodities, and suppressing disloyalty. Since many of the state councils were employed to promote the sale of federal Liberty Bonds and to elicit other formal support, such as collecting contributions to the Red Cross, their agents put pressure on citizens to show their loyalty and patriotism by contributing to the cause. The South Dakota Council of Defense, for example, sent a circular letter to the county councils in which it noted that some persons had refused to subscribe to the number of Liberty Bonds which had been apportioned to them by committees. "Such persons," the letter stated, "come under our classification as 'slackers,' and where they can afford to take certain amounts of bonds, can justly be suspicioned as being in opposition to the policy of our government." The letter went on to state, "there is no law upon our statute books governing such cases, but in these times there is a recognition of authority that has the right and power to inquire into the general conditions and reasons." [125] The county councils were thus advised to subpoena the delinquents and interrogate them about their ability to buy bonds. In Iowa "kangaroo" or "slacker" courts were set up, and special summonses were sent to people who had not subscribed to their imposed quota of bonds. In Missouri saloon-keepers who did not purchase bonds were threatened with revocation of their licenses. In Wisconsin a number of towns threatened to place the names of recalcitrants on a "Dishonor Roll," which would be exhibited in a prominent place.[126] Michigan merchants were threatened with classification

125. Council of National Defense Papers, April 30, 1918. National Archives.

126. The politics of the Wisconsin situation are interesting and not atypical. The Republican governor had packed the state council of defense with friends and supporters out to use it to embarrass the Demo-

as "pro-Germans" or "slackers" if they refused to take bonds in the amounts fixed by the local committee. In such an atmosphere, the vigilantes were not far behind. A Seattle citizen who did not buy bonds had his telephone line cut and yellow paint splashed on his house. In Wentworth, South Dakota, a man who refused to buy bonds was horsewhipped, his hair cut off, and his head painted red. In one community, where a group of Mennonites had refused to buy bonds because of their religious hostility to war, their cars were seized and sold at auction and the proceeds applied to Liberty Bonds.[127] Antiwar expression, whether verbal or symbolic, had little chance in the face of such coercion.

"Loose talk" was also carefully monitored by council agents.[128] In New Mexico, the state council sent a circular letter to the county councils, strongly hinting that the latter should send letters to certain individuals, informing them that they had uttered remarks unbecoming to a person "enjoying the liberty and protection of the United States," and stating emphatically "that such conduct will not be tolerated." [129] A second complaint would bring such remedy "as is necessary to counteract seditious conduct." Similar action was widely reported elsewhere. The criteria for what constituted "unbecoming remarks" was the province of the enforcing officer. In Missouri, some of the county

crats. The latter then moved into the Wisconsin Loyalty Legion as a body through which to retaliate. Lorin L. Cary, "Wisconsin Patriots Combat Disloyalty" (M.A. thesis, University of Wisconsin, 1965), pp. 65–68.

127. For a litany of such episodes, see Peterson and Fite, *Opponents of War*, pp. 141–46.

128. Frederick Lewis Allen, writing in *Century Magazine* 95 (December 1917), pp. 264–65, stated: "As time goes on, it becomes evident that no obligation lies more heavily upon the state councils than that of mobilizing public opinion, of spreading the gospel of a war to win peace for the world. Missouri and Iowa do not compromise with sedition. When disloyal utterances are reported to Mr. Young, chairman of the Iowa Council, he writes to the supposed traitor and asks him point-blank to declare whether he is for the United States or for Germany."

129. Council of National Defense Papers, August 25, 1917.

councils of defense sent out "Red, White, and Blue Cards" of warning to people accused of uttering antiwar sentiments. The results, as the state council reported, were gratifying:

The person to whom the first warning card is sent, generally takes it as a warning that they are being watched and immediately becomes very careful in their expressions. It has been found necessary in only a few cases to send a blue card to anyone and the red card has never been sent. The red card is simply a statement from the Council of Defense that the recipient will be reported immediately to the United States Secret Service.[130]

German-Americans were logical targets for such activity. Chronic victims of bond sellers, their language and their publications were also fair game. Harrassment of anyone or anything German clearly enhanced the loyal image of the harrasser. Many state councils agitated against the German language and in several cases effectively prohibited its use in the schools or other public places. The governor of Iowa prohibited the use of all languages except English in schools, churches, and in other public places. The South Dakota Council prohibited the use of German in public places, with one exception: It would issue permits for its use at funerals. Similarly, pressure from government officials, aided by various state councils, forced many German language newspapers to suspend publication.[131]

Western governors were particularly anxious to use state councils, or any other machinery available, to strike at the IWW. Although ultimately they succeeded in drawing various agencies of the federal government in to spearhead the attack on the organization, many state officials were prepared to use troops

130. Ibid., December 16, 1917.
131. Leubke, *Bonds of Loyalty,* pp. 215–17; Peterson and Fite, *Opponents of War,* pp. 195–96. An extreme example of such pressure occurred in Montana, where the state council ordered the public schools to cease using a textbook on ancient history written by Professor Willis Mason West because he gave too favorable a treatment of the Teutonic tribes prior to A.D. 812. At the time West was an active member of Creel's Committee on Public Information. Council of National Defense Papers, May, 1918.

to deal with them at the local level. Generally, the federal government followed a hands-off policy in these local situations. No operational precedents existed within the nation's legal and constitutional structure at the time to suggest that the federal government had any formal obligations to protect the rights of federal citizens against violation or abrogation by the states. The Fourteenth Amendment, which had been enacted as an instrument through which to achieve that end, had been so interpreted by the Supreme Court in the late nineteenth century as to deny its original purpose. Thus, the legal authority to intervene to prevent the state from trampling upon Bill of Rights protections did not exist. The converse was not true, however. State authorities were in no way reluctant to demand that the federal government do its duty in rooting out at the local level subversive activities and utterances which they deplored. Local hostility to the controversial antiwar figure, Robert M. LaFollette, after his September 1917 speech in St. Paul makes an interesting example. Numerous state councils of defense flooded Washington with demands that LaFollette be removed from office. The Wisconsin state council of defense drew up resolutions condemning the senator and sent them to president Wilson. While not going as far as one correspondent (who wrote to the Senate Committee on Privileges and Elections suggesting that a patriotic committee of the Senate and House investigate utterances by Senator LaFollette and others and that he should be "shot at once, without an hour's delay" if found guilty of traitorous statements), many council members made clear in their communications that failure of federal action to oust the senator would, in their eyes, constitute a disappointing endorsement of disloyalty.[132] Implicit in such arguments was the assumption that local standards of permissible freedom of expression should be implemented by federal authorities.

The response of the federal government to such arguments was cautious, especially toward the latter portion of the war

132. Belle C. and Fola LaFollette, *Robert M. LaFollette* (New York, 1953), pp. 763–78.

period. By then federal officials increasingly felt the need to consider growing demands that it take action to protect the rights of local citizens from unrestrained local superpatriots. John Lord O'Brian summarized the government's dilemma poignantly in a January 1919 speech to the New York State Bar Association in which he pointed out that:

a great strain was placed upon those charged with the administration of justice, whether federal or local officials. It was particularly troublesome to the federal authorities because of the incessant pleas on the one hand for the protection of these people in the exercise of what they claimed was legitimate political agitation and, on the other hand, the demand of their political opponents for indiscriminate prosecution. The duty of the federal officers was to enforce the law, but the great difficulty presented was that of obtaining unprejudiced statements of fact, and disentangling fragments of evidence from statements highly colored with partisan emotion.[133]

This sense of frustration experienced by federal officials extended to the patriotic voluntary bodies, which were eager and willing to use what little legal authorization they had to mobilize all citizens into unquestioning acquiescence to their particular version of 100-percent Americanism. Again, resultant policies flowed not from formal authorization, or even from the orders of organization officers, but from the mood of the self-appointed patriots involved and the level of hysteria of the moment.

These primarily self-appointed agents of coercion evinced little, if any, sensitivity to the civil liberties implications of the new wartime relationship between government and the citizen. They were equally insensitive to the fact that heavy-handed quasi-vigilante tactics employed to compel full compliance with governmental policies and programs might embarrass the government and raise civil liberties issues regarding this type of activity. Concern for the legitimacy of the means used, which came to trouble more sensitive administrative officers—and even at times the president—seemed scarcely to trouble such citizens

133. O'Brian, "Civil Liberty in Wartime," p. 13.

at all. The end was their only concern, so they proclaimed, and those who would divert attention from that end by carping about the implications of the means being used to attain it were obviously suspect in their patriotism. When administration officials moved to restrain the activities of such patriots, they were quick to charge the government with being weak-kneed in its wartime zeal and, in some extreme cases, with violating their constitutional rights to criticize both it and its enemies. The constant possibility that this type of retaliation could also tarnish the administration's professed liberal image made national leaders highly reluctant to apply the same criteria of permissible freedom of expression to such people as those that they professed to be employing in monitoring and restraining left-wing critics. Clearly, the patriots chose to view the government's hesitancy to restrict their actions as an informal sanction for their activities.

Various examples are pertinent. One of the ways in which the federal government acted most directly upon American citizens at this time was through national conscription. The turn to conscription early in the war raised a variety of concerns regarding the relationship of government to the citizen. The government, failing to recruit adequate military personnel through a voluntary system, reluctantly agreed to a plan developed by the General Staff to draft Americans into the army. Aware of Americans' resistance to being coerced into military service, Secretary of War Newton D. Baker was hesitant to have the draft administered by the army. He therefore agreed to a plan whereby administration of the Selective Service System was to be conducted through "neighborhood" civilian draft-boards, hoping thereby to create the illusion that the process was "democratic" and free of overt government interference.[134] The draft bill, which was signed into law by the president on May 18, 1917, called for full-scale registration of all able-bodied American adult males. There were certain designated

134. Carl B. Swisher, *American Constitutional Development* (Boston, 1954), pp. 600–01.

exemptions, including a narrowly defined category for conscientious objectors, but even those exempted were required to do noncombatant duty.[135] The draft was launched with much patriotic fanfare, a national "Registration Day" was designated, and despite the fact that Woodrow Wilson had quietly instructed his attorney general to prosecute any "slacker" who failed to report, with the penalty to be a year in prison, the registration for the draft was presented as an opportunity for Americans to demonstrate their patriotic citizenship. Compliance was generally good, the number of overt "draft dodgers" constituting a negligible segment of the eligible population.[136] But the situation afforded a tantalizing opportunity to patriots in the American Protective League, the National Security League, and the American Defense Society, especially, to take out after "slackers" and alleged slackers and to force patriotic citizenship upon them. Furthermore, such a mission opened up other opportunities for "constructive coercion."

All three of the major organizations were highly conservative in orientation, anti-alien in ideology, pro-business and anti-union in their politicoeconomic bias. The APL's membership consisted primarily of bankers, businessmen, successful attorneys, factory owners and foremen, chamber of commerce leaders, and insurance company executives, men with means and leisure to devote to the cause—men, who in many instances became members of draft boards, war bond sale committees, food- and fuel-rationing units, and state defense councils. From these positions they were frequently able to obtain illicit information about "troublesome" citizens, particularly those for

135. Exemptions included: officials of federal, state and most local offices; subjects of Germany and aliens without first citizenship papers; ministers of recognized religions and bona fide theological students; all military and naval personnel; persons engaged in essential industry and agriculture; men with dependents; the physically and morally unfit; and all members of recognized religious sects whose principles were opposed to war. See Warren S. Tryon, "The Draft in World War I," *Current History* 54 (June 1968): 344.

136. Ibid., p. 368.

whom conscription might be a sobering experience.[137] Attorney General Gregory, hoping to channel the energies of these people into something constructive, found that one obvious assignment for them was to assist in the conscription process. At the request of the provost marshal general, at least one APL member sat on "each local and district exemption board [in the country] to accomplish the location and apprehension of delinquent registrants." [138]

The role of the National Security League and the American Defense Society was less formal but at times more coercive and intimidating. The more powerful National Security League was organized in December 1914 to promote military preparedness and universal military training. It attracted the support of prominent pro-Ally politicians, military figures, and wealthy industrialists and financiers.[139] Ostensibly nonpartisan, the NSL failed to satisfy the political appetites of some of its frankly anti-Wilson members, who withdrew in August 1915 to form the American Defense Society. The new organization became a more tightly Republican, though less influential, version of the NSL, despite Theodore Roosevelt's prominent association with it as honorary president. With the war both bodies turned their energies to forging national unity through systematic propaganda efforts. This included vigorous, wide-scale pamphleteering and vigorous assaults upon everything German within this country: One of the American Defense Society's more widely distributed pamphlets was entitled "Throw Out the German Language and All Disloyal Teachers." [140] Both organizations lost no time in denouncing purveyors of dangerous radical ideologies such as the IWW, the Socialists, and the Non-Partisan League as in-

137. On the APL see Joan M. Jensen, *The Price of Vigilance* (Chicago, 1968).

138. Harold M. Hyman, *To Try Men's Souls* (Berkeley, 1959), p. 290.

139. Robert D. Ward, "The Origin and Activities of the National Security League, 1917–1919," *Mississippi Valley Historical Review* 47 (June 1960).

140. Leubke, *Bonds of Loyalty*, p. 216.

hibiters of the war effort. One ADS pamphlet, *AWAKE, AMERICA,* published in 1918 by a trustee of the organization, warned the reader to "Beware of organized German-pacifists; pro-German Socialists, pro-German anarchists, and venomous I.W.W.'s." [141] The latter super-patriots lacked the authority to harrass such enemies legally. The conscription system provided a possible route.

Here Attorney General Gregory found himself in a peculiarly uncomfortable position. By 1918 the excesses of these groups were beginning to produce considerable negative feedback. Unpopular citizens and groups were being subjected to a variety of forms of harrassment, ranging from simple intimidation to beatings and lynchings.[142] By June, President Wilson, Gregory, Creel, and a number of lesser national officials were conducting energetic public relations campaigns deploring the mob spirit abroad in the land and charging that intemperate patriotism was providing critics of the country with a growing body of propaganda with which to assail American democracy as a sham. In June Gregory warned the Council of National Defense, the state councils, and all the APL locals in the country that:

The suppression of sedition . . . rests entirely with the Department of Justice. It is a technical and difficult task which outside agencies are likely to confuse and obstruct. . . . undertake no work for the detection and repression of sedition except such as is expressly requested or authorized by . . . the U.S. Department of Justice and done on its behalf.[143]

Such warnings went virtually unheeded, despite their position as official doctrines. In order to direct the energies of such groups into more constructive activity and to disarm public criticism of the Justice Department for its failure to arrest men

141. Thomas A. Lawrence, "Eclipse of Liberty: Civil Liberties in the United States During the First World War," *Wayne Law Review* 21 (1974): 55–57.

142. For the Herbert Bigelow incident, see Chapter 5. An equally infamous example of vigilante tactics was the Frank Little lynching in Montana. For details see Peterson and Fite, *Opponents of War,* pp. 57–60.

143. Quoted in Hyman, *To Try Men's Souls,* p. 289.

avoiding the draft, Gregory set out to employ the American Protective League to stage a series of "slacker raids" throughout the country. The league plunged into this assignment with the greatest enthusiasm. In dozens of cities government agents and their volunteer auxiliaries raided theaters, hotels, restaurants, train and bus depots, factories, union halls, offices, and even private homes, herding thousands of young men into over-crowded detention centers to check their draft cards. When admittedly only 5 percent of the men so detained turned out to be genuine draft dodgers, public response—already some-what negative—became particularly stormy.[144]

The raids in New York City, thought by many to be the national haven for slackers and deserters, finally brought the civil liberties violations implicit in the behavior of the raiders into national focus. The New York raids were massive in scope and carried out—with particular insenitivity—largely by APL agents in early September 1918. But the high-handedness of many overly zealous raiders produced an adverse reaction across the country which opened the door to Woodrow Wilson's critics for vigorous and loud charges that his administration had no respect for the basic civil liberties of citizens. The *New York World,* a pro-Wilson newspaper, charged that the raiders had no warrants for arrest or any official standing and concluded, in an editorial entitled "Amateur Prussianism in New York," that the arrest of any number of slackers "could not excuse this rape of the law—this ravishing of the very spirit of American institutions." [145] In the meantime, anti-Wilson senators were pre-paring a resolution to denounce the action. Wilson, anxious to head off criticism and avert public controversy, promptly an-nounced that he was launching an investigation of the Justice Department. Attorney General Gregory immediately promised full cooperation, admitting that the APL, which had been en-couraged by the department to involve itself in the raids, had been led into breaches of propriety "by an excessive zeal for the

144. Jensen, *Price of Vigilance,* pp. 188–218.
145. *New York World,* September 6, 1918, p. 8.

public good." [146] He acknowledged, however, that "this does not excuse their actions." He then sent John Lord O'Brian to New York to investigate. O'Brian, clearly the most concerned civil libertarian in the department, publicly stated that he intended to determine whether the raids constituted interference with the personal liberties of citizens. He took pains in his public statement to disassociate the department from the APL, which he characterized as a "private concern." [147] The action proved effective for Wilson's purposes. It communicated the administration's immediate concern for civil liberties to the public and in the process undercut mounting Republican criticism. By the end of September, the particular civil liberties issues raised by the episode had largely been deflected, to the President's considerable relief and comfort.

The members of the National Security League and the American Defense Society were never afforded similar authorization for their activities from the federal government, although they frequently claimed that their activities were carried out to implement the policies of the state councils of defense, which were agents of the National Council. The administration disputed such claims when the organizations' zeal drew public reaction, and especially when they engaged in bitter criticism of the president. George Creel was particularly caustic regarding these groups, and in later years characterized them as "the most obnoxious of the hysteria manufacturing bodies, whose patriotism was, at times, a thing of screams, violence, and extremes." They were chiefly responsible, Creel charged years later, "for the development of a mob spirit in many sections." [148]

Any empirically precise analysis of public reaction to the whole national pattern of repression is impossible. Attitudinal surveys were not carried out at the time, nor were public opinion polls taken. Impressionistic and anecdotal evidence, however, tends to suggest a number of things. By and large, the country's

146. Jensen, *Price of Vigilance,* p. 210.
147. *The New York Times,* September 8, 1918, p. 9.
148. Creel, *Rebel at Large,* p. 196.

collective political conscience regarding civil liberties was not sufficiently well developed to make a meaningful general response. By and large the public was less likely to react to the steady expansion of the government's formal repressive policies and mechanisms than to specific episodes and outrages with which they could identify in a highly personalized way. Regrettably, for the scholar, little satisfactory documentation remains which affords any accurate contemporary group response to the wide range of nationally reported episodes which punctuated the war period. Reciting some of the more colorful, however, affords a flavor of wartime behavior. Consider the following:

- Five hundred citizens of Collinsville, Illinois, who had decided that a fellow townsman, Robert Prager, was a German spy, dragged him into the street, wrapped him in the flag, and then murdered him.

- Beethoven's music was banned in Pittsburgh for the duration of the war.

- The Los Angeles Board of Education forbade all discussions of peace, even the program of the League to Enforce Peace headed by former President William H. Taft, in the schools of Los Angeles.

- Will H. Hicks, a former minister, was seized by a mob at Elk City, Oklahoma, and given a coating of tar and feathers for alleged propaganda against Liberty bonds.

- E. V. Hanegan, of Washington, D.C., began a crusade for melting down the statute of Frederick the Great at the national capital, making two million nails from the metal, and using them to drive into "Koffins of Kultur" to be set up in countless American cities.

- J. M. Ellis, a black Baptist preacher, was beaten by a mob at Newport, Arkansas, for alleged treasonable utterances which were regarded as unproved by a grand jury after he had been kept in jail for ninety-six days.

- Aliens were barred from holding licenses and permits to do business within the city limits of Cleveland, Ohio.

- Former United States Senator R. F. Pettigrew's law offices at Sioux Falls, South Dakota, were daubed with yellow paint. He had opposed America's entry into the war.

- The conservative American *Review of Reviews,* edited by Dr. Albert Shaw, was barred from the New York high schools for publishing an article to the effect that "the Entente's arrogant declaration of a patchwork program of spoils and conquests" prevented a peace without victory before the United States entered the war.

- At Mount Olive, near St. Louis, Missouri, a mob led by prominent businessmen compelled P. Hein, a leading merchant charged with making disloyal remarks, to kneel on the icy sidewalk in his night clothes and kiss each of the forty-eight stars on the flag.

- At Salisbury, Pennsylvania, Charles Klinge was beaten and made to walk across the street with a dog chain around his neck, was forced to kiss the flag, and was then ducked, for alleged disloyal remarks.

- At Marysville, Nebraska, a mob broke into a school, removed all books and material either written in German or about Germany, including Bibles in German, piled them outside and burned them.

- In Detroit, Louis Rafelburge, who was said to have made unfavorable remarks about the Red Cross, was taken from his home in his night clothes, given a haircut and had his mustache trimmed by members of a mob which for a while threatened to duck him in the river.

- After being tarred and feathered, George Koetzer, a brewery worker of San Jose, California, was chained to a brass cannon in the city park. He was charged with having made pro-German remarks.

- Clarence Nesbitt, of Thetford Township, Michigan, was tarred and feathered by a group of men who were displeased because he bought only $1,500 worth of Liberty Bonds instead of the $3,000 that they thought he ought to have purchased.

- The Austrian-born violinist, Fritz Kreisler, and the famous Swiss-born conductor of the Boston Symphony, Dr. Karl Muck, were denied access to American music halls.

- In Columbus, Ohio, school teachers were required to meet after school to paste in school music books blank sheets of paper covering "The Watch on the Rhine" and "The Lorelei."

- In 1917, Emma Goldman, anarchist writer and editor and militant feminist, was arrested for obstructing the draft and sentenced to two years in prison in Jefferson City, Missouri. Upon her release she was deported to Russia.

- In July 1917, 1,200 striking IWWs and their sympathizers, in Bisbee, Arizona, were corralled in a ball park by armed businessmen and mine officials, herded into cattle cars, and shipped into the Arizona desert and left to shift for themselves in a situation where they were wholly without an adequate supply of food and water.

- Victor Berger, Milwaukee Socialist editor, whose newspaper, the *Milwaukee Leader,* was indicted for violating the Espionage Act, was denied his seat, with only one dissenting vote, following election to the House of Representatives. One congressman summarized the opposition position, "The one and only issue in this case is that of Americanism."

- A South Dakota farmer who opposed the war received a five-year sentence for advising a young man not to enlist in the army, and saying "that it was all foolishness to send our boys over there to get killed by the thousands, all for the sake of Wall Street."

- Charles A. Schenck, a Philadelphia Socialist, was arrested under the federal Espionage Act, and sentenced to fine and imprisonment for distributing literature critical of the draft.

- Joseph H. Odell, pastor of the First Presbyterian Church of Troy, New York, charged in an article in the *Atlantic Monthly* that preachers were to blame for the whole world situation. "The Kaiser is what he is because preachers are what they are," Odell claimed. "They, with their German theology, have taken all the supernatural element out of the Bible under the inspiration of the Kaiser himself."

- In Montana, Ves Hall was arrested and charged with espionage for having stated that he would not go to war, that Germany would win, that President Wilson was crooked, and that the war was being fought for the benefit of Wall Street millionaires.

- John White, an Ohio farmer, was sentenced to twenty-one months in the penitentiary for stating that soldiers in American camps "were dying off like flies" and that the "murder of innocent women and children by German soldiers was no worse than the United States' soldiers did in the Philippines."

- In Texas, three organizers of the Non-Partisan League were arrested and jailed for disloyalty. When M. M. Offut, state office manager, protested, he was seized and had his hair and beard cut off with sheep shears before he was driven out of town. The three men were taken by a mob and given a severe whipping. The *Greenville* (Texas) *Banner* stated that this was evidence that "Americanism" is not to be tampered with around Mineola."

- A Minnesota man was arrested under the Minnesota Espionage Act for criticizing women knitting socks for soldiers, in stating, "No soldier ever sees these socks."

- Carl Wold, a small-town Minnesota newspaper editor, was physically assaulted and his presses wrecked as a result of his refusing to publish editorials critical of the Non-Partisan League.

- Fred Boyd was beaten up in Rector's Restaurant in New York City for not standing up when the National Anthem was played.

- Women in charge of the Emergency Peace Federation, headquartered in Washington, D.C., were ordered by militiamen to close the office and "beat it," or they would be "raided and raped."

- Six farmers in Texas were horsewhipped because they had not subscribed to the Red Cross.

- George Maynard of Medford, Oregon, a member of the International Bible Students' Association, had an iron cross painted on his chest, and was driven out of town.

- In Baltimore, the day before Wilson's war message, rioters broke up a meeting at which David Starr Jordan, president of Stanford University, was to talk under the auspices of the American Union against Militarism, chanting "We'll hang Dave Jordan to a sour apple tree." *The New York Times* noted that the mob was led by "men socially prominent," including "college professors, students, bankers, and lawyers."

- The producers of a film *The Spirit of '76* which dealt exclusively with the American Revolution but showed scenes unflattering to the British army, was convicted of attempting to cause insubordination in the armed forces of the United States and sentenced to prison for ten years.

- D. T. Blodgett was sentenced to twenty years in prison for circulating a pamphlet urging the voters of Iowa not to re-elect a congressman who had voted for conscription.

- Twenty-seven South Dakota farmers were convicted for sending a petition to the government objecting to the draft quota for their county and calling the war a "capitalist's war." [149]

149. For an attempt to quantify similar episodes in one state, see John D. Stevens, "Press and Community Toleration: Wisconsin in World War I, *Journalism Quarterly* 46 (Summer 1969): 255–59; and "When Sedition Laws Were Enforced: Wisconsin in World War I," *Wisconsin Academy of Sciences, Arts and Letters* 58 (1970): 39–60.

5

Faltering Efforts
to Make Civil Liberties
a Legitimate
National Agenda Item

WHILE MANY AMERICANS reacted negatively to wartime excesses in the curtailment of individual freedom, such reactions produced little constructive counter-action to secure the protection of those freedoms. Clearly, there was not, as yet, a sufficient collective consciousness regarding the importance of protecting civil liberties to generate vigorous, broad-based citizen participation programs on their behalf. As Zechariah Chafee, Jr., later observed, "the First Amendment had no hold on people's minds, because no live facts or concrete images were then attached to it. Consequently, like an empty box, with beautiful words on it, the Amendment collapsed under the impact of Prussian battalions, and terror of Bolshevik mobs."[1] To Americans of the World War I era, little was to be gained by active crusades for civil liberties. At a time when government leaders were emphasizing the citizen's obligation to sacrifice certain freedoms in order to secure victory and a liberal society, involvement in a movement which seemed to place people against their government smacked of disloyalty and a lack of patriotism.

1. Zechariah Chafee, Jr., *Thirty-Five Years with Freedom of Speech* (New York, 1952), p. 4.

There was, however, a small but aggressive minority of Americans who felt differently. Apprehensive about the repression which war was bringing to the country, these citizens saw ominous implications in the troubling new relationships evolving between the federal government and the citizen. Power arrangements of an earlier era, in which national leadership was vested in the great entrepreneurs and financiers, were being supplanted by the leadership of a directorate of capitalist managers in the government bureaucracy. Where business leaders' power over citizens had been informal, subtle, and indirect, the new bureaucrats sought to act directly with legal sanctions. This new legal relationship between the government and its citizens involved the creation of precedents for the limitation of citizens' rights which posed a long-term threat to their continued existence. But the situation had even more ominous overtones. What the government seemed to be saying was that the very act of dissent was not a legitimate mode of political behavior, since the motives of those who engaged in such behavior were necessarily devious, dubious, and destructive. Whereas previously the government had protected, or at least been neutral toward, unorthodox political thought and expression, it now felt an obligation to punish it. Such a view incorporated some aspects of Progressive paternalism. But to some, it also incorporated some disturbing aspects of Prussianism as well.

Civil libertarian activists perceived a pressing need to counter these developments, and to do so quickly, in order to prevent a hardening of these new and allegedly temporary institutional arrangements—with the restrictive civil liberties assumptions which they embodied into a permanent new system highly threatening to the rights of citizens in a democracy. This entailed bringing these risks to the attention of millions of Americans, most of whom had little interest in having their consciousness raised on these questions. It meant inducing citizens to embrace the idea that civil liberties was a legitimate, debatable issue; that to disagree with the government regarding the permissible limits of free speech, free press, and peaceful assemblage in a wartime period was a defensible action; that in a democracy there were at least two sides to public issues. The permissible limits of the curtailment of civil liberties was one of those questions, and a vital one. For the government to claim that the issue of permissible limits of free speech, free press, and peaceable assembly was not debatable was to betray its lack of faith in the capacity of the American people to make an intelligent, rational, and patriotic policy choice on an issue directly affecting their well-being. Such civil liberties activists were calling for an elementary faith in the democratic process and were rejecting the theory and practice of progressive leaders who wished to manage these issues so as to insure unquestioned acquiescence to the formal national "party line." That taking such a position threatened them with charges of disloyalty and lack of patriotism struck the libertarians as ironic. Why should it be risky, in a democracy, to argue for the proper protection of Bill of Rights freedoms? Why should it be suspect to argue that people who disagreed with the government and went too far in the use of their freedoms should at least have a fair trial? And why, above all, should people who insisted that such arguments were legitimate subjects for public discussion, be identified as hostile to governmental security policies in wartime and subjected to repression themselves?

It was on these grounds that civil libertarians hoped to draw support behind their cause, but the wartime situation made this difficult. Since they had little expectation of reaching people through their consciences, they hoped to personalize the civil liberties situation by presenting concrete evidence of what the government was doing. Repression of immigrants, radicals, suspected hyphenates, and slackers could clearly become a precedent for the same type of repressive activity against the doctrines, attitudes, or behavior of others who were in any way out of tune with the dominant majority in power. If Americans could be made to see that the massive repressive mechanism which the government had created could actually be turned against them, it was hoped that such an appeal to self-interest might make an enduring impression on patriotic minds.

Implicit in the civil libertarian position was the assumption that once their countrymen were convinced that they had a personal stake in this debate they might be persuaded to embrace the abstract notion that the American tradition of civil liberties encompassed a concept of equal rights for all. Universal civil liberties presupposed that the law applied equitably and fairly to all citizens in all places and at all times. To achieve this end it was essential to educate people to see that embracing an abstract commitment to universal civil liberties had benefits for them, as well as for the general society. Such a view was certainly not compatible with American history, nor current in the American society of 1917 and 1918. The traditional operation of American institutions, to say nothing of the assumptions on which they proceeded, in no way presupposed such a version of what Bill of Rights freedoms did and should mean in American society. Thus, the situation in 1917 was hardly a hopeful one, despite the ardor which hard-core civil liberties advocates were prepared to bring to it.

There were a number of groups to whom civil liberties activists hoped that they might turn for sympathetic support. In each case either the behavior of the group suggested that it valued civil liberties principles, or the wartime harrassment that the group was experiencing suggested that it should. At the national level Republican leaders in the Congress and prominent party figures with national support such as Theodore Roosevelt devoted considerable wartime energy to criticizing Wilson for his dictatorial behavior, charging him and his lieutenants with unwarranted abuse of free speech and press. Their motives, however, were thoroughly partisan and politically self-serving. They were in no danger of having their own expression suppressed by any of the wartime legislation or by any of the federal officials implementing it. Yet their ability to charge, as they did whenever it seemed politically advantageous, that the Wilson administration's attempts to place itself above criticism, that its call for suspension of partisan politics and its insistence that certain of its policies were not debatable, were unjustified gave them civil liberties issues with which to denounce its excessive repressiveness to the voters. The appeal of such tactics was underlined by the substantial gains the Republicans made in the elections of 1918.[2] But to get such partisan manipulators of the civil liberties issue to see that the administration behavior which they were deploring was an unwarranted and unjustified threat to the freedom of aliens, radicals, pacifists, conscientious objectors, and other opponents of the war, was something else. There were few Republican votes to be gained from such elements, and the political costs of supporting their full Bill of Rights protections were too high. In fact, to the extent that the Republican party at this point represented American business, it was highly desirable to have Wilson and his lieutenants utilizing the wartime emergency to suppress such critics of the American business system as the IWW, the Non-Partisan League, the Socialists, and other enemies. Thus, such leaders could have their cake and eat it too. They could criticize the Wilson government for being too repressive, while reaping the benefits of that repression in seeing business critics tamed, if not eliminated. Further, with civil liberties spokesmen such as Roger Baldwin and Norman Thomas insisting that the struggle for civil liberties was very largely a struggle against the evils of industrial capitalism, there was little incentive to affiliate with such an "enemy."

The behavior of the leaders of the nation's press was similar to that of Republican and business leadership and thus, they offered equally discouraging prospects as recruits to the civil liberties cause. The conservative press was frequently an adjunct of big business and was generally Republican. It had little hesitancy to blast away at Wilson, his liberalism, his periodic arbitrariness, and especially his administration's censorship policies. This not only made good critical copy and points for conservative causes, but enabled editors to "run up the flag" of press freedom in such a way as to serve their own self-

2. Seward W. Livermore, *Politics Is Adjourned: Woodrow Wilson and the War Congress* (Middletown, Conn., 1966), explores the elections and their results.

interest and sell newspapers. As the spokesmen for a very influential segment of society, there was very little likelihood that they would become targets for suppression. But when liberal or radical journals were suppressed or banned from the mails, or their editors harrassed, very little conservative press support was expressed for those so victimized. As Sally Miller has pointed out in her study of Victor Berger, the Socialist editor, whose *Milwaukee Leader* was excluded from the mails: " . . . the popular press saw no cause for alarm. Outside of a number of former radicals, current radicals, and those still suffering the birth pangs of radicalism, few defended the constitution. [New York Socialist Congressman] Meyer London's voice was nearly the only one heard in Congress demanding the absolute right of freedom of expression." [3]

A greater potential for support seemed to lie within victimized groups. Previously, left-wing critics, from anarchists to agrarian collectivists, had been free to criticize all aspects of the American system, and even to launch extensive recruiting campaigns in an effort to bring about a major and generally socialistic restructuring of the American political and economic structure. However, the war changed all this. Now such activity was formally open to proscription through legal criminalization. To continue it meant risking heavy legal sanctions, not only for the leaders, but even for rank and file followers. Thus, for such Americans to participate actively in the more formal civil liberties movement was to ask them to add an additional stigma to their already substantial vulnerability, particularly since participation in the civil liberties movement was seen by many as a concrete form of wartime disloyalty. Further, in a practical sense, members of such organizations could not see civil liberties as a useful vehicle for obtaining their ends. Granted, the upgrading of such liberties as speech, press, and assembly might reopen a useful path toward their goals, but this seemed unlikely in a period when national security was a prime and central value. The only possible utility which embracing civil liberties

3. Sally M. Miller, *Victor Berger and the Promise of Constructive Socialism, 1910–1920* (Westport, Ct., 1973), p. 195.

might have was symbolic. Deploring the government's repressive path might throw some doubts on policies adverse to their self-interest. Manipulating the civil liberties issue, in other words, might elicit sympathy and support for antigovernment activities, and make government agents more cautious in the enforcement of particularly repressive statutes.

The price of such action, however, was totally different for left-wing victims than for the "haves" of society. No one questioned the loyalty of business, despite its frequent grumbling about government policies. Business, after all, was the cornerstone of the capitalist system. If advocates of social reconstruction and industrial democracy were to criticize the Wilson administration too vehemently for its undue repressiveness, they simply enhanced their own vulnerability by revealing their lack of patriotism. And in the minds of various of their leaders, this was to add a needlessly harmful impediment to the attainment of the sharp, social and political changes which they were seeking.

Specific examples of this dilemma are revealing. From its inception, the IWW had been unpopular, not only with the American business establishment, but with traditional labor organizations such as the American Federation of Labor (AF of L), whose conservatism and lack of concern for the unskilled worker made them targets of the IWW's stinging criticism. The Wobblies had long been intrigued with the possibility of manipulating civil liberties symbolism to advance their cause. The most obvious example was the "free speech fight" in which Wobblies would enter a community to stage public demonstrations, usually speaking on busy street corners from soap boxes—in defiance of local ordinances—and thereby invite arrest. When one Wobbly speaker was hauled off by the police, another would take his place, until the local jail was overflowing. It was initially hoped that such arrests would make martyrs of the speakers and generate publicity for the "cause." [4] By 1916, however, the IWW

4. Paul F. Brissenden, *The I.W.W.: A Study of American Syndicalism* (New York, 1920), pp. 260–64. See also Donald M. Barnes, "The Ideology of the Industrial Workers of the World: 1905–1921" (Ph.D. dissertation, Washington State University, 1962), pp. 147 ff.

had abandoned the free speech fight in recognition of its limited usefulness and its potentially negative impact. Their use of the tactic had been cynical from the outset. They had little interest in constitutional principles, per se, but in expanding the ranks and the power of the organization. By flaunting their own repression by those in power they hoped to prove that bourgeois society's alleged commitment to freedom was meaningless. This aided their attempt to demonstrate that the symbols of the system were sheer hypocrisy and that it was time to call for the destruction of the system. In the meantime, as free-speech fight after free-speech fight saw their most courageous members "murdered, maimed, beaten, and starved," and as the fights created as much adverse as favorable publicity and seemed to stimulate vigilantism against the Wobblies, they reached a point where further manipulation of civil liberties symbolism seemed not only futile but counterproductive.[5] They came into the wartime period seriously disillusioned by their prior attempts to utilize civil liberties consciousness to advance their ends.

When the federal government launched massive prosecutions of the leaders of the organization under the new wartime espionage and sedition legislation, the IWW felt even less like reviving earlier free speech arguments in their own defense. Further, they fatalistically accepted the fact that their antimilitarist, anticonscription, and wartime strike activities would make them vulnerable to suppression by a government seeking to mobilize a citizens' fighting force and to insure a steady flow of materials for the military forces. When, on September 5, 1917, federal officials raided various IWW headquarters and union offices across the country and seized all available records, documents, correspondence, and literature, the Wobblies were outraged but not surprised. In the aftermath of these raids, they were less concerned with pursuing civil liberties violations in the courts than with finding legal counsel which would attempt to save what remnants of the body's cohesiveness and authority

5. William Preston, "Shall This Be All?" *Labor History* 12 (Summer 1971): 446–47.

still existed. They turned their attention largely to urging those liberals with a civil liberties conscience to engage in fundraising activities on their behalf. Ironically, those civil liberties types who agreed to do so found themselves stigmatized by such association, which put them in the uncomfortable position of having to reevaluate whether specific involvement in immediate civil liberties crises would advance the broader cause of attaining abstract civil liberties or undermine it.

The situation of the Socialists was a variation, although an important one, on the same theme. If the IWW was a hated and feared minority of rowdy, Rabelaisian itinerants, the Socialist party was very much the opposite. By 1916 the organization had a membership running into the hundreds of thousands and its political strength, especially in local elections, was growing steadily—and, in some cases, dramatically. Up to this time, the party had suffered no overt repression, either in being denied access to the ballot or in censorship of its publications and the speeches of its leaders. It thus had not felt any necessity to utilize civil liberties arguments as devices to gain access to the political process. When the war broke out in Europe in 1914, American Socialists had issued an antiwar manifesto replete with anticapitalist rhetoric, a position which was endorsed in a mail referendum vote by a large majority of its membership in September 1915. The party, however, was generally more concerned with rhetoric and doctrine than direct action. Daniel Bell has written: "The American Socialist Party was heavily a doctrinaire Socialist Party, more so than most of its European counterparts, because of its lack of commitments to the labor movement. With none of the strings of responsibilities which held the European socialists, the party, reacting by formulas, branded the war 'imperialist' and then stood apart from it."[6] With American entry, the party promptly held an emergency convention in St. Louis and announced its opposi-

6. Daniel Bell, "The Background and Development of Marxian Socialism in the United States," in Donald D. Egbert and Stow Persons, *Socialism and American Life* (Princeton, 1952), 1:266.

tion. Its antiwar declaration restated a classic Marxist analysis of war, emphasizing that war was inherent in competing capitalist-imperialist drives for markets and insisting that American entry was instigated by the predatory capitalists' of the United States, who were out to profit from the manufacture and sale of munitions and war supplies and from the exportation of American food stuffs and other necessities. Its authors, Morris Hillquit, Algernon Lee, and Charles Ruthernberg, went on to brand the war "a crime against the people of the United States," and pledged that "we will not willingly give a single life or a single dollar." [7] This St. Louis Proclamation was ratified by the national membership by a margin of 10 to 1.

The result was twofold. On one hand, a group of prominent conservative intellectual Socialists (Allan Benson, W. J. Ghent, Gustavus Myers, J. G. Phelps-Stokes, Charles Edward Russell, A. M. Simons, Upton Sinclair, John Spargo, and William English Walling) deserted the cause, thereby depriving the party of some of its aura of respectability and widening the gap between progressives and radicals.[8] In publicly denouncing the party as "un-neutral, un-American, and pro-German," former Socialist leaders clearly provided ammunition to those patriots seeking an excuse to suppress it. Within this spectrum only Upton Sinclair seemed conscious of the potential for abrogation of the civil liberties of antiwar Socialists which this action opened up. While he supported the war, with important qualifications, he insisted that Socialists had a right to oppose the war and that the government was defeating the ends which it was supposedly fighting for when it stifled criticism.[9]

7. James Weinstein, *The Decline of Socialism in America* (New York, 1965), p. 125.

8. Simons became director of the Bureau of Literature of the Wisconsin Loyalty League during the war. Myers, after offering his services to Woodrow Wilson, was assigned by George Creel to the League for National Unity, a right-wing patriotic group headed by Ralph M. Easley of the National Civil Federation. David Shannon, *The Socialist Party of America* (New York, 1955), p. 100.

9. Upton Sinclair, *The Autobiography of Upton Sinclair* (New York, 1962).

The second consequence of the party's wartime stand was to enhance its strength and popularity with antiwar groups and individuals. Because it was the only political party which was antiwar, it found mounting support in Northern industrial and foreign-language centers. In the local elections of 1917, the Socialist party vote reached an all-time high. In New York City, Morris Hillquit ran for mayor and polled 22 percent of the city's vote. The party sent ten assemblymen to Albany, seven aldermen to the city hall, and even elected a municipal court judge. In Chicago the party received nearly 34 percent of the vote; in Buffalo, 25 percent; and even in conservative Ohio, significant totals were registered in every major city: Dayton, 44 percent; Toledo, 34.8 percent; Cleveland, 19.3 percent; and Cincinnati, 11.9 percent.[10] Such success, along with exposés by party defectors, made it thoroughly suspect and highly vulnerable to wartime suppression. Most of its major antiwar leaders were indicted under the Espionage or Sedition Acts before the conflict was over, virtually the entire Socialist press was closed down by Postmaster Burleson, and doubts were raised publicly as to whether duly elected Socialist officials should be allowed to take their seats and serve in the offices for which they had been chosen.

As with the IWW, while civil liberties violations in these circumstances were overt, massive, and relentless, the possibility of alleviating such oppression by active involvement in formal civil liberties work seemed both remote and fruitless. Although Socialists like Sinclair (or, later, Norman Thomas) did become involved in the defense of civil liberties in certain cases and circumstances, the antiwar elements of the party could see few advantages to be gained from such action.

The record of the Non-Partisan League provided yet another variation on this theme. Harrassed by conservative state authorities in Minnesota and the Dakotas, the league's leaders saw little hope of drawing the federal government into local affairs to protect their civil liberties when it was prepared to

10. Bell, "Background and Development," pp. 314–15.

proclaim neither its legal authority nor its desire to intervene at the state level on behalf of Bill of Rights guarantees. Although the league utilized civil liberties rhetoric far more heavily during the war period than either the IWW or the Socialists and its counsel, Arthur LeSueur, became an early convert to and laborer in the civil liberties movement, the commitment of rank-and-file membership to abstract civil liberties as a viable and vital cause was minimal.[11]

The American Federation of Labor's civil liberties concerns were well illustrated in that body's relationship to the Wilson government. It early adopted a "no strike" pledge, promised complete compliance with the orders of the War Labor Board, and welcomed the responsibility to assist in repressing the alleged "enemies" of the Wilson government, be they pacifists and antiwar agitators or left-wing labor bodies. In the latter case, its antagonistic relationship with the People's Council of America for Democracy and Peace, an antiwar body made up of groups and individuals connected with the labor movement which did not share the prowar views of the AF of L's leadership, is revealing. The People's Council drew its support from antiwar Socialists, some Wobblies, some German-American and Irish-American workers, and some Russian-Jewish workers attracted by the Russian Revolution and its peace proposals. At a meeting in New York City on May 30, 1917, representatives of these groups endorsed the peace terms of the Russian Revolution and the maintenance of minimum living standards for American workers. They also called for the repeal of conscription and the defense of civil liberties while denouncing the AF of L for its support of the war. At that point it proposed to establish a permanent national People's Council, with branch organizations known as Workmen's Councils. By the end of June, the People's Council claimed that 284 organizations were

11. On the civil liberties aspects of the NPL, see Carol Jenson, "Agrarian Pioneer in Civil Liberties: The Non-Partisan League in Minnesota" (Ph.D. dissertation, University of Minnesota, 1968), and Carol Jensen, "Loyalty as a Political Weapon," *Minnesota History* 43 (Summer 1972): 43–57.

affiliated with it, and of these almost a hundred were trade unions. The rest were local Socialist, peace, or fraternal organizations.[12]

Seeing the movement as a challenge both to his leadership and to his prowar posture, AF of L President Samuel Gompers reacted with alarm and annoyance. He therefore urged the formation of an American Alliance for Labor and Democracy to support the United States government, encourage Americanization, and foster loyalty.[13] When the People's Council announced an organization convention in Minneapolis on September 1, 1917, alliance leaders announced that they would meet in the same city at the same time. At that meeting, alliance conference delegates resolved that anyone who publicly opposed the government in arms was taking undue advantage of civil liberties and "should be repressed by the constituted authorities."[14] But Gompers and the constituted authorities had already out maneuvered the People's Council. Prior to its September 1 meeting, the Gompers group sent the alliance's secretary, Robert Meisel, to Minneapolis to rent all the available halls so that the People's Council would have no place to convene. The governor of Minnesota, J. A. A. Burnquist, proclaiming vigorously that freedom of speech did not apply to traitors, issued a proclamation forbidding any meeting of the council in any city in Minnesota. And although this action drew criticism—the conservative *Milwaukee Free Press* denounced the governor's behavior as "one of the most abominable infringements of the constitutional rights of American citizens which the record of this country has to offer"[15]—the People's Council did not meet in Minnesota. Rather, it retreated to Chicago, at the invitation of

12. C. Roland Marchand, *The American Peace Movement and Social Reform, 1898–1918* (Princeton, 1972), pp. 294–98.

13. See Frank L. Grubbs, Jr., *The Struggle for Labor Loyalty: Gompers, the A.F. of L., and the Pacifists, 1917–1920* (Durham, N.C., 1968).

14. Samuel Gompers, "Labor and Democracy," *American Federationist* 24 (October 1917): 840.

15. Quoted in Louis P. Lochner, *Always the Unexpected* (New York, 1956), p. 69.

the outspokenly anti-British mayor, Big Bill Thompson, who agreed to see to it that the body could meet undisturbed in his city. There the council drew up a constitution defining its objectives in terms anticipating Woodrow Wilson's later Fourteen Points, including its intention "to defend our constitutional rights of free speech, free press, peaceful assemblage, and the right to petition the government. . . ."[16] Gompers, however, was determined to have the last word. At the AF of L's 1917 convention, he demanded a full endorsement of the American Alliance for Peace and Democracy and its program as an act of loyalty. The action did not escape debate. One delegate even complained that "the Alliance was hand in glove with a government that was unjustifiably suppressing free speech."[17] Such a view proved to be a minority one, however, and ultimately not only was endorsement achieved but the delegates' patriotism carried over to the next AF of L convention, when they endorsed both the Espionage Act of 1917 and its Sedition Act amendment of the following May.[18] No campaign to win the support of such labor patriots in the effort to make civil liberties a serious public policy concern ever came to fruition.

The lack of support from the above groups disappointed but did not surprise the civil libertarians. They were aware that neither powerful industrialists and financiers nor the working classes had ever assumed any important role in prior reform movements in America. They were also aware that revolutionary anarchists, socialists, and syndicalists had little commitment to the values of the system, preferring to replace it with a new order. Libertarians did hope, however, that the radical and rebellious sons and daughters of the upper middle class, frequent participants in earlier reform, might again be recruited. These expectations were sometimes fulfilled and sometimes thwarted. The prewar youthful intellectual radicals took some

16. Ibid., p. 71.
17. Mark Karson, *American Labor Unions and Politics, 1900–1918* (Boston, 1965), pp. 104–05.
18. Ibid.

delight in criticizing Progressive pomposity and paternalism. They also enjoyed the troubled apprehensions which their cries for artistic, spirtual, and social revolution and for the liberation of the free spirits of America created among their elders and the establishment generally.[19] There was little doubt as to their sincerity regarding tolerance, generosity, and freedom for unpopular ideas. How far they would go in working for the achievement of those views, and what concrete steps they would take in their pursuit, was not clear. Literary and cultural radicals such as Randolph Bourne, Max and Crystal Eastman, and *The Masses* group seemed recruitable allies. As the extreme left of intellectual radicalism, their ongoing ability to advise their public of the hypocrisy and repressiveness of official and traditional political and social orthodoxy depended upon continued access to uninhibited public communication. The same was true for the Chicago poets and the denizens of Greenwich Village and Bohemia generally. High expectations also existed for the original *New Republic* people, such as Herbert Croly, who consciously sought to join *The Masses* and the *Seven Arts* in speaking for youthful iconoclasm by bridging the moderate relativism of the older pragmatists to some of the ideas of the young intellectuals.[20] The divergent elements in this youthful rebellion were ideologically empathetic in many ways to antimilitarism, anticonscription forces, and certainly to anticensorship sentiment in the pre-entry years. The groups thus found themselves thrown into a state of severe intellectual and emotional ambivalence by Wilson's war declaration, by the results of American entry, and particularly by the growing orthodoxy which seemed to link disagreement with government policies with disloyalty.

The behavior of certain of the group's role models, John Dewey, Thorstein Veblen, Charles A. Beard, and George Santayana, had an impact on its ultimate decision regarding wartime

19. Henry F. May, *The End of American Innocence* (New York, 1959.

20. Henry F. May, "The Rebellion of the Intellectuals, 1912–1917," *American Quarterly* 8 (Spring 1956): 114–26.

behavior. Dewey's response was watched with particular interest. Unlike the Progressive moralists, for whom entry into the war against evil Prussianism made logical sense, and the cultural Progressives, who were committed to the triumph of Anglo-Saxonism at home and abroad, such pragmatic Progressives faced more difficult problems. Spokesmen of relativist social science and philosophy, they could not make up their minds about the war by simple moral or cultural generalizations. But many were susceptible to persuasion by Dewey as he moved to consider how such concepts as force and liberty might best be adapted to wartime exigency. And when Dewey embraced the view that both terms were ethically neutral, and that their value was dictated by the use made of them, it was a short step from there to the rationalization of a prowar position.[21] Proper use of force, in this case as part of a well-planned war-effort, could secure desirable and liberal results with a minimum of undesirable side effects. In such circumstances, liberty was not highly practical, not being the most efficient use of means for ends. Pacifists and antiwar spokesmen were using the concept obstructively. And since "it is as an efficiency factor that its value must ultimately be assessed," its use in this fashion was obviously unwarranted.[22] Thus, Dewey was largely prepared to jettison liberty as a value worth serious concern during the war period and hold those who embraced it above other values as either confused or misled. He later admitted that wartime suppression was probably extreme, even though it was inevitable, given the irrational fears at the time of the success of Old World autocracy. In an article in *The New Republic* in October 1919, he contended that any alternative approach that sought, through positive liberal and radical exhortation, to elicit sympathetic and intellectual support for Wilson's liberal

21. John C. Farrell, "John Dewey and World War I: Armageddon Tests a Liberal's Faith," *Perspectives in American History* 9 (1975): 299–340.

22. May, *End of American Innocence,* p. 373. See also Alan Cywar, "John Dewey in World War I: Patriotism and International Progressivism," *American Quarterly* 21 (Fall 1969): 590–93.

war aims would have failed, given the eagerness of the American people to "grovel in the sacrifice of their liberties" as a way of supporting the cause.[23] Dewey's principal wartime gesture toward civil liberties constituted too subtle and, some argued, too cynical an argument for many to embrace. The problem with repression, he contended, was not so much its effect upon its victims, who could legitimately be expected to make certain wartime sacrifices, but upon the minds of the suppressors themselves as they dutifully carried out repressive policy. "Absence of thought, apathy of intelligence, is the chief enemy to freedom of mind. And these hasty ill-considered attempts to repress discussion of unpopular ideas and criticism of governmental action foster general intellectual inertness."[24] Such a cost was troubling but not ultimately so debilitating as to warrant withholding support of the war. Dewey thus eased the way for many of the young radicals to support the war, although some—Randolph Bourne being a prominent example—vigorously denounced both his logic and his integrity.[25] Dewey's not atypical action in taking Jane Addams to task for her pacifism did not sit well with many, nor did his frequent allusion to the wrongness of those contending that liberty had a positive value and that wartime destruction of liberty had ominous and long-range overtones.

Veblen's position was less complicated, although the logic which he used to defend it seemed tortured to some. Placing his hopes for the future in the insubordination of citizens, he saw less opportunity for iconoclasts to function should Germany win and rule the West. He concluded that, on balance, this warranted support of an Allied victory. Beard came down on the Allied side as well, and even before American entry took the position that the United States should "eliminate Prussianism

23. John Dewey, *Characters and Events* (New York, 1929), 2: 633–34.

24. Cywar, "John Dewey," p. 592; Dewey, *Characters and Events*, 2:568–69.

25. Randolph S. Bourne, *War and the Intellectuals, Collected Essays, 1915–1919* (New York, 1964), pp. 63–64; Christopher Lasch, *The New Radicalism in America, 1889–1963* (New York, 1965), pp. 205 ff.

from the earth." [26] For him, if Americans believed in their own freedom, they had to contribute to the defeat of its greatest enemy, Germany. Santayana, while hostile to Germany, remained hostile to the Allied cause as well, feeling that neither side offered much hope for the survival of the kind of mature, classic European culture to which he was committed.

Thus, the older leaders of American thought whom the young intellectuals most respected, generally tended to favor the Allied cause, as did the leading men of letters, the college presidents, the old-line publishers, the editors of standard magazines, and their friends.[27] The result was both to reduce the appeal of a strident antiwar posture and to undermine any enthusiasm which might exist for joining in a positive and aggressive assault upon those actively involved in the suppression of various forms of personal freedom and liberty. The pattern, however, had interesting variations.

Max Eastman and many of the contributors to *The Masses,* continued to raise the antiwar, antimilitarism flag. However, after the famous episode in which the journal's mailing privileges were revoked, and after Eastman came close to being lynched for an antiwar speech in North Dakota, much of his enthusiasm for aggressive antiwar action diminished. Similarly, some of the more bitter war critics of *The Masses* group capitulated as the war progressed. George Bellows moved from drawing antiwar cartoons to provictory posters. Floyd Dell, after initially facing trial for praising conscientious objectors, ultimately enlisted in the army.[28]

26. *The New York Times,* February 17, 1917, p. 2. For a recent controversial view, see John P. Diggins, *Thorstein Veblen and Modern Social Theory* (New York, 1978).

27. Many academics were put in a difficult dilemma. With many of their peers involved in "patriotic" war work, and with the young AAUP capitulating badly in the academic freedom area to wartime pressures, any controversial posture left them vulnerable and virtually unprotected. See Carol S. Gruber, *Mars and Minerva* (Baton Rouge, La., 1975), pp. 164–72.

28. Max Eastman, *Love and Revolution* (New York, 1964), pp. 62–63. After the North Dakota episode, Eastman wrote to Woodrow

The *New Republic* crowd was almost instinctively prowar and from the moment of Wilson's war message became unabashedly so. Convinced by Wilson's war message and by the participation of liberal intellectuals and progressives in the direction of the war effort that a more sane world order would emerge from the conflict, they flayed pacifism, remained skeptical about atrocity stories and the alleged excesses of domestic repression, and believed that reason would lead all advanced countries, including Germany, to join a postwar league which would administer the backward areas of the earth.[29] In September 1917, the journal published a piece by John Dewey on "Conscription of Thought," stating that he was "not . . . seriously concerned that 'liberty of thought and speech' would 'seriously suffer . . . in any lasting way.' All that troubled him was that 'conscription of thought . . .' was not the most efficient means of promoting social solidarity," since it gave rise to resentment among its victims.[30] The journal generally continued to embrace this posture, even as wartime repression intensified, resisting, like other war liberals, the conclusion to which events seemed to point. Numerous comparable examples could be cited. *The Forum,* for example, a stronghold of the rebellion until 1916, yielded early to wartime pressure. When a change of management occurred on the eve of American entry, its readers were quickly subjected to two slogans, "Public Service" and "America First," as well as to frequent orthodox attacks on those who would tolerate radical dissent in wartime.[31] This posture was clearly symptomatic of what lay ahead for all

---

Wilson, arguing that the policies and officials of his administration were a "grave danger" to our "civil liberties." Wilson replied that in wartime many things which are normally innocent "may be very dangerous to the public welfare" and subject to legitimate restraint.

29. Charles Forcey, *The Crossroads of Liberalism* (New York, 1961), pp. 276–86. On Lippmann's wartime free speech views, see John Luskin, *Lippmann, Liberty, and the Press* (University, Ala., 1972), pp. 36–37.

30. John Dewey, "Conscription of Thought," *The New Republic* 12 (September 1, 1917): 129.

31. May, *End of American Innocence,* p. 392.

writers of liberal to radical opinion pieces. After America's entry into the war, the freedom of these writers was further restricted as editors grew wary of contributors whose antiwar opinions might either offend readers or make their publication susceptible to the stigma of wartime censorship.

The cultural radicals responded with equal antipathy to the civil libertarians' overtures. With American entry and serious wartime resoluteness, Greenwich Village and Bohemia generally —which had previously lived by the media—began to die by it. Wartime society was little amused by the antics of a youthful counterculture. Large circulation publications that had been titillated by radicalism and had provided outlets for avant garde works now backed away. Thus, a journal such as the *Seven Arts* ceased publication in December 1917 after publishing vigorous antiwar pieces by Randolph Bourne and the outspoken John Reed, who from the point of American entry had taken the public position that "this is not my war . . . and I will not support it. This is not my war, and I will have nothing to do with it." [32]

Given the apparent persuasiveness of this composite of philosophical assumptions, pragmatic logic, Wilsonian idealism, the dangers of pacifistic and antiwar postures, and the general hostility of a no longer amused middle-class support group, it is not surprising that a majority of the young radicals were untouched and unmoved by the appeal to join a group of civil libertarians who associated themselves with pacifism and radicalism. This did not mean complete capitulation to strident wartime patriotism. Even those in the *New Republic* camp were prepared, on occasion, to speak out and deplore individual episodes of outrageous vigilantism and repressive overkill. But such behavior was generally reactive and individualistic, not carried out in concert with those seeking positive and aggressive counter-action on behalf of civil liberties principles.

The nature and personality of the young intellectual radicals

32. Robert A. Rosenstone, *Romantic Revolutionary: A Biography of John Reed* (New York, 1975), p. 265.

is also pertinent. Long-time uncommitted critics of much of the American system, and of progressivism generally, they had previously been carefree and cynical, clearly enjoying the semi-irresponsibility of their gadfly role and their success in offending their elders. With a sharply changed emotional and intellectual climate, it was easy to withdraw in silence, to wallow morosely in self-disillusion, and to yearn with a certain bitter nostalgia for the tolerant climate in which their earlier activities had been conducted. This was not only easier but safer than becoming actively involved with the formal civil liberties types, an action which few could see as having any potential as a palliative for the pessimistic cynicism which most of them, whether they supported the war or not, now clearly felt.[33]

The group which ultimately came to represent the one definable element within the American structure sufficiently alert to the dangers inherent in the repression being conducted by the new bureaucratic managers of the country, and sufficiently committed to begin some kind of consciousness-raising activities to oppose them, emerged from the old American Union Against Militarism. Roger Nash Baldwin was the spearhead behind the creation of the original Civil Liberties Bureau (CLB) of the AUAM.[34] Born into a Wellesley, Massachusetts, Unitarian family of some means, Baldwin might have become an abolitionist or followed his grandfather into religious charities in an earlier era. But by the time of his graduation from Harvard in 1905, the old Protestant callings had faded, and Baldwin, in casting about for a career, was almost instinctively drawn to social work. Taking a position managing a St. Louis settlement house in 1906, he also taught sociology at Washington University and a year later took a third job as chief probation officer for the juvenile court. Volunteering as an unpaid secretary for the

33. The same syndrome carried into the postwar years. See Paul L. Murphy, *The Meaning of Freedom of Speech* (Westport, Ct., 1972), p. 123.
34. On Baldwin's background see Peggy Lamson, *Roger Baldwin: Founder of the American Civil Liberties Union* (Boston, 1976), pp. 1–66.

National Probation Association, he helped write one of the association's reports, "Juvenile Courts and Probation," for many years recognized as a central work in its field. Chided by his colleagues about his New England conservatism he went to hear a speech by the eloquent anarchist Emma Goldman. Entranced and conscience-shaken, he quickly realized the overly ameliorative quality of social work and began an intense study of socialist and anarchist literature. This led him to embrace certain postures regarding extreme individualism and the right of every person to exercise his own free will. But Baldwin was not a total anarchist. Government, if properly organized, he felt, could be useful in protecting the rights of individuals and their general freedom. Only when it turned to arbitarary control of the individual was it to be resisted. Under such conditions citizen counter-action was quite justified. In 1916 he joined the local AUAM in St. Louis and moved to New York in April of 1917. There he assumed leadership in fighting the conscription bills then in Congress and was soon appointed associate director of the AUAM. With the war declaration, he began urging the creation of a special civil liberties bureau in the organization,[35] a bureau which he quickly came to head. Looking back at these developments in 1970, Baldwin wrote:

All great struggles for liberty have been conducted against the forces opposed to change and determined to protect the status quo and the privileges of its most powerful elements. Every minority that has won its rights has battled the powerful, the ignorant and the apathetic and overcome them. Every struggle is fought against a background of majority indifference, prejudice and sometimes open hostility, hate and fear. The A.C.L.U. [survivor of the CLB], as a defender of rights in these minority struggles, has always faced the

---

35. The term "civil liberties" itself was a product of this period. Baldwin recalls: "I don't think anyone had ever called anything civil liberties in the United States before we did." Lamson, *Roger Baldwin,* p. 72; Roger Baldwin, "Recollections of a Life in Civil Liberties," *Civil Liberties Review* 2 (Spring 1975): 48, 53. John Haynes Holmes, *I Speak for Myself* (New York, 1959), p. 189, recalls that "disarmament was a lost cause, but . . . there suddenly came to the fore in our nation's life the new issue of civil liberties."

same opponents as the 'clients' it serves. But its appeal to American principles of law and fair play has given it a leverage on public opinion and on the agencies of government to which it turns to vindicate the Bill of Rights.[36]

The creation of the Civil Liberties Bureau was itself achieved against considerable opposition, both within the AUAM and from the public at large. In arguing the importance of such an agency, Baldwin initially emphasized the need to provide legal counsel and advice for the defense of conscientious objectors. But he also stressed the necessity to challenge the constitutionality of the conscription act and to lobby for a new and more liberal law. His proposal was distressing to a good many of the pacifists, and particularly the social worker element in the AUAM, a number of whom—particularly members of New York's Henry Street Group, including Lillian Wald, Paul Kellogg, and Alice Lewisohn—threatened to resign.[37] AUAM leader Crystal Eastman, however, saved the day, suggesting that actions for the protection of civil liberties of far more than conscientious objectors were certainly in order and arguing that no one would quarrel with the importance of protecting civil liberties.[38] The bureau gained official status on July 2, 1917, and promptly set out to play a multifaceted role, continuing to defend conscientious objectors, but also challenging Espionage Act prosecutions, publicly deploring the mob violence which the war was eliciting, and finally, attempting to provide or secure support for victims of wartime repression in their struggle for a fair trial and due process.

As this process unfolded, civil liberties leaders quickly came to realize that various approaches were open to them in pur-

36. Roger Baldwin, "The Meaning of Civil Liberties," introduction to the *American Civil Liberties Union Annual Reports* (New York, 1970), p. xx.
37. Marchand, *American Peace Movement,* pp. 256–57.
38. Charles Chatfield, *For Peace and Justice: Pacifism in America, 1914–1941* (Boston, 1973), p. 29. A *New York Times* editorial on July 4, 1917, made clear that Miss Eastman's hopes were a bit optimistic. To the *Times* the whole process of protecting civil liberties was at best a tricky and more clearly a dubious business.

suing these ends. With considerable sympathy in the War Department and with ready access to the White House and to
congressmen, it proved possible to address the conscientious
objector issue through lobbying, personal appeals, and political
manipulation at a fairly high level. However, with Espionage
Act and other censorship enforcement in the hands of unsympathetic administration lieutenants, from Burleson and Lamar
to Gregory and Bielaski, such techniques were soon found to
be ineffectual in this area. In recognition of the special problems
posed by the Espionage Act, the Civil Liberites Bureau, which
became officially the National Civil Liberties Bureau in October
1917, assumed the role of a propaganda agency, rather than
that of an advisor or quiet negotiator, issuing pamphlets, cam-
paigning openly against censorship, and bringing to light various
outrages committed under the act, in the hope of reaching the
public's conscience. At one point they even tried to hold a
nationally publicized mass meeting to deplore the situation
which wartime hysteria had created. Crystal Eastman was an
early proponent of an aggressive program of confrontation politics designed to highlight civil liberties denial. She advocated
defying local authorities by convening public meetings for the
discussion of a negotiated peace, or "some other controversial
subject," to test rights of free speech in areas where attempts to
hold antiwar meetings had been denied, or where federal authorities had been especially arbitrary. Either free speech would
be vindicated, she argued, or a case for an appeal to the courts
would be established.[39] She was persuaded by others, however,
that with minimal national tolerance for personal liberties, especially in wartime, militant action in behalf of Bill of Rights
freedoms would arouse reprisals instead of sympathy and might
thoroughly discredit the Civil Liberties Bureau as an agent of
rational democratic values.[40] The bureau acknowledged this

39. Blanche Wiesen Cook, "Democracy in Wartime: Antimilitarism
in England and the United States, 1914–1918," *American Studies* 13
(Spring 1972): 60–61.
40. Marchand, *American Peace Movement,* p. 258.

danger and sought to defuse it in a publicity statement issued in November 1917. Setting forth the established policies and procedures of the body in securing legal aid wherever constitutional rights were violated, the statement concluded:

While the bureau is active chiefly in behalf of persons organizations and publications which are working for peace and for the conscientious objector, it announces that it is not adopting a policy of obstruction or attempting to embarrass the government in any way—it stands for the preservation of constitutional rights on general principle in the interest of democratic institutions—and its work is done in close cooperation with government officials both local and federal.[41]

The leaders of the AUAM soon viewed the government's deliberate prosecution of radical groups, and especially the IWW, as a symbolic action which demanded symbolic response. Its move to assist indicted Wobbly leaders through its Civil Liberties Bureau arm, while clearly a public relations gesture, was motivated by a desire to awaken the IWW to the newly-forged link between leaders of industrial capitalism and formal government power. As Baldwin was later to admit, the bureau's participation in the defense of Wobbly leaders (who had their own counsel and needed no such assistance) was calculated not simply to defend civil liberties but to "put the whole industrial system on trial"[42] by pointing out the way that private capital was exploiting workers and using the federal government as a willing agent in that process. This form of consciousness-raising was still tied closely to broader bureau goals of alerting people to the dangers inherent in the new government-to-citizen relationship. Previously, Wobblies had been dealt with either through local authorities or through the overt use of private economic power. Now the federal government was becoming the instrument for imposing restrictive sanctions against them, sanctions which, if applicable to such a definable group of dis-

41. The statement appeared in *The Survey* 39 (November 3, 1917): 130–31.
42. Quoted in Donald Johnson, *The Challenge to American Freedoms* (Lexington, Ky., 1963), p. 92.

senters, could be turned against similar groups at a later time.

The success of tactics during the wartime period varied. Despite setbacks in specific instances, all of these paths continued to be pursued. Baldwin, along with Norman Thomas and other conscientious objectors, initially hoped to convince Secretary of War Baker, who was reputed to be a pacifist, that the principle of conscientious objection went well beyond simply exempting members of well-recognized religious sects and organizations. They contended that this was a highly personal matter and turned upon individual conscience and people's general attitude toward war. Thomas suggested at one point that exemption from combatant service should be available to anyone "who is conscientiously opposed to engaging in such service." [43] When the Selective Service Act passed, without recognizing individual conscience or altering the exemption clauses, Civil Liberties Bureau people had little choice but to attempt to formulate a suitable policy for objectors which would protect their right to refuse to serve and to express their views about it. When Baldwin offered to cooperate in the formulation of such a policy, he was surprised and pleased that the War Department cordially accepted his offer. Misunderstandings arose concerning Baldwin's position that "absolutist" conscientious objectors (who opposed war in such an "absolute" sense that they would not comply with any military order whatever) should be exempted from military service entirely and be allowed to take "essential" jobs in agriculture or industry. In the wake of Woodrow Wilson's executive order of March 20, 1918,[44] which implied that political objectors would be able to choose noncom-

---

43. Ibid., pp. 15–16. Thomas was particularly involved in the question, as his brother Evan, an "absolutist" conscientious objector, suffered terribly as a result of wartime incarceration. Evan W. Thomas has prepared a sensitive evaluation of his great-uncle's wartime experience, "Evan Thomas: A Case Study of Conscientious Objection in the First World War" (Honors thesis, University of Virginia, 1977).

44. Newton D. Baker, *Statement Concerning the Treatment of Conscientious Objectors in the Army* (Washington, D.C., 1919), pp. 18, 38–39.

batant service, Baldwin assumed that the War Department would acquiesce to this proposal. He quickly became disillusioned as army leaders callously disregarded such distinctions in implementing the policy. Absolutists were court-martialed for refusing to accept noncombatant work within the army. Despite Baldwin's protests and a clarifying order from Secretary Baker, such leaders showed no willingness to change their course. At this point military intelligence reports revealed the organization's activities in collecting funds for the IWW and *The Masses* and its association with other groups of war obstructionists.[45] With the War Department increasingly convinced that the Civil Liberties Bureau was aiding draft dodgers and slackers and encouraging conscientious objectors, Frederick P. Keppel, one of Baker's special assistants and a former Columbia University dean, informed Baldwin in May 1918 that the department could no longer "cooperate in any way with the Civil Liberties Bureau."[46] Despite further appeals to higher officials, the CLB lost its internal influence as it became stigmatized as a body principally concerned with obstructing the war.

Circumstance required that the Civil Liberties Bureau shift its focus, but it did so willingly. By this time even supporters of the war were becoming distressed by the brutal treatment afforded conscientious objectors by the army in various camps into which they were herded. Secretary of War Baker, again anxious to avoid having his department gain an image of excessive brutality, promised to investigate the situation and persuaded the bureau to give him time to solve the problem internally. But when no action was forthcoming and news of more distressing episodes leaked out, the bureau broke its no-publicity pledge and began releasing information about the incidents. The War Department was infuriated by the publicity, promptly charging that bureau leaders were defending traitors and suggesting that such action might well be prosecuted under

45. Johnson, *Challenge,* pp. 36–37.
46. Ibid., p. 38.

the Espionage Act.[47] Refusing to be intimidated by such threats the CLB continued to expose the brutality meted out to conscientious objectors through the end of the war.

By this time, Baldwin had decided, as a matter of conscience and as a way of dramatizing the broader question, to challenge the whole conscription system by refusing to enter the army after being drafted himself. Since his violation of the draft law meant he would go to jail, he resigned the directorship of the CLB. Baldwin's action and trial had considerable symbolic importance and drew national attention at the time. He had written to his draft board in September 1918, indicating his personal opposition not only to direct military service but to war itself, and particularly to the principle of conscription. When he appeared on October 30 before Federal Judge Julius M. Mayer, he used the occasion to make more explicit his general posture and, by implication, that of the body which he had previously directed. He told Judge Mayer:

The compelling motive for refusing to comply with the Draft Act, is my uncompromising opposition to the principle of conscription of life by the state, for any purpose whatsoever, in war-time or peace. . . . I regard the principle of the conscription of life as a flat contradiction of all our cherished ideals of individual freedom, democratic liberty, and Christian teaching. I not only refuse to obey the present conscription law, but would in future refuse to obey any similar statute which attempts to direct my choice of service or ideals.[48]

Judge Mayer, in responding to Baldwin's position, took the typical legalistic posture that whether one likes the law or not, obedience to it was an obligation of citizenship. "He who disobeys the law," Mayer contended, "knowing that he does so with the intelligence that you possess, must, as you are prepared to do, take the consequences."[49] Baldwin was prepared to do

47. Ibid., p. 41.
48. *The New York Times,* October 31, 1918, p. 11. Baldwin's statement is reprinted in Lillian Schlissel, *Conscience in America* (New York, 1968), pp. 142–48.
49. Ibid., p. 149.

so, feeling that his action and its consequences made a statement regarding the new relationship which the federal government was now forcing upon American citizens at large, a relationship which involved unwarranted encroachments by the state upon the sphere of civil liberties and personal ideals.

Ironically, Baldwin's action drew wide commendation from a surprisingly large number of groups which were in no way prepared to associate themselves with the CLB but were apparently prepared to speak out regarding the justice or injustice of individual episodes. Among these were the American Association for Organized Charities, the National Municipal League, the Society for Prevention of Cruelty to Animals, the Liberal Club of Harvard, the League for Amnesty for Political Prisoners, the National Popular Governmental League, the Society of St. Vincent de Paul, and the League for Democratic Control.[50]

One final incident of the Baldwin incarceration again suggested new areas of government activity of concern to civil libertarians. One of Baldwin's friends, George Foster Peabody, appealed to Woodrow Wilson for his pardon. Wilson turned the question over to Attorney General Gregory, who indicated that this would be unadvisable. Wiretaps on Baldwin's phone conversations, he indicated, had revealed "his opposition to the course of the government in the war" and also that he was "not leading a moral life." In Gregory's opinion an individual like Baldwin, "one of a very dangerous class of persons," should have been sentenced for an even longer period.[51] Wilson, in turn, refused the pardon. The Justice Department subsequently warned American citizens, as a result of Baldwin's example and his identification with the CLB, not to contribute to so-called "civil liberties," "liberty defense," "popular council," "legal advice," or antiwar organizations unless they expected their contributions to be used by other organizations which would seek to hinder prosecution of the war.[52]

50. Lamson, *Roger Baldwin,* p. 111. The list may well reflect Baldwin's elderly propensity for "shoring up" the past.
51. Johnson, *Challenge,* pp. 46–47.
52. *The New York Times,* November 20, 1918, p. 24.

Bureau leaders had considerably less impact on espionage, sedition, and censorship legislation. As the Espionage Act was moving relentlessly toward passage, Gilbert E. Roe, an AUAM attorney long active in the Free Speech movement, warned that the censorship clause of the measure was ruinous, leaving, as it did, discretion as to what should be censored in the hands of enforcement officers. It encouraged administrators and bureaucrats to make decisions regarding First Amendment rights before they could ever reach the courts, thus preventing a legal ruling which might open up questions regarding the constitutionality of the measure itself. The president quickly moved to allay such suspicions, indicating that he would endorse no system which would deny to the people "their indisputable right to criticize their own public officials." [53] Nonetheless, the final bill left these broad but disputed discretionary powers in the hands of the postmaster general and it was used for the very purpose which Wilson repudiated.

CLB officials protested the enactment of the two other censorship measures with the same disheartening result. When leaders picked up the clause in the Trading-with-the-Enemy Act forbidding foreign-language newspapers from printing any article about the war unless they first submitted an English translation to the postmaster general, Baldwin wired the president that this new censorship clause would destroy any semblance of free speech in America. It would allow Burleson to "suppress any article about the war, and consequently to exclude any material which criticized war policies . . . even Burleson's censorship policies." [54] Osward Garrison Villard, editor of *The Nation,* wired the president, demanding a hearing on the bill. Wilson, following his usual procedure, asked Attorney General Gregory if he had any objections to the bill. When Gregory

53. Gilbert E. Roe to Roger Baldwin, March 30, 1917, ACLU Papers, New York Public Library, New York City; Wilson to Arthur Brisbane, April 25, 1917, Wilson Papers, LC.

54. Harry N. Scheiber, *The Wilson Administration and Civil Liberties* (Ithaca, N.Y., 1960), p. 20.

replied that he could not find any flaw in the measure, Wilson signed it into law.[55] By the time the Sedition Act Amendment had reached the Congress in April 1918 the bureau was losing the will to continue the battle. In this case Baldwin attempted to appeal to the president through his close advisor, Colonel House. Both he and Norman Thomas wrote to House emphasizing that the bill threatened free discussion, that in threatening even political critics of the administration, such as Republicans, it was "inexpedient politically" and that it could backfire on its sponsors. While House sympathized with these views, he was reluctant to speak to the president about them, pointing out that on espionage matters the president listened principally to Gregory. Since Gregory had written large parts of the bill, there was little point in trying to work through him. Baldwin ultimately came to feel that it made little difference. As he wrote to a friend, "hysteria and intolerance will get its victims, regardless of the legislation. If the authorities don't do it, a mob will, and the authorities will act with or without the law."[56]

The enforcement practices proved the repressiveness of these measures. Here the bureau put its confrontation and exposé tactics into play. When Burleson banned *The Masses* and fifteen other major liberal and radical publications from the mails, the bureau called an emergency conference and decided to send four of its lawyers—Clarence Darrow, Frank Walsh, Morris Hillquit, and Seymour Stedman—to visit the postmaster general and plead for the adoption of a more reasonable policy. In that confrontation, however, the four attorneys got a taste of Burleson's insensitivity and arbitrariness: He branded the attitude of the attorneys "impertinent" and insisted that the best general guide for editors was to follow the Espionage Act to the letter.[57] The attorneys then turned to the president, who, although he refused to see them, did suggest to Burleson that

55. On Villard and Wilson see Michael Wreszin, *Oswald Garrison Villard* (Bloomington, Ind., 1965), pp. 94–95.
56. Johnson, *Challenge*, p. 71.
57. Ibid., pp. 58–59.

his department be sensitive on censorship matters. To Max Eastman he wrote that the government was trying to establish a sensitive distinction between liberty and license without partisanship.[58] This posture seemed to have the effect of making Burleson, and his deputy, Lamar, even more defensive and arbitrary.

But Burleson and Lamar were punitive as well, and were particularly piqued by the Civil Liberties Bureau. They now began denying bureau pamphlets mailing privileges as a way of silencing criticism of Post Office Department policies.[59] Baldwin now hoped to take the issue to the public and needed a sufficiently appalling episode to show the type of behavior that such blind intolerance was fostering. On October 28, 1917, he was unexpectedly rewarded. Herbert S. Bigelow, minister of the People's Church and Town Meeting Society of heavily German Cincinnati, was seized by a group of masked men as he entered a hall in Newport, Kentucky, to speak at a Socialist antiwar meeting. He was taken across the county, stripped to the waist and beaten extensively with a blacksnake whip. His hair was then cut off and he was covered with crude oil. As the mob was leaving he was told, "You are to be out of Cincinnati in thirty-six hours and remain away until the end of the war." [60] The fact that Bigelow had been a leading Progressive in Ohio, a prominent single-tax advocate, a friend of Ohio reformers Tom Johnson and Brand Whitlock, a one-time associate of Newton D. Baker, and an opponent of the Boss Cox machine in Cincinnati [61] heightened interest in the situation. So, too, did the fact that Bigelow had been under Justice Department surveillance. His sermons had been monitored, and he had been labeled by department agents as a "dangerous enemy of the war effort," despite the fact that he had publicly disagreed with the Social-

58. Eastman, *Love and Revolution,* p. 63.

59. Johnson, *Challenge,* pp. 60–61.

60. Daniel R. Beaver, *Herbert Seely Bigelow, a Buckeye Crusader* (Cincinnati, 1957), pp. 41–44.

61. Herbert Shapiro, "The Herbert Bigelow Case: A Test of Free Speech in Wartime," *Ohio History* 81 (Spring 1972): 108–109.

ists' antiwar St. Louis Declaration and had publicly spoken in support of Wilson and Wilson's peace goals.

National response to his flogging was strong and widespread. Although some patriotic journals and leaders suggested that he got what he deserved—the *New York Herald* suggesting that this was an appropriate way for Americans to deal with seditionists —the lion's share of the response was one of outrage, although more at the technique employed than out of sympathy with the victim. Woodrow Wilson used the episode as an occasion to deplore mob action generally. Speaking to the AF of L convention in Buffalo on November 12, he stated, "I have no sympathy with the men who take their punishment into their own hands; and I want to say to every man who does join such a mob that I do not recognize him as worthy of the free institutions of the United States." [62] Some readers of the Buffalo speech, however, were quick to pick up on the fact that it significantly lacked any commitment to take federal action in protection of the First Amendment in the Bigelow case. Two days after the incident, the *Cincinnati Enquirer* reported from Washington that federal officials did not like mob action but they did not want to do anything that would encourage opposition to the war.[63] The Justice Department's policy was clearly outlined in a memorandum by O'Brian to Attorney General Gregory. Charging that Bigelow had been properly regarded as thoroughly disloyal since the declaration of war, O'Brian recommended that "nothing further be done by us." [64] Implicit in his position was the notion

62. Ray Stannard Baker and William E. Dodd, *The Public Papers of Woodrow Wilson* (New York, 1926), 4:120–23. Newton D. Baker also deplored the episode. "The cause of the United States is not aided, but hurt, by that kind of thing. No night riders are needed, and when the country is at war for liberty and justice, they make a humiliating contrast to our national ideals and aims." ACLU microfilm collection, Reel 1, New York Public Library, New York City.

63. *The Cincinnati Enquirer,* November 1, 1917, p. 7; Shapiro, "Herbert Bigelow," pp. 115–16.

64. John Lord O'Brian memorandum to Thomas W. Gregory, November 30, 1917, Department of Justice file no. 188455, National Archives, Washington, D.C.

that government would seek to protect the exercise of free speech only when it approved of what was being said. The United States Attorney for the Southern District of Ohio, Stuart R. Bolin, was even more blunt: "Our courts are not permitting persons who have taken a stand against the Government in this war to seek shelter behind the Constitution. . . . The Constitution is being virtually suspended during the time when America is facing this tremendous crisis." [65]

Sensing that the response to the episode signaled that it was time to muster liberals of all persuasions against press censorship, mob violence, and suppression, Roger Baldwin set out to hold a public meeting in Carnegie Hall to discuss the Bigelow case. Invitations to join in sponsoring the event were sent to a number of liberal organizations including Socialists, pacifists, labor groups, the Non-Partisan League, and various religious bodies. The returns were almost universally disappointing, with bodies such as the NAACP and the Single Tax Association—which Baldwin felt were likely supporters—categorically declining and others doing so with specific reservations. Theodore Schroeder, founder of the Free Speech League and, prior to 1917, probably the nation's best known civil libertarian, refused to have anything to do with the case or with the meeting. In response to Baldwin's invitation, he replied that he felt Baldwin "was using free speech for an improper end" in attempting to turn it into a device for advancing pacifism and not for itself and that he would not "have the issue narrowed to economic liberty with a maximum pacifist leaning." [66] Failing to get group sponsorship, Baldwin set out after individual sponsorship. A variety of well-known and self-proclaimed liberals were approached. Again, however, the majority declined. Assistant Secretary of Labor Louis F. Post, a critic of mass deportation of radicals whom Baldwin hoped would preside, indicated that he

65. Quoted in Shapiro, "Herbert Bigelow," p. 116.
66. Murphy, *Meaning of Freedom of Speech*, pp. 31–32. Theodore Schroeder to Roger N. Baldwin, November 27, 1917, ACLU microfilm, Reel 1, New York Public Library, New York City.

would not endorse speakers who "sympathized with the enemy." Charles E. Russell thought the meeting was "anti-American and anti-democratic," and William English Walling believed that the real purpose of the meeting was "not the protection of free speech, but the propaganda of an immediate or German-made peace." [67] Charles W. Eliot called it "inexpedient"; Charles A. Beard thought it sounded more like "an anti-war than a pro-liberty meeting." Nonetheless, Baldwin persevered. Denied the use of Carnegie Hall, he succeeded in securing the Liberty Theatre. Mrs. Mary Ware Dennett, the bureau's executive secretary, then set up a rough agenda with the goals that it was hoped the meeting might achieve. These included protesting the general suppression of liberty; exposing the efforts to crush the labor movement by putting the IWW tag on all radical labor movements; rallying support for the abolition of post office censorship; educating public opinion on the rights of minorities; fostering popular control of the machinery of government; and revealing the misuse of public officers by business interests in their fight against labor. The meeting was also meant to show the public why civil liberties issues should be taken up by Congress during the war. Admitting that "restrictions have got to be made in talk which directly interferes with the war," [68] leaders still hoped to nail down the point that this did not justify suppressing discussion of peace terms, domestic policies directly related to the war, the crushing of labor, or mob violence.

The meeting was finally held on January 13, 1918, before a capacity audience. Among the ranks of the speakers were Lincoln Steffens, Joseph McAfee, Herbert S. Bigelow, Harry F. Ward, James H. Maurer, and Norman Thomas. The proceedings attracted a good deal of attention in the press. The *New York Call* was particularly intrigued with Steffens's statement, "Accept this war but do not accept the consequences of it. Underneath this war there are forces fighting against the liberty and

67. Donald Johnson, "The American Civil Liberties Union: Origins, 1914–1917" (Ph.D. dissertation, Columbia University, 1960), p. 119.
68. Shapiro, "Herbert Bigelow," p. 117.

welfare of the entire world." Bigelow's moving statement, "the whip left no scar of malice on my soul . . . but it did burn into my being an implacable hatred of the system that could make such fiends of men," was widely picked up by the press, as was his hope that the war effort could achieve the president's liberal war aims. The meeting was significant as a public reaffirmation in belief in free expression.[69] It afforded some evidence to civil libertarians that some concerned Americans would publicly protest flagrant vigilantism. But it also provided evidence that in the context of World War I, civil libertarians could not develop a widely inclusive mass movement that would ignore the war and focus on the threatening overtones of the new government-to-citizen relationship for civil liberties which now was woven into the nation's structure. It was a clear signal to Baldwin to move quickly to other tactics. The bureau never again attempted to hold a mass meeting during the war period.[70]

The episode also had the effect of intensifying federal suspicion of NCLB action. By May 1918, all of the bureau pamphlets had been denied mailing privileges, including one on *Freedom of Speech and of the Press.* In ordering its suppression, the postal inspector who read it made clear that the subject of free speech was not an appropriate issue for public debate, that the government's wartime policy on it was not to be questioned, and that any organization which did so was disloyal. Meanwhile, the Justice Department had ordered a full-scale investigation of the NCLB, and on August 31 its New York offices were raided by a federal agent and a number of "volunteer" operatives from New York's Union League Club, who proclaimed it their patriotic duty to investigate an organization propagandizing against the

69. Ibid., p. 119.
70. Other concerned individual civil libertarians did attempt to reach national consciousness through the media when outrages with strong civil liberties overtones occurred. Villard used *The Nation* vigorously for this purpose, at times finding himself under fire for so doing. See Wreszin, *Villard,* pp. 97–98. The Rose Pastor Stokes episode especially drew civil libertarian wrath from people ranging from William English Walling and John Spargo, to the *New Republic,* to the *New York Tribune.* See *Literary Digest* 57 (June 15, 1918): 13.

war.[71] Baldwin promptly set out to take legal action against the raiders, contemplating at one point retaining Republican attorney Charles Evans Hughes to defend the Bureau "against the tyranny of a Democratic administration."[72] He decided against this course of action when he discovered that federal officials had learned of his strategy through the wiretapping of his telephone. The bureau then retained a conservative Southern Democrat, George Gordon Battle, as counsel. By September, Battle had persuaded the government that the material which the raiders had seized could not sustain an indictment of the NCLB. This was a great disappointment to District Attorney Francis G. Caffey, who had felt he had a sure case under the Espionage Act since the bureau had defended the IWW, advocated unlimited free speech, and encouraged conscientious objection.[73] The failure to pursue an indictment was related to some significant actions in Washington. Upon learning of Caffey's position, O'Brian advised him that there was nothing wrong in the advocacy of civil liberties and free speech; these, in fact, were official government policies. Even "the organization of defense of persons accused of crime," O'Brian declared, was not "in and of itself a crime."[74] In the meantime, Walter Nelles, an NCLB attorney who had struggled bitterly with the Post Office Department to get Bureau pamphlets released, succeeded in getting Federal Judge Augustus Hand to direct the Post Office Department to deliver all of the Bureau's "suppressed" pamphlets through the mails.[75] The action represented one of the few successful appeals to the courts against post office censorship during the war period.

O'Brian's statement regarding the legitimacy of defending persons accused of crime could profitably have come earlier for

71. Baldwin "Recollections," pp. 62–63. See also Walter Nelles, *A Liberal in Wartime* (New York, 1940), pp. 145 ff.

72. Baldwin, "Recollections," p. 62. Lamson, *Baldwin,* pp. 85–86.

73. Johnson, *Challenge,* p. 77.

74. John Lord O'Brian to Francis G. Caffey, October 15, 1918, Justice Department Archives, Washington, D.C.

75. Johnson, *Challenge,* p. 78.

the bureau. It clearly alluded to the body's support of the IWW. However, the bureau's involvement with harrassment of the IWW had had other kinds of payoffs about which certain members of its central board felt positively. The IWW, while stormy and controversial, had been tolerated by the Justice Department as a legitimate labor union prior to American entry.[76] With the failure of that body to embrace any "no strike" position after American entry into the war, its prior activities came to be viewed as antiwar action. Its strike activity, especially, began to be looked on by many as a deliberate attempt to obstruct the war effort. Civil Liberties Bureau leaders watched the situation with growing interest and concern. Roger Baldwin had admired the IWW for many years. He also knew that the IWW had taken no official stand on the war because it was essentially interested in economic gain. But he sensed that many employers who had suffered from Wobbly harrassment for years would now make strong attempts to gain formal government support against them. This would be done by casting Wobbly action for better wages, working conditions, and living conditions (many of the Wobblies were migrants) in an antiwar light and arguing that the federal government now had the authority and obligation to stop them on the grounds that they were jeopardizing the war effort.

The episodes in the Arizona copper districts at Jerome and Bisbee proved a self-fulfilling prophesy for bureau leaders. Wobblies had struck but had promptly been subjected to mine owner and local enforcement harrassment, and their strike efforts had been violently terminated. The mine owners in the area utilized their control of the local telegraph offices to transmit their own dispatches describing developments. Focusing exclusively on IWW violence, they suggested that this kind of "terror" was a threat to the war effort and ultimately to the whole nation.[77] The Civil Liberties Bureau promptly replied

76. Michael R. Johnson, "The I.W.W. and Wilsonian Democracy," *Science & Society* 28 (Summer 1964): 257–74.

77. The literature on Bisbee is vast. See John H. Lindquist and James Fraser, "Sociological Interpretation of the Bisbee Deportation," *Pacific Historical Review* 28 (1968): 402.

through pamphlets that the copper companies were trying to capitalize on war hysteria to break strikes and that Wobbly leader William D. "Big Bill" Haywood had himself stated that neither he nor his men were attempting to obstruct the war in any way. However, the governors of eight western states quickly urged President Wilson to suppress the entire IWW.[78] Attorney General Gregory was highly sympathetic to the plight of the mine owners, and suddenly activities which the Justice Department had previously considered legitimate became "a grave menace to the nation."[79] The Bureau of Investigation was quickly instructed to investigate the IWW, in the belief that its activities were being financed by Germany. By September Gregory was convinced that he had adequate evidence to prosecute the entire organization for violation of the Espionage Act. And on September 5, 1917, the government began a spectacular nationwide round-up of IWW leaders, with federal agents and local police raiding IWW offices, ransacking halls, confiscating papers and pamphlets, and smashing equipment. Baldwin protested to the Justice Department against the lawlessness of these actions. Bruce Bielaski, director of the Bureau of Investigation, replied that the raids were uncovering data and equipment which was "clearly linking the IWW with a variety of secret anti-war communications."[80]

Since the IWW had its own attorneys, NCLB leaders decided that their role was largely one of public education. The bureau set out to alert the public to the fact that governmental harrassment and prosecution of the organization involved serious violations of the rights of free speech, free press, and free assembly, to say nothing of the guarantee against unreasonable search and seizure. IWW leaders were presumed guilty before their trial had even begun. Roger Baldwin dramatically pro-

78. July 10, 1917, July 14, 1917, (Wilson Papers, LC).

79. Thomas W. Gregory to Charles Warren, July 11, 1917. Justice Department Archives, Washington, D.C.

80. Bruce Bielaski to Roger N. Baldwin, January 22, February 4, March 11, 1918, ACLU Papers.

claimed that this was "probably the most important labor case in history." [81]

Central to much of the Bureau's campaign was a pamphlet entitled *The Truth About the I.W.W.*, which Baldwin had spent four months preparing "to be absolutely certain that every detail in it was correct." [82] Marshaling the evidence to show that the IWW was working legitimately for the welfare of its membership, it concluded by charging that the government was wantonly seeking, through its prosecution of IWW leaders, to destroy a legitimate labor organization. Wilson administration officials moved rapidly to suppress the pamphlet. Both the Justice Department and the Post Office Department used formal sanctions to kill it. When the IWW sought to raise money for its defense by placing ads in liberal journals such as *The New Republic, Outlook,* and *Atlantic Monthly,* government pressure was such that these organs refused to accept the advertising. Furthermore, all money mailed to the IWW headquarters for trial expenses was stopped, as the Post Office Department refused to deliver the mail to that address. In the meantime, Montana Senator Thomas Walsh introduced a bill into Congress outlawing the IWW and making it a crime to belong to the organization. Even the conservative *Christian Science Monitor* called the measure "more severe and drastic in character than anything hitherto proposed." [83] Fearing charges of deliberate suppression, Wilson administration leaders maintained a discreet silence on the measure, letting it ultimately die in the Congress. By this time the government had largely won its case in court against the organization, convicting 96 of 113 IWW leaders who had been charged with violating Espionage Act provisions. Baldwin accepted the action as "another war verdict." [84] Judge Kenesaw Mountain Landis also echoed semiofficial governmen-

81. Johnson, *Challenge,* p. 92.

82. Ibid., pp. 94–95.

83. *The Christian Science Monitor,* June 4, 1919.

84. *New York Call,* August 19, 1918. See also *Literary Digest* 58 (August 31, 1918): 14.

tàl policy. He sentenced Haywood to twenty years' imprisonment and a $30,000 fine and gave most of the other leaders from one- to fifteen-year terms. In so doing, he stated: "When the country is at peace, it is a legal right of free speech to oppose going to war and to oppose even preparation for war. But when once war is declared this right ceases." [85] Baldwin, seeking to the end to enlighten the public on the ominous implications of the whole episode, wrote an open letter to President Wilson on September 23, 1918. In it he deplored all aspects of the government's action, from raiding and confiscating to harrassing IWW leaders, dispersing union meetings, threatening to arrest persons who testified for the defense, intimidating the press, tampering with the mails, and suppressing freedom of information on the subject. In conclusion he demanded in the name of justice that the president stop persecuting the body.[86] Wilson carefully ignored the communication. The president knew that there were virtually no restrictions growing out of case law which afforded him any guidelines for imposing practical restraints on his underlings. He was further aware that few, if any, judges were prepared to set forth such legal guidelines during the war. He also knew the limits of his own authority and sensed the unpopularity of the cause in which Baldwin was calling upon him to use it. Wilson's animosity toward the organization was manifested most clearly after the armistice, when he ordered that virtually all of the government's espionage cases be dropped except those against the IWW.

No body of aggregate data is available enabling students of this period to evaluate the precise impact of the wartime activities of the civil liberties activists. Yet certain conclusions seem clear from the informal evidence. There would seem to be little question that by and large, the civil libertarians failed in their attempts at wartime consciousness-raising and agenda-setting. At no time, from April 1917 to November 1918, did the civil

85. *The Survey* 40 (September 7, 1918): 632.
86. Roger N. Baldwin to Woodrow Wilson, September 23, 1918 (Wilson Papers, LC).

liberties issue emerge as a legitimate public policy question. Despite the efforts of Roger Baldwin and the National Civil Liberties Bureau, there was no broad-scale public discussion of the government's wartime suppression of civil liberties or of the rights of citizens to contest such policies. Even the much milder contention of the civil libertarians that there should be guidelines defining the permissible limits of both expression and repression fell upon deaf and frequently hostile ears. In the tradition of Progressivism, these distinctions, particularly during wartime, were left to government leaders, who bore the responsibility of seeing to it that the policies they evolved in this area fit in with plans to mobilize the nation for victory.

Ironically, as J. A. Thompson has argued, the progressives, who so trusted mastery and efficiency, were in some ways antielitist themselves. They opposed big-business-crowned-head elitism and had a great faith in popular government and direct democracy. But progressivism was also republican in many of its aspects. Once the people had elected their "managers," and once those managers had decided upon a salutary and viable public policy for the achievement of social needs, the populace had an obligation to support such proper authority fully.[87] In this respect Roger Baldwin, Norman Thomas, Oswald Garrison Villard, and a substantial number of the activist civil libertarians were not progressives at all. Villard was an old-fashioned Jeffersonian and an opponent of much of progressive reform and agitation, on the grounds that it constituted a form of important state coercion.[88] Baldwin was antistatist in the extreme, seeing as much danger in the abuse of "proper" laws and "proper" authority as in the power of the conservative business elite which had controlled the country since the Civil War. Unsympathetic to Progressivism's emphasis upon efficiency, scientific manage-

87. J. A. Thompson, "American Progressive Publicists and the First World War, 1914–1917," *Journal of American History* 58 (September 1971): 369–70.

88. For a current assessment of Villard, see Ronald Radosh, *Prophets on the Right* (New York, 1975), pp. 67–85.

ment, and bureaucratization, and upon the welfare of the group above the rights of the individual, he saw this carried exactly where he feared, as national authorities more and more acted to manage defenseless members of the lower class and those outside the system whom he identified primarily in economic terms. Many such people were actually being exploited more callously then ever under the new arrangement and particularly in its wartime form. Civil liberties provided potential remedies from a government grown too powerful and irresponsible. If civil liberties were available to both protect and enhance the economic status of have-nots, such citizens would be better able to guard their own rights against the insensitive governmental monolith which bureaucrats and businessmen had so skilfully created on the dubious grounds of wartime exigency.

Thus, many of the most influential civil libertarians came out of a tradition of American individualism, a tradition of negative freedom—freedom from government's arbitrary authority. Their public postures were based on assumptions growing out of a Thoreau-like, quasi-anarchistic, nineteenth-century libertarianism. To a Woodrow Wilson such a posture—particularly during a world war—was both practically and ethically unacceptable and intolerable, given the type of positive planning which he was convinced a modern government must undertake.

But the civil liberties position behind which National Civil Liberties Bureau leaders were seeking to line up Americans also went against the grain of other traditional and contemporary values. Americans were being asked by suspect nonconformists to subscribe to principles that few Americans had previously embraced. This entailed the protection of the civil liberties of the "undeserving,"—those who did not have a respectable stake in American society and who were in no way ready to use these "rights" responsibly. Despite civil libertarian arguments, few could see what would be gained by defending the civil liberties of the undeserving. There had to be further assurances that those who received such rights would use them for constructive purposes (as defined by the so-called majority). What social purpose was to be served in demanding full rights for opponents of the war, conscientious objectors, slackers, disloyal aliens, radical labor agitators, and those who would abuse the power of the press? To give such citizens further "license" would simply be to encourage them to further undermine the stability of the American social fabric and to encourage the further disruption of normal, efficient capitalist development.

Few Americans with any power or authority could seriously entertain the argument that the denial of rights to a minority established precedents by which similar rights could be denied to a majority. They had very little sense that repressive wartime laws and their arbitrary enforcement had anything to do with them. They would not be the victims of such action. And if they were, they were in positions of sufficient power and influence that they could gain quick redress and exemption.

An indifferent "establishment" had trouble seeing any sincere virtue in either the arguments or the behavior of civil libertarians. Instead, traditionalists saw these people openly assailing the American government, sharply and scurrilously criticizing valid capitalist institutions, and failing to appreciate the way in which the war was fostering efficency, modernization, and social engineering. They perceived their behavior as obstructing and interfering with the war effort in the guise of civil liberties. Civil liberties were being prostituted in support of unpatriotic left-wing activities. In so misusing the civil liberties issue libertarian activists invited and warranted repression themselves.

At the institutional level, fundamental and abstract constitutional disagreements contributed to a split along traditionalist and realist lines regarding public law. Basically, both the wartime repressionists and the wartime civil libertarians disagreed as to the proper approach to the doctrine inherent in the Bill of Rights. The repressionists took the position that because constitutionalism embodies value choices and political preferences which are opposed to the arbitrary coercion characteristic of an undemocratic state, there should be no questioning of the way valid constitutional officers of that state decide to deal with Bill of Rights freedoms. Government leaders, as democratic agents charged with preserving the system, must be free to evolve the most practical ways to perform their function.

Civil libertarians took the opposite position. The very doctrine which was at stake invited questioning and discussion, particularly when the official positions became arbitrary. Since that doctrine addressed the vital question of the essential use of governmental authority to coerce wartime loyalty along certain lines, it was imperative that the people should have a significant voice in formulating the pertinent public policies. It is not surprising that the dichotomy between those traditionalists who viewed the Constitution as an immutable body of first principles which the government should protect at all costs—even if this meant temporarily destroying them in order to save them— and those who viewed the Constitution as an instrument through which the people could impose their own sense of moral imperatives upon the society through popular participation was not resolved in the wartime atmosphere.

The controversy survived the war and took on new meaning in the postwar period. In the reconstruction days of 1919 and the Red Scare days of early 1920, it became apparent that many ambitious national leaders had no intention of dismantling the mechanisms for wartime repression and planned to extend them into peacetime America. In that context many Americans were prepared to consider the possibilty that the wartime civil libertarians had had more objective and selfless ends than wartime obstruction. Americans were also beginning to see how important it was that someone other than the traditional power elite have a hand in shaping the meaning of Bill of Rights freedoms. The idea that the civil liberties issue was a valid one which should concern the nation and be a national agenda item —the central aim of the wartime civil libertarians—garnered some converts with the winding down of the wartime hysteria. Many who felt that a legitimate national war crisis might justify a temporary suspension of personal freedom were less trusting and passive in the face of a contrived postwar crisis. This was especially true because it was not clear the lengths to which its sponsors were prepared to exploit it for private purposes. Those prepared to blow the whistle on such opportunism thus stood to gain new credibility.

6

The Reaction of the Legal Community to a Wartime "Government of Men"

THE REACTION of the bench and bar to the civil liberties implications of the new government-to-citizen relationship which evolved during the war years was central to the immediate status of Bill of Rights freedoms and to their postwar future. Important shifts and reallocations of formal authority and real power were occurring. The new wartime legislation afforded the federal government and the states new opportunities to shape private institutions as well as the conduct of private citizens and thereby, indirectly, patterns of social, political, and economic development. Further, this new arrangement impacted upon private power structures and the ways in which private relationships impinged on both federal questions and upon the liberties of individual citizens. The legal community had to react to this development, since the judiciary was responsible for interpreting the law and thereby for validating, modifying, or challenging these new arrangements. Its response turned on the predilections of its members, on their awareness that the nation's public policymaking authority was being drawn into the hands of a wartime bureaucracy, and on their understanding of the immediate and long-term implications of that development. At stake here, at the most abstract but basic level, was the concept of the rule of law, a principle central to the preservation and future of American constitutionalism.[1]

The legal community of 1917 and 1918 had little perspective for seeing such implications clearly. There was no way that its members could anticipate that in emulating the Wilson government's example, Franklin Roosevelt and New Deal leaders might further stretch federal authority in their efforts to solve a depression and win a second world war; that Harry Truman might claim inherent presidential prerogatives in coping with cold war exigencies; that Lyndon Johnson might maneuver Congress into granting him virtually complete discretion to confront a deteriorating situation in Southeast Asia; or that Richard Nixon might finally turn a swollen federal bureaucracy into a clandestine surveillance state in order to preserve and extend his own power and authority.

On the other hand, as the "guardians of the temple," under oath to preserve and defend the Constitution of the United States, there is reason to expect that they might have been alert to the fact that a "government of men, not of laws," even if a wartime development, represented a serious threat to the constitutional system. Solutions which created a precedent for solving future crises simply by applying the will of the strongest, with the rights of the minority expendable to the majority's view of the purpose at hand, should have raised the legal eyebrows of the more sensitive. There were, after all, a number of lawyers in the Congress, in the courts, in the law schools, and involved with specific organizations who were sensitive to the implications of what was taking place and warned, through one medium or another, of its potential danger. Granted, there was strong temptation and strong pressure to see the massive steps toward extending governmental power over the lives of citizens

1. I am defining constitutionalism here in terms of Thomas Paine's aphorism that "whereas in England, the King is law, in America, the law is king" or, to be more precise, as the sanctity of process and a process which applies alike to rulers and ruled, at all times and in all circumstances, and serves to curtail the rule of force or the rule of the shrewdest and strongest.

at the time as an extraordinary and temporary development, essential to coping with a national emergency which potentially threatened a liberal society. But legal training, then as now, turned on the central role of precedent and *stare decisis* in American public law (the concept that precedent should be followed in all but exceptional circumstances). It should have enabled its recipients to recognize that what did take place during the war years would have an impact upon legal doctrine and legal procedure of long-term significance.

What was taking place—for the first time since Lincoln, at least—was that the principles of the rule of law were being pushed aside for the rule of men in positions of governmental power, men suddenly given a new blanket authorization to use power with very few guidelines specifying the type of discretion that they could exercise in its use. The situation should have been far more disturbing to legalists than it was. Clearly the government was entering new fields of private action, developing criminal penalties to apply to forms of behavior previously conceded to be permissible, and thereby setting forth a chain of new relationships with citizens. With virtually no case law available to serve as a guideline for defining such relationships, it was obvious that judges could deal with free speech, free press, free assembly, and various aspects of criminal procedure in a variety of discretionary ways. Such a situation raised the broader question of what responsibilities legal leaders had in such circumstances and what kind of action they, as professionals, should be taking. Would they quickly attempt to evolve a body of case law in such a way as to temper the government's power with the rule of law? Or would they assume the judicial self-restraint role of deferring slavishly to the legislative branch and merely applying the new statutes dutifully and unquestioningly, so as to condone the optimum use of federal coercion against the citizens in a variety of contexts?

Another ingredient intruded. This was the semiofficial public policy which argued that the rule of law question should not be framed in this context. The question was not whether judges should work to assure the continuation of a rule of law in this country during the war period; rather, it was whether the country could return to a rule of law once the war was over. The answer to that turned wholly upon who won the contest. If Germany won a rule of force would be imposed and the future of the rule of law in America would be dim. If the allies won it would be possible to get back to the rule of law again in a peacetime situation. Thus, to many legal patriots the domestic situation regarding the rule of law simply involved recruiting the legal community behind wartime victory and applying the battery of federal statutes and the doctrines embodied in them—the Espionage, and Sedition Acts, the Conscription Act, and the various censorship rules—in such a way as to minimize the impediments to that process. State sedition, criminal anarchy, and red flag laws should be handled similarly. As a leader of the American bar, Charles Evans Hughes wrote in 1918, "lawyers have a stake in the outcome of the struggle since they are 'fighting the battle of the law, the battle for the rule of reason against the rules of force.' "[2] Or, as Elihu Root added, the protagonists in the current battle are "divine right" and "individual liberty."[3]

Starting with the legal community's "role models," the justices of the Supreme Court, the pervasiveness of this posture emerges sharply. In April 1917 the high bench was in firm conservative hands and the civil liberties attitudes of its members, while previously little displayed, were relatively predictable. The dominant and senior member of the bench was Chief Justice Edward D. White. White, a successful Louisiana businessman, and a former Confederate soldier, had, in his later career, a compelling need to validate his nationalism, reject any states' rights taints, and demonstrate his total loyalty to the nation. The war afforded him an excellent opportunity to do all three. In this regard his positive attitude toward governmental power

2. Charles E. Hughes, "New Phases of National Development," *American Bar Association Journal* 4 (January 1918): 93.
3. Quoted in Jerold S. Auerbach, *Unequal Justice* (New York, 1976), p. 103.

was pertinent. In the earlier Progressive years, he had supported state police power as a valid exercise in the curtailment of rights of property. To White, even property's sanctity was clearly qualifiable when the curtailment was in the public interest. This applied to federal regulations as well. For example, in sustaining the Wilson-sponsored Adamson Act of 1916 imposing rigid wage and hour restrictions on railroad workers, White upheld the principle of emergency legislation in a period of national crisis, contending that while an emergency could not be made the source of new constitutional power, it could furnish a proper occasion for the exercise of power already enjoyed.[4] With such a patriot heading the bench, prepared to find ways to underwrite legally the expansion of wartime authority, the hopes of realistic civil libertarians obviously had to be placed elsewhere.

The senior justices following White, Joseph McKenna and William R. Day—both relatively progressive Republicans—also were frequently prepared to support positive governmental intervention in the economy. McKenna had sustained the federal Mann Act, as well as various police power measures, and ultimately dissented from Day's contrary opinion throwing out the federal Child Labor Law. He thus emerged over time as committed to a broader concept of the use of federal police power than his collegue. His few civil liberties rulings had given him the reputation as a liberal in the area of Bill of Rights guarantees, although in most of these cases, the litigants were conventional Anglo-Saxon Americans.[5] A Californian, McKenna's attitude toward the Chinese was possibly more revealing. Originally elected to Congress on a Republican platform which strongly advocated Chinese exclusion, he had urged that the government compile a record of all Chinese in America, issue identification cards, and, upon trial and conviction, deport or imprison all those found without cards on their persons. After

4. Wilson *v.* New, 243 U.S. (1917). On White, see Marie C. Klinkhamer, *Edward Douglas White* (Washington, D.C., 1943).

5. Matthew McDevitt, *Joseph McKenna* (Washington, D.C., 1946).

his appointment by President Harrison to the Ninth Circuit Court of Appeals in 1892, he affirmed all official decisions to exclude or deport Chinese laborers. And as United States Attorney General in 1897, he vigorously enforced the anti-Chinese laws.

Day, a close personal friend of fellow-Ohioan William McKinley—who had appointed him to the Sixth Circuit Court of Appeals—was strongly affected by McKinley's assassination. Blaming it largely upon anarchism and the alien philosophies which reached America with the massive immigration of the 1890s, he came into the war period with an increasingly hostile attitude toward alien and foreign-born dissenters—the people who, as it turned out, were frequently involved in wartime civil liberties cases. Further, his attitude toward Bill of Rights procedures was far less indulgent than McKenna's. In a postwar case involving alleged illegal search and seizure by a corporate official of evidence that enabled the government to prosecute another such official, Day saw nothing violative of Fourth Amendment guarantees. No reason existed for illegally seized material to be inadmissible in a court, Day held, if it helped to convict a culprit and get at unwarranted behavior.[6]

Willis Van Devanter was appointed to the bench by Taft in 1910, as a result of his reliable party service and his correct positions on the issues.[7] His entire career was built upon a conservative, property conscious intellectual and political philosophy. When the popular majority called for suppressing dissent during the war, it did not occur to Justice Van Devanter either to stand in the way or to question that policy.

Mahlon Pitney's track record was clearer and more precise. He had been involved intimately in the notorious prewar Leo Frank case in Georgia, in which Frank, a New York Jew and an "alien" (at least to Georgia culture) had been accused in

6. Joseph E. McLean, *William Rufus Day* (Baltimore, 1947).
7. Maurice P. Holsinger, "The Appointment of Supreme Court Justice Van Devanter: A Study of Political Preferment," *American Journal of Legal History* 12 (1968): 324–35.

1913 of assaulting and murdering a young Southern woman. His trial had taken place in an atmosphere of mob violence and hysteria so extreme that the judge, in the presence of the jury, conferred with the Atlanta police chief and the commanding colonel of the fifth regiment of the Georgia National Guard about security measures and eventually delivered the sentence in Frank's absence because his safety could not be guaranteed.[8] When Pitney was called upon to deal with the issues of the case, he flatly refused to examine pertinent facts surrounding the trial. His only concern was whether judicial procedures had been followed, not whether fairness had been achieved. Such behavior proved to be an accurate prediction of his attitude toward wartime cases, where unpopular minorities were frequently involved and where hysteria was a major factor affecting the treatment of such citizens.

James McReynolds had been Wilson's "trust busting" attorney general and had been moved to the Supreme Court early in Wilson's first term. Despite an image of being prepared to support the exercise of government power against miscreants, McReynolds generally was a believer in economic laissez-faire and had highly traditional nineteenth-century libertarian views regarding freedom and liberty. This largely meant "freedom from" government. As he wrote later in ruling unconstitutional a Nebraska statute which forbade teaching any subject in any school in the state in any language other than English, liberty protected by the due process clause of the Fourteenth Amendment includes not merely freedom from bodily restraint but the right of the individual to enjoy those privileges long recognized at common law as essential to the orderly pursuit of happiness by free men.[9] However, it turned out that this did not include wartime dissent, nor was McReynolds prepared to alter the law in any way to achieve that purpose.[10]

8. Frank *v.* Mangum, 237 U.S. 309, 345 (1915).
9. Meyer *v.* Nebraska, 262 U.S. 390 (1923).
10. McReynolds viewed government's positive duty to serve the citizen with a totally jaundiced eye. Typical was his action as acting attorney general. Responding to a distraught father's plea for aid in locating his

John H. Clarke of Ohio in some ways represented the most stereotypically dutiful Progressive position on the court at the time. Clarke, a friend of Cleveland's reform mayor, Tom Johnson, and Attorney General Gregory, was also a protégé of Secretary of War Baker, who had urged his appointment to the lower federal bench. Wilson had elevated him to the Supreme Court in 1916, largely as a result of Baker's recommendation that he could be relied upon for "a liberal and enlightened view of the law." [11] This he possessed (by Progressive standards), supporting economically and socially progressive measures and programs. But Clarke was also, like so many Progressives, an advocate of judicial restraint, feeling that it was not the place of judges to place their views above those of elected representatives. It was natural that he would support Wilson's wartime goals and the wartime Congresses' programs and find ways to adapt them to the exigencies of those times. This in turn was to lead him to support the suppression of speech which had a tendency to subvert the established order or to interfere in any way with the war effort.

This left only Oliver Wendell Holmes, Jr., and Louis D. Brandeis as flickering rays of hope for some judicial sensitivity to rule-of-law abrogations. In neither case was that hope fully justified. Holmes's prior judicial career had been marked strongly by a spirit of permissive majoritarianism and a commitment to judicial self-restraint. A general advocate of permitting the federal government and the states to use power positively to confront a variety of situations and to impose social control where necessary, Holmes's rulings, in the free speech area particularly, betrayed no great civil liberties concern prior to the wartime period or, as it turned out, during it. Stating at one

---

kidnapped daughter, he wrote, "You should furnish me with the names of the parties holding your daughter in bondage, the particular place, and the names of witnesses by whom the facts can be proven." Homer Cummings and Carl McFarland, *Federal Justice* (New York, 1937), p. 374.

11. H. Landon Warner, *The Life of Mr. Justice Clarke* (Cleveland, 1959), p. 63.

point that the rights enjoyed by individuals were social and not natural rights, Holmes was fairly well in tune with the growing tendency in twentieth-century America toward community control, with its corresponding limitation upon individual freedom.[12] His ruling in *Patterson* v. *Colorado* [13] in 1907 set forth a theory on permissible expression from which he did not depart appreciably until well after the war. The case involved the conviction of a Colorado publisher for articles and cartoons critical of Colorado's supreme court. The defendant had maintained that the statements in the articles were true and that under the First Amendment, truth was a defense for an alleged libel. Holmes rejected this contention, maintaining that the main purpose of the First Amendment was to prevent prior restraint by the government of private publications. Once printed, statements "deemed contrary to the public welfare" might be punished, whether true or false. Such a restricted view of First Amendment freedoms hardly took Holmes much beyond the old law of criminal attempts, which emphasized the permissibility of striking at individual freedom when the intent of the party involved seemed willful and malicious and when the expression of opinions seemed as if it might clearly create some measurable danger.

On the other hand, Holmes's commitment to fair procedure was noteworthy. The elderly justice had protested sharply against Pitney's callousness in the Leo Frank case, objecting to his colleague's unwillingness to review the facts of the case in light of the mob hysteria which surrounded the earlier trial. Observing in his dissent that "any judge who has sat with juries knows that, in spite of forms, they are extremely likely to be impregnated by the environing atmosphere," [14] he went on to contend that the hysteria which had surrounded the earlier trial was indeed a part of the facts of that case, facts "we must

12. Oliver Wendell Holmes, Jr., *The Common Law* (Cambridge, Mass., 1963), pp. 360-67.
13. 205 U.S. 261 (1907).
14. Frank *v.* Mangum, 237 U.S. 309, 349 (1915).

look in the face" and which clearly affected the outcome of the ruling. It is our duty, Holmes wrote, "to act upon total reality, and to declare lynch law as little valid when practiced by a regularly drawn jury, as when administered by one elected by a mob intent upon death." [15]

Louis D. Brandeis had just ascended the high bench on the war's eve after a bitter confirmation struggle over his appointment which had included anti-Semitic overtones, assaults upon his character, and a questioning of his prior legal career.[16] Wilson had gone to bat for Brandeis, a close acquaintance and advisor, and generally his commitment to Wilsonian liberalism was one of the factors which led the "interests" to fear him on the Supreme Court. Brandeis's record as a civil libertarian could be inferred from his general concern for the "little man" and from his open attacks on the "curse of bigness." More specifically, as early as 1890 he had called for the creation of a constitutional right of privacy, basing this call upon a concern for the inherent dignity of the individual.[17] His "sociological" briefs before the Supreme Court had probed the way in which society generally had deprived its minority members of much of their integrity as individuals. But, on the other hand, he was also committed to community welfare and social control, which advanced the general cause of upgrading the status and condition of citizens. In this respect, he was a creative constitutionalist and a potential judicial activist looking for new ways to guarantee new rights and prepared to experiment with constitutional mechanisms in the pursuit of the purpose. Wartime suspension of the rule of law went against his instincts and views of law as a social instrument for the service of all classes.

As a group these nine justices felt little obligation to mediate

15. Ibid., p. 350.

16. Alden L. Todd, *Justice on Trial* (New York, 1964).

17. Samuel D. Warren and Louis D. Brandeis, "The Right to Privacy," *Harvard Law Review* 4 (December 15, 1890): 193–220. On Brandeis generally see Alpheus T. Mason, *Brandeis: A Free Man's Life* (New York, 1946).

for citizens in assisting them to gain their civil liberties. Generally insensitive to the issue, they turned a deaf ear to exhortations from the small group of civil libertarians that swollen governmental power and a largely uninhibited new bureaucracy created a new need for civil liberties vigilance. There was not, as yet, either a well-defined judicial role regarding the question or a sense that there was a civil liberties constituency to which they had to be sensitive and accountable. On the contrary, with the possible exception of Brandeis, most seemed to feel natural and comfortable with the idea that the judiciary's wartime function was one of seeking out ways to afford constitutional legitimization to the government's new role.

The attitude of the members of the lower federal judiciary, where cases coming under the new battery of federal criminal laws would be instigated, are in no way as clearly definable as those of the Supreme Court. However, the federal bench of this time tended to reflect the conservatism of the legal profession, the attitudes of the American Bar Association, and the political orientation which had led to the appointment of most of the jurists. The majority of judges chosen to serve in that capacity were men who could be expected to conform with popular demands for suppression of foreign sentiments, doctrines, and dissenters.[18] Almost all native-born Americans, impatient with "alien" ideas such as socialism or pacifism, the conservative monotony of the federal bench was relieved only occasionally by a sensitive judge with sufficient vision to see his role as including something beyond simply applying law in an unquestioning fashion. Those few dissenters, as it turned out, paid heavily for their actions, particularly as their behavior was perceived by the administration and by substantial segments of the public as a form of obstructionism which impeded wartime victory. Thomas A. Lawrence has characterized the lower federal

18. Holmes in 1919 characterized the behavior of the lower federal judiciary as "hysterical." Mark De.W. Howe, ed., *The Holmes-Laski Letters* (Cambridge, Mass., 1953), p. 190.

judiciary during the war as "intent upon meting out quick justice and severe punishment to the disloyal' and no provision of the first amendment was thought to stand in the way." [19]

Similar pressures made the state judiciaries highly pliant and supportive of suppression as well. In those states where criminal syndicalism and sedition laws were enacted, their application was carried out with few deviations from the most restrictive views of the time regarding the permissible limits of freedom of speech and press. As Carol Jensen has pointed out in her study of the government's harrassment of the Non-Partisan League in Minnesota, the state courts, in dealing with league indictments for criticism of the war and opposition to the war effort, inevitably interpreted the state's vaguely drawn suppressive laws in the broadest possible fashion—thereby inviting their further use and making them a powerful weapon against the organization.[20]

Similarly, a large body of informal evidence suggests that juries were swayed by wartime hysteria. Jurymen were reported by one judge to have regarded verdicts of guilty as a means of demonstrating their own loyalty. In case after case, the severity of the sentence recommended by jurors reflected their desire to contribute to wartime patriotism through demonstrating their "toughness on traitors," a posture which many judges were hesitant to take any steps to ameliorate.[21]

The United States Department of Justice also helped to set the tone for the war period and to shape the attitudes of those called on to deal with the wartime legislation. Attorney General Gregory wanted to create the impression that the depart-

19. Thomas A. Lawrence, "Eclipse of Liberty: Civil Liberties in the United States During the First World War," *Wayne Law Review* 21 (1974): 70.

20. Carol Jensen, "Agrarian Pioneer in Civil Liberties: The Non-Partisan League in Minnesota" (Ph.D. dissertation, University of Minnesota, 1968), pp. 274–75.

21. Harry N. Scheiber, *The Wilson Administration and Civil Liberties* (Ithaca, N.Y., 1960); James R. Mock, *Censorship, 1917* (Princeton, 1941), pp. 197–200. Zechariah Chafee, Jr., *Free Speech in the United States* (Cambridge, Mass., 1941), pp. 70–73.

ment was greatly concerned with the important distinctions between permissible and disloyal behavior;[22] in so doing he apparently hoped to counteract the reputation of the Post Office Department for insensitivity to the rights of the individual. The edicts and the orders which the department sent out early in the war to federal attorneys emphasized the importance of adhering to strict legal rules, urging fairness in prosecutions and careful line-drawing regarding the permissible limits of open discussion. The Justice Department, he stated in his *Annual Report* for 1918, "is not only responsible for law enforcement, but, in a larger sense, is responsible for the protection of civil liberty."[23] A number of the department's key officials—O'Brian, Herron, and Bettman—were fair-minded in their approach, as long as they were not subject to pressure to compromise in doubtful cases involving allegedly disloyal action.

However, Gregory also engaged in other forms of communication which suggested that he was prepared to condone broad discretion regarding enforcement of the new laws. To United States attorneys, eager to prosecute vigorously under that legislation and anxious to secure convictions from juries, further encouragement was unnecessary. In a speech to the executive committee of the American Bar Association in early 1918, Gregory made clear that he felt that existing disloyalty legislation was inadequate, because it provided no punishment for a variety of treasonous acts. He further indicated that when it came to alleged German spies, "we are going to urge capital punishment in any case where the facts justify it" and commended those states which had strong laws punishing antiwar activities. He wished that Congress would go further in enacting federal legislation and encouraged "dramatic enforcement of the law against idlers" in all cases. The greatest menace to the

22. Such a view was undermined by the effort of the department to resurrect the doctrine of seditious libel early in the war. See Fred D. Ragan, "Justice Oliver Wendell Holmes, Jr., and Zechariah Chafee, Jr.," *Journal of American History* 58 (June 1971): 25.

23. *Report of the Attorney General* (1918), p. 16.

country, he concluded, was not the German spy but the "respectable" pacifist. The male pacifist is a "physical, or moral degenerate," he contended, urging the association to "in every way set its face against the pacifist and his propaganda." [24] In terms of procedural rights, Gregory was equally categorical. Alluding to an Illinois Bar Association resolution that condemned a lawyer's defense of a draft evader as unpatriotic and unprofessional, he told the committee: ". . . speaking not as a lawyer but as an American citizen, I wish to express my admiration for the action taken." [25]

Later in May 1918, Gregory issued a circular about the new Sedition Act amendment to the Espionage Act to all United States attorneys. Although his general order regarding its enforcement stressed again that this new measure should be administered with proper respect for strict legal processes and "should not be permitted to become the medium whereby efforts were made to suppress honest, legitimate criticism or discussion of government policies, or for personal feuds or persecution," [26] he also called for prompt and aggressive enforcement by the district attorneys, the very government officials who were not, in the nature of their assignment, expected to be impartial. In practice this situation got so out of hand that a month before the end of the war, Gregory had to issue a further circular directing district attorneys to send no more cases to grand juries under the espionage legislation without first submitting a statement of facts to the attorney general and receiving by wire his opinion whether or not the facts constituted an offense under the act. This circular, wrote O'Brian, who distributed it, "is suggestive of the immense pressure brought to bear throughout the war upon the Department of Justice in all parts of the country for indiscriminate prosecution

24. "Suggestions of Attorney General Gregory to Executive Committee in Relation to the Department of Justice," *American Bar Association Journal* 4 (1918): 309–16.
25. Ibid., p. 314.
26. Chafee, *Free Speech in the United States,* p. 68.

demanded in behalf of a policy of wholesale repression and restraint of public opinion." [27] But as Zechariah Chafee, Jr., later pointed out, until this order was issued, "all persons who were opposed to the war were practically at the mercy of the local district attorneys, and under the District Court test of the 1917 Act [set forth in The *Masses* case] or the express language of the 1918 Act, prosecution almost invariably resulted in conviction." [28]

The war situation also played into contemporary concerns of the American bar, with anti-civil liberties consequences. Admission to the bar at the time was relatively open, even though it was controlled by the American Bar Association. That body, in turn, was dominated by the conservative elite of the American legal community. For some years leaders of that community had deplored the declining professional and educational standards in the law, especially with the persistence of the practice of "reading" law, the growth of night law schools, and other newer institutions. In response to growing demands for higher educational and admissions standards in the prewar years, the ABA urged that a number of steps be taken to achieve these ends, including the requirement of three years' attendance at a law school to qualify for the bar. With the war, and the accompanying hysteria which swept the country, legal leaders, much like their counterparts in higher education, jumped aboard the wartime bandwagon, making their talents available to the war effort and showing their patriotism by expressing their distaste and, in some cases, hostility to opponents of the war of all stripes. Bar associations organized preparedness committees to care for the practices of attorneys in military serivce, to provide legal assistance to dependants of military personnel, and to defend American war policy. Conversely, lawyers who criticized the war effort or who defended war critics frequently encountered punitive professional sanctions. A particular variation on this theme, according to Jerold Auerbach, was to

27. Ibid., p. 69.
28. Ibid., p. 69.

capitalize upon the wartime hostility against those who were not 100 percent American by urging that such types be kept out of the profession in the future.[29]

Wartime attitudes emerge more revealingly from the anecdoctal literature. A radical Pennsylvania attorney was disbarred for associating with groups whose views conflicted with those of the American government and for organizing opposition to the Selective Service Act. Lawyers were disbarred for speaking publicly under the auspices of the IWW. In Texas, a German-born lawyer was disbarred for saying ". . . Germany is going to win this war, and . . . I hope she will." When a Chicago attorney acting on behalf of his client challenged the constitutionality of the draft law, the *Central Law Journal* accused him of subversion, contending that although an individual enjoyed the right to his own opinions, he could not delegate that right to his attorney, to whom, presumably, the client's views were imputed.[30]

The ABA itself seemed generally to endorse and encourage this behavior. Members teaching at a number of major law schools not only supported war policies but rationalized the suppression of civil liberties as a justifiable policy during wartime. The working bar, which tended to dominate the eleven thousand members of the body, took an early stand in April 1917 by unanimously endorsing a recommendation introduced by Elihu Root to the effect that:

We condemn all attempts in Congress and out of it to hinder and embarrass the government of the United States in carrying on the war with vigor and effectiveness. . . . Under whatever cover of pacifism or technicality such attempts are made, we deem them to be in spirit pro-German and in effect giving aid and comfort to the enemy.[31]

In January 1918 its *Journal* reprinted an address entitled "The Socialist Menace to Constitutional Government," in which the speaker branded Socialists as "agents out to destroy America's

29. Auerbach, *Unequal Justice,* pp. 104–05.
30. Ibid., pp. 105, 326.
31. "War Resolutions," *American Bar Association Journal* 3 (1917): 577.

court's function as protector of life, liberty and property" because Socialists advocated judicial recall and elimination of the Supreme Court's power of judicial review.[32] Charles Evans Hughes, in the same *Journal*, lauded the Conscription Act as a "needed lesson of duty in a democracy," since it taught "a new appreciation of the power of our government." [33]

At a more doctrinal level, W. R. Vance, dean of the University of Minnesota Law School, argued that the First Amendment embodied only the 1790 common law of freedom of speech and press, contending that this reduced the problem to a determination of the scope and extent of the existing right of free publication and free speech at the time of the adoption of the Constitution. Since those rights at that time were highly limited and included simply freedom from prior restraint, there was little restriction on the liability which people incurred for improper expression. In fact, Vance contended, the only real check on the government's power to control speech and the press was public opinion, arguing further that jurors interpreting the often vague provisions of the various wartime statutes should decide whether the defendants' words were seditious "according as they think the defendant blamable or not. . . . Thus a sedition law, supported by public sentiment, will be enforceable, while one violating the public sense of justice and freedom will register its unfitness in verdicts of acquittal." Vance did not mention that the logical outcome of this attitude, in the context of wartime hysteria, would be to make any critical statement "blamable" and would effectively terminate dissent during the wartime period.[34] Such a widely held intractable attitude toward civil liberties and those who would defend them

32. Rome G. Brown, "The Socialist Menace to Constitutional Government," *American Bar Association Journal* (1918): 54.

33. Hughes, "New Phases of National Development," p. 107.

34. W.R. Vance, "Freedom of Speech and Press," *Minnesota Law Review* (1918): 260. Legal education and the general nature of American legal culture as partial products of the Langdell-inspired shift to the case method coming from the Harvard Law School, contributed to much of the attitude of the bench and bar at the time. See John W. Johnson, "Adaptive Jurisprudence: Some Dimensions of Early Twentieth-Century Legal Culture," *The Historian* 40 (November 1977): 16–35.

was an overt threat to the rule of law. Surprisingly, it was troubling to only a minority fraction of the legal community.

Three examples of the effect that these attitudes had upon the law in action illuminate the wartime civil liberties situation. The first involves an early coming-to-terms with the restrictive and discretionary parts of the 1917 Espionage Act, and especially its controversial Section XII.

The case of *Masses Publishing Co.* v. *Patten* [35] has been discussed earlier with regard to the parties involved in the case. From the standpoint of the lawyers and the judges involved, other factors intrude. When Postmaster General Burleson, after a conference with the attorney general and the judge advocate general of the Army, ordered the postmaster of New York City not to accept the August 1917 issue of *The Masses* for mailing, the publishers went into Judge Learned Hand's court and asked for a restraining order. Hand promptly issued an injunction preventing the postmaster from excluding *The Masses* from the mail. He was particularly anxious to establish the point that the test for suppression in a democratic government was "neither the justice of its substance, nor the decency and propriety of its temper, but the strong danger that it would cause injurious acts." In this case, he pointed out, no crime had been committed, since the publication in question had not, in so many words, directly advised or counseled a violation of the Espionage Act. He further attempted to set forth an interpretation of that measure which he hoped would provide a liberalizing test for heading off further such efforts to quash legitimate public expression:

If one stops short of urging upon others that it is their duty or their interest to resist the law, it seems to me one should not be held to have attempted to cause its violation. . . . If that not be the test, I can see no escape from the conclusion that under this section [XII], every political agitation which can be shown to be apt to create a seditious temper is illegal. I am confident that, by the

35. 244 Fed. 535; 245 Fed. 102; 246 Fed. 24 (1917).

language of the statute, Congress had no such revolutionary purpose in view.[36]

But Hand's confidence in the persuasiveness of the open democratic process was shared by few in positions of power. Attorney General Gregory promptly charged that Hand had "taken the teeth" out of the 1917 Act and urged their restoration. Chafee branded the charge "absurd." [37] The "teeth" that the government wanted, he wrote in his postwar volume, *Freedom of Speech,* were never there until other judges put in false ones in decisions fraught with misdirected patriotism and fervor. Under such circumstances it is not surprising that Judge Hand's position was not only rejected but its implications deplored. In granting a stay of his injunction until the case could be heard in the court of appeals—a highly irregular procedure—Judge Charles Hough also addressed the issue regarding where and what kind of expression could be proscribed. Alluding to the fact that *The Masses* had admired the "sacrifices" of conscientious objectors and praised anarchists Emma Goldman and Alexander Berkman as "friends of American freedom," he candidly expressed his opinion that "it is at least arguable whether there can be any more direct incitement to action than to hold up to admiration those who do act." [38]

Circuit Judge H. W. Rogers, who overturned Hand's earlier ruling, went further. Rejecting Hand's distinction ("This Court does not agree that such is the law"), his attitude was even more restrictive than Burleson's or Hough's. Anything that impeded, hindered, retarded, restrained, or put an obstacle in the way of recruiting, he ruled, was sufficient to warrant criminal penalty under the Espionage Act. He thereby made available to district judges everywhere the old "remote bad tendency" doctrine. Rogers then went on to state:

36. See Chafee, *Free Speech,* pp. 44–49, for a discussion of Hand's posture.
37. Ibid, p. 49.
38. Masses Publishing Co. *v.* Patten, 246 Fed. 24, 27 (1917).

Courts have nothing to do with the wisdom or unwisdom of a legislative act. It is the function of the legislative department to enact law, and of the judicial department to construe and apply it. The judges cannot pass upon the wisdom or the justice of the statute, but are simply to ascertain the intent of the law makers as expressed in the enactment, and to give effect thereto.[39]

Dutiful and unquestioning compliance was obviously the proper prescribed wartime behavior for the legal community. District judges knew now that they could ignore entirely the first element of criminal attempt and solicitation—that the effort to commit a crime, though unsuccessful, must approach dangerously near success. They could also comfortably ignore Hand's test of guilt—that the words must in themselves urge a duty or an interest to resist the law. All that had to be shown to sustain conviction was that words uttered or written had a tendency to cause unrest among soldiers or to make recruiting more difficult. They were also encouraged to view as pertinent any evidence of intent to induce questionable overt action. This new standard of guilt allowed conviction for any words which indirectly discouraged recruiting and the war spirit, if only the intention to discourage existed. Intention thus became the crucial test of guilt in any prosecution of opposition to the government's war policies, and this requirement became a mere form, since it could always be inferred from the existence of the indirect injurious effect.

Only a handful of federal district judges failed to embrace the message implicit in this ruling. Two dissenting members of the judiciary balked, however, and their behavior further crystalized attitudes which affected subsequent wartime prosecutions. One such figure was Federal District Judge George M. Bourquin of Montana. Bourquin and United States District Attorney Burton K. Wheeler found themselves caught up in a situation which saw the Anaconda Copper Mining Company, the dominant economic and political power in Montana, at-

39. Department of Justice, *Interpretation of War Statutes,* Bulletin No. 7 (Washington, D.C., 1918), p. 7.

tempting to use wartime hysteria to strike at its critics and opponents. Anaconda was particularly anxious to capitalize on the wartime atmosphere to gain mass indictments against those considered "slackers" and "seditionists," and Bourquin and Wheeler were equally adamant in their intention of heading off just such a process.[40]

Bourquin, a 1912 Taft appointee and a rugged individualist, heard a case in late January 1918 involving the first alleged violation of the Espionage Act in the region. Ves Hall, a rancher from Rosebud County, had been arrested for making seditious remarks. Hall, clearly a hothead, had made statements in a small Montana town of sixty people, sixty miles from the nearest railroad, in a hotel kitchen, at a picnic, in the street, and in a "hot and furious saloon argument" to the effect that he would flee the United States to avoid the draft; that he hoped Germany would defeat the United States; and that he felt that President Wilson was "a British tool, a servant of Wall Street millionaires, and the richest and crookedest —— ever President." [41] On January 27, Bourquin directed the jury to return a verdict acquitting Hall. He then explained his ruling, since, he maintained, he felt that it was necessary to interpret the Espionage Act "to the end that a precedent be established." Admitting that he found Hall's slanderous statements "unspeakable," he nonetheless contended that they could not justify a verdict of guilty. In his opinion, the Espionage Act was not intended "to suppress criticism or denunciation, truth or slander, oratory or gossip, argument or loose talk." [42] Loose talk and slander of the president were not federal crimes, he maintained, and thus Hall could not be punished for them.

This strict interpretation of the Espionage Act and Bourquin's jealous protection of individual rights and free speech infuriated local supporters of the war. They quickly set out both

40. Arnon Gutfeld, "The Ves Hall Case, Judge Bourquin, and the Sedition Act of 1918," *Pacific Historical Review* 37 (May 1968): 164.
41. U.S. *v.* Ves Hall, 248 Fed. 150 (1918).
42. Ibid., p. 141.

to drive Bourquin out of office and to forestall the reappointment of District Attorney Wheeler because of his expressed approval of Bourquin's position and his failure to prosecute more vigorously under the measure. Governor Sam V. Stewart called a special session of the Montana legislature to urge the passage of new legislation to stop the activities of the disloyal element in Montana. "Feeling is running high, and I really expected some killing as a result of the construction of the law in the Hall case," he stated.[43] The editor of the influential Helena *Independent* wrote an open letter to Senator Henry L. Myers, asking him to look into the possibility of having Bourquin removed from the state for the duration of the war. "Men . . . are determined to rid the state of Wobblies, slackers, disloyalists and traitors. . . . I am ever expecting . . . trouble . . . in the state where sedition runs wild."[44] Guy E. LaFollette, managing editor of the same newspaper, stated that impeachment of Bourquin would prove too long a process. He asked that the Department of Justice transfer Bourquin to another district because "Montana is fed up with Bourquin."[45] He also forecast the lynching of those whom Bourquin had set free.

At the special session, Governor Stewart spoke at length about the vigilantism which had been fomented by Bourquin's narrow ruling. Given such an interpretation of the federal sedition statute, there was no way, within the law, of punishing treasonable and disloyal utterances within Montana. This would undoubtedly lead the people of the different communities to engage in unwarranted and illegal violence. Therefore, a state law punishing seditious expression was clearly in order. The legislature responded with the Criminal Syndicalism Act, thereby affording Montana authorities a law with which to deal with disloyal elements. The special session also entertained joint resolutions which called for the resignation of Bourquin and Wheeler. The strongest of these was defeated by one vote. The

43. Quoted in Gutfeld, "The Ves Hall Case," p. 170.
44. Ibid.
45. Ibid.

judge and the district attorney, however, fared better than Judge Charles L. Crum of the Fifteenth Judicial District of Montana. Crum had acted as a character witness for Ves Hall. The Montana Senate felt that he was guilty of aiding and abetting draft dodgers and criticizing American participation in the war. He was impeached. It is more likely that Crum's real crime was his German heritage and his lack of public enthusiasm for the war.[46]

Federal response to the Bourquin situation also affected wartime attitudes toward civil liberties and those who would defend them. In the wake of the Ves Hall ruling, the Justice Department received a large number of communications, as had Montana congressmen, criticizing Bourquin and asking whether his decision could be appealed. O'Brian, in investigating the matter, wrote to Attorney General Gregory that the way to dispose of Judge Bourquin's interpretation would be through an amendment to the federal Espionage Act, spelling out more clearly the kind of crimes of expression which fell under it. At the same time, however, he indicated somewhat resignedly that such an amendment would probably not dispose of the attitude of Judge Bourquin. "The record of his rulings in our files," O'Brian wrote, "show unmistakably that the real trouble with him is that he is distinctly against the proper enforcement of any of the war statutes, and is out of sympathy with their purpose." [47] At this point military intelligence also entered the scene.[48] Colonel F. G. Knabenshue, an intelligence officer in the western department, wrote to the Justice Department that "Judge Bourquim [sic] should be transferred and a man 500

46. Burton K. Wheeler, *Yankee from the West* (Garden City., N.Y., 1962), p. 155.
47. John Lord O'Brian to Thomas W. Gregory, February 27, 1918. Department of Justice Files.
48. Although the Bureau of Investigation was beginning to take over much of the federal government's investigatory work, information concerning alleged illegal activities was also gathered by the military intelligence section of the War Department and the postal, internal revenue, customs, immigration, and naval intelligence services, many of which pooled their information to promote speed and efficiency in detection.

percent American be sent to Butte." [49] He also urged that the reappointment of Wheeler be killed. Senator Thomas J. Walsh of Montana also inquired repeatedly whether the decision in the Hall case could not be appealed. Gregory answered that in such a case a judge's action in directing the jury to acquit could not be appealed. O'Brian explained to Walsh that to appeal the case would mean reopening. This would place the defendant in jeopardy of being tried again on the same charge. The most appropriate course of action, the department indicated, was a new Sedition Act amendment, something that Walsh supported strongly and finally saw enacted in May 1918. In supporting that measure, Senator Myers argued that the bill was essential to stop mob rule. If seditionists could be dealt with effectively through the courts and convictions could be assured, the tendency of local citizens to take law into their own hands would be greatly diminished. Thus, the attitude of Montanans and the response of a judge seeking sensitive application of the federal repressive legislation led to even more repressive federal legislation. The Justice Department, recognizing the broad scope of the measure and the danger to individual liberties inherent in its wholesale and insensitive use, urged district attorneys to enforce it with discretion. Regrettably, the attempt to instill that attitude into law enforcement practices was largely futile.

Aspects of the rule-of-law issue in the Bourquin controversy are complex. Clearly, Bourquin saw himself utilizing the law as a way of heading off the frivolous abuses of private power during the war period. Those who deplored his actions did not see them as such. Rather, they saw Bourquin injecting his own views of public dissent into the process in such a way as to condone the behavior of people who were not themselves dutifully adhering to wartime policy. Further, they saw his actions as ones which would further induce private noncompliance and flouting of formal legal processes. Those who rushed the state criminal syndicalist law through the Montana legislature and urged the passage of the Sedition Act amendment to the

49. Gutfeld, "The Ves Hall Case," p. 175.

federal Espionage law felt that they were formalizing legal structures in such a way as to insure uniformity and presumably fairness. They did not, however, acknowledge that the substance of the laws which they were supporting tended to underwrite a wartime policy destructive of objectivity and fair legal process for those who legitimately opposed what the government was doing and sought to correct it, not out of malice, but from a desire to protect democratic processes.

Judge Charles Fremont Amidon of the Eighth Circuit, based in North Dakota, was a progressive friend and supporter of Theodore Roosevelt. Amidon met some similar reactions when he attempted comparable forms of liberalization. Yet a number of aspects of his career contain important and revealing variations. Whereas Bourquin had sought repeatedly to prevent the prostitution of the federal Espionage Act into a device to "wreak private vengeance, and work for private ends," [50] Amidon set his face much more firmly against a broad federal use of the act to subvert democratic processes, deploring particularly the surrender to hysteria of judges on the federal bench and hoping, by setting an example of calm and detached judgment, to prove that such action was not only desirable but viable. Amidon was distressed from the outset with the Espionage Act of 1917, feeling that it was too general and should probably have been condemned on that ground alone. He was even more upset by the 1918 Amendment, which he felt "has in it every evil of the old definition of treason," comparing it to the old English law which made it criminal to "imagine the King's death." He was especially vitriolic in his assessment of the attorney general's instruction circular for the later measure. "No comment upon it could add to its language," he wrote to Zechariah Chafee, Jr., after the war.

It converts every U.S. Attorney into an angel of life and death, clothed with the power to walk up and down in his district, saying, this one will I spare, and that one will I smite. If the law leaves it to the district attorney to determine when an act shall be prosecuted

50. *Ex parte Starr*, 263 Fed. 145, 147 (1919).

as a crime, and when it shall not be, how is the citizen to know when he is exercising his constitutional right, and when he is committing a crime? Of course . . . such conduct in administering criminal law, punishable by imprisonment for twenty years, simply converts the government into a government of men and not of laws.[51]

His reaction to the conviction of Rose Pastor Stokes, who was sentenced to ten years in prison for seditious expression by the United States District Court of Missouri, contained poignant observations about the behavior of his fellow judges. "You got no notion from the opinion," he wrote to Chafee later, "of the violence of Judge Van Valkenburg's language in submitting the case to the jury . . . Judge Van Valkenburg is one of the ablest judges in the Eighth Circuit, yet it was like the charge of soldiers on the battlefront in France, and illustrated how far the war passion could sweep a very able Judge from his moorings." [52]

Amidon's record on the bench in Espionage Act cases was courageous and judicious. However, certain of his own strong personal attitudes and values impacted on that record. This was especially true of his tolerance for reform, on the one hand, and his impatience and intolerance with clinging to foreign and alien sympathies on the other. One contributed healthily to the public dialogue by validly introducing new and unorthodox proposals as potential vehicles for problem solving. The other became a vehicle for the retention of archaic and inapplicable views and impeded democratic social progress. This helps to explain the apparent contradiction between his bitter denunciation of a German-American preacher who sympathized with the fatherland and his refusal to let a jury decide on the guilt or innocence of a rabid socialist agitator in the employ of the Non-

51. Charles F. Amidon to Zechariah Chafee, Jr., August 29, 1919, Amidon Papers, University of North Dakota. The best study of Amidon's career is I. Kenneth Smemo, "Progressive Judge: The Public Career of Charles Fremont Amidon" (Ph.D. dissertation, University of Minnesota, 1967).
52. Amidon to Chafee, June 5, 1920 (Amidon Papers).

Partisan League. Amidon had no quarrel with the suppression of genuine hyphenate disloyalty, and his most emotional and didactic opinions from the bench during those years dealt with this issue. Alluding frequently to the "melting pot failure," he nonetheless blamed the ongoing ethnicity of these groups, and their failure to respond to Americanization, on selfish, exploiting industrialists who had brought them to this country originally and had kept them "foreign" in order to keep them tractably exploitable. Amidon wanted them to be Americans, and thereby to appreciate and understand the true meaning and utility of American rights and freedoms. He saw their antiwar posturing as a disappointing symptom of the failure of that process, revealing the extent to which they were still being duped by their exploiters. Therefore, he had no trouble supporting the national program of George Creel, which he felt "had done more to educate the American people in the duties of citizenship than a thousand universities." [53] This, he hoped, would open the eyes of the unassimilated to the folly of their manipulatability.

With regard to socialists and agrarian radical reformers, however, the situation was very different. To such people who had analyzed problems carefully and were prepared to work to eliminate major flaws in the system, he was prepared to afford maximum leeway. As he stated in his instructions to the jury in the case of Job W. Brinton, a Non-Partisan League leader who had spoken bitterly in opposition to war-profiteering and had been charged with attempting to set class against class:

I have never known any great reform being carried through where the people whose established condition would be disturbed by the carrying out of the reform not to say that the people who were trying to bring about the reform were stirring up class against class. That argument . . . is repeated in every effort to change an existing condition . . . the only way you can produce a change in any political or economic condition is for the people who suffer from that con-

53. Charge to jury, U.S. *v.* Wishek (D.N.D., 1918), U.S. Department of Justice, *Interpretation of War Statutes,* Bulletin No. 153. Washington, D.C., 1919.

dition to say that the people who are inflicting the sufferings are doing wrong, and speak right out plainly on that subject.[54]

Amidon's overall wartime record reflects these alleged ambivalences. On one hand, he dismissed over 50 percent of the cases brought before him for alleged Espionage Act violations in a district which had seen more persecutions per capita under the act than any other section of the country. On the other hand, in cases in which he had sustained conviction—usually involving German-American opponents of the war—he was sharp and unbending. In both circumstances, Amidon was dealing with United States Attorney Melvin Hildreth, whose eagerness to prosecute all forms of disloyalty under the act was highly indiscriminate.

The Justice Department quickly labeled Amidon and his court a trouble spot: Its concern was reflected in the explosive and nationally publicized case of Kate Richards O'Hare, a Socialist stump speaker employed by the Non-Partisan League. Mrs. O'Hare had been one of the sponsors of the antiwar resolutions at the Socialists' St. Louis convention in 1917. She was subsequently arrested for a speech to a small crowd in Bowman, North Dakota, and charged with obstructing enlistment under the Espionage Act by telling the mothers of North Dakota that they were no better than brood sows if they let the government send their offspring to fight in Europe and become fertilizer.[55] Normally, Amidon would have been the circuit judge presiding in the case. But as a result of Justice Department pressure, he was removed in favor of Judge Martin Wade, a "Bourbon, anti-Bryan Democrat . . . with a mania for denouncing 'traitors' on all possible occasions."[56] After

54. Charge to jury, U.S. *v.* Brinton (Unrep., D.N.D., 1918), U.S. Department of Justice, *Interpretation of War Statutes,* Bulletin No. 132. Washington, D.C., 1919.

55. Robert L. Morlan, *Political Prairie Fire* (Minneapolis, 1955), p. 148. See also Kate Richards O'Hare, *In Prison* (Seattle, 1976).

56. H. C. Peterson and Gilbert Fite, *Opponents of War* (Madison, 1957), p. 36.

Wade's vicious, emotional charge,[57] the jury quickly found Mrs. O'Hare guilty, sentencing her to five years in a federal penitentiary. Wade later revealed that he had received a letter from the Justice Department's St. Louis office prior to the trial which said, in part, "nothing would please this office more than to hear that she got *life*." [58] The successful conviction of Mrs. O'Hare helped set the tone of conservative expectations for espionage prosecutions in subsequent cases involving Non-Partisan League activists. Amidon viewed the action with bitter resignation. He also viewed with alarm increasing prosecutions under the new Sedition Act amendment, which he felt betrayed a misunderstanding of the restrictive implications of that measure for legitimate criticism. The first case to reach him under that measure afforded him the opportunity to make his point from the bench.

The case involved E. H. Schutte, a farmer alleged to have stated publicly that "this is a rich man's war and it is all a damned graft and swindle," and "if you don't believe it, just look at the price of wheat." He was indicted under Section 3 of the 1917 act, prior to amendment, and the charges were based on the fact that among those who heard the words were men who might be subject to the draft. Amidon sustained a demurrer to the indictment, thereby dismissing the action. To do so, he applied a narrow interpretation of the act of 1917, arguing that the fact that Congress found it necessary to amend and broaden that clause in 1918 proved that the proper interpretation of it as first enacted was restricted to actual interference with recruiting and enlistment. He wrote: "As the indictment in the present case fails wholly to state that the language complained of was spoken to named persons belonging to one of the classes mentioned in the act, or to an audience at which such persons were present, it is fatally defective, and

57. The charge is printed in Walter Nelles, ed., *Espionage Act Cases* (New York, 1918), pp. 46–47.
58. Quoted in Smemo, "Progressive Judge," p. 264.

the demurrer must be sustained." [59] He did point out, however, for the public's guidance, that the amended act had far broader application.

The immediate effect of this ruling was twofold. District Attorney Hildreth, seeing little further hope for conviction in peripheral cases, promptly, if grudgingly, withdrew ten other indictments for statements similar to those made by Schutte. The action demonstrated that a forceful and courageous judge could set a tone from the bench which could undermine sharply the atmosphere which produced indiscriminate indictments. [60] However, people hostile to any wartime tolerance came to view Schutte and two similar subsequent rulings as evidence of Amidon's questionable and potentially dangerous views.

In one of these subsequent decisions, the subject was John H. Wichek, a North Dakota banker of German ancestry known for his pro-German sentiments, who had stated that "banks having large holdings of Liberty Bonds are unsafe to keep money in. . . ." He had subsequently been indicted under the Espionage Act. Amidon, in instructing the jury, pointed out that Wichek was not directly affecting the attitude of anyone eligible for service in the Army and Navy. He urged jury members to determine the facts in strict accordance with the law, while disregarding the emotional currents running through the entire situation. The jury ultimately voted nine to three for acquittal, and although Hildreth swore he would bring the suit up for trial again in the fall, he ultimately did not do so. Amidon's charge, as it turned out, served as a precedent for a narrow interpretation of the 1917 act as a military rather than a sedition statute. The Justice Department reported it in its *Interpretations Bulletins,* which were issued to guide federal attorneys and the courts. [61]

59. U.S. *v.* Schutte, 252 Fed. 212 (1918).

60. Ultimately, Justice Brandeis cited the Schutte decision as an example of proper Sedition Act interpretation in his dissent in Schafer *v.* U.S., 251 U.S. 466 (1920).

61. Justice Department, *Interpretation of War Statutes,* Bulletin No. 153. Washington, D.C., 1919.

This ruling, plus Amidon's statement in the Brinton case on the legitimacy of class protest, produced a storm of local criticism. The Department of Justice was quick to pick it up and exploit it, reproducing the charge to the jury in the Brinton case and disseminating it to the major North Dakota newspapers. They lost no time in catching the cue, pillorying Amidon in their editorial columns. The following month Frederick P. Cuthbert, president of the North Dakota Bar Association, denounced Amidon and the practice which enabled federal judges to talk politics from the bench. Ultimately, Theodore Roosevelt joined the chorus, insinuating that his former friend and supporter was encouraging indefensible class warfare in the upper Midwest in wartime.[62]

Amidon suffered more than simply verbal abuse. His former friends and associates ostracized him; friends and neighbors crossed the street in order to avoid speaking to him; and he received numerous threatening letters and phone calls. Such behavior only subsided when late in the war he upheld the conviction of John Fontana, a pro-German minister charged with stating to his "flock" in his heavily German community that he was proud of the noble fight the Germans were making, that the United States had no reason to take up arms against them, and that he was praying for victory for the fatherland. In sustaining his indictment for sedition, Amidon used the occasion to deliver one of his most impassioned and widely quoted opinions, castigating alien ideals and "hyphenism" in a thoroughly Rooseveltian fashion. Characterized by *The New York Times* as a verbal condemnation more severe than any except those that the basest criminals ever hear from the bench,[63] the statement was widely reprinted and distributed for nativist purposes in the late war and immediate postwar periods. While Amidon later regretted the use that was made of the statement, he still felt that it had helped to fuel the fires under the melting pot in the

62. *Fargo Forum,* October 7, 1918, quoted in Smemo, "Progressive Judge," p. 282.
63. *The New York Times,* September 17, 1918, p. 12.

North Dakota area. As a result of this reestablished credibility and his careful explanation to the jury of the provisions of the Sedition Act, the grand jury returned only 13 valid indictments in over 150 cases during the fall term of North Dakota's district court session, beginning in October 1918. Amidon in turn was gratified that his tactical maneuvering had enabled him once again to temper by the rule of law the excessive zeal of those who still continued to utilize war hysteria as the basis for criminal conviction.

Hand, Bourquin, Amidon, and a few other scattered judges such as John E. Garland and Kimbrough Stone of the Eighth Circuit Court [64] seemed to be the rare exceptions among members of the lower federal judiciary prepared to see wartime dissent as something more than simply individual interest. For these judges free expression also had a vital dimension as a process contributing to social interest: If speech was serving that purpose, repression of it was to be done with great reluctance, and only if it was clearly demonstrable that its continuation was purposely and irresponsibly threatening the rights and the security of others. The massive majority of their brethren simply took the position that dissent was solely a matter of personal interest which had to give way, like other personal desires, the moment it interfered with the broader interests of the nation. To have maintained that the nation might benefit from preserving First Amendment rights intact was beyond both their conception and comprehension and that of most other First Amendment thinking at the time.

The behavior growing out of these rabid nativist and patriotic attitudes emerges from the judicial record of the war period. Well over two thousand prosecutions occurred under the war-

64. Garland and Stone reversed Amidon in the case of Henry Von Bank, a naturalized citizen from Luxembourg indicted under the Espionage Act for refusing, as president of a district school board, to put the flag of the United States upon the schoolhouse in the district and for stating that he would "just as soon see a pair of old trousers hanging over the school house as the American flag." Von Bank *v.* U.S., 253 Fed. 641 (1918).

time Espionage and Sedition Acts. Over a thousand convictions resulted.[65] There is a striking correlation between those United States district attorneys gripped by war hysteria and the number of prosecutions in various districts. Prosecutions in thirteen of the eighty-seven federal districts accounted for almost half of the total number of prosecutions, with areas such as northern Illinois, North Dakota, eastern Missouri, and Arizona heading the list. However, there is far more to wartime judicial behavior than simply a counting of the cases. For an understanding of the factors contributing to the pattern of wartime repression, one must also look at the tone which was being set in the early wartime decisions, particularly notorious ones in the higher courts.

Emma Goldman, a Russian-Jewish immigrant, radical, spell-binding speaker, and, with Alexander Berkman, the central figure of American anarchism since the turn of the century, had suffered no overt federal repression because of her views or her radical activities in the prewar period. A bitter opponent of war, a fact evident to the readers of her frequently strident anticapitalist and antiwar publication *Mother Earth,* she was particularly upset with American entry into the European conflict, and especially with the idea of conscription—a policy and program which to her constituted the ultimate affront to individual conscience. As she stated freely and often in the early weeks of the war, she could not understand how professed liberals could in one breath denounce Prussian militarism and in the next propose conscription. She joined with other anarchists and radicals in founding the No Conscription League and set out to hold a series of well-publicized public protest meetings in New York to speak out against the practice. The meetings quickly became the target for patriot vigilantism, as well as police and governmental surveillance and frequent violence. When it became clear that the authorities were using the meetings to trap young men in attendance who had not

65. Scheiber, *The Wilson Administration and Civil Liberties,* pp. 46–47, 61–63.

registered for the draft, Goldman and her associates decided to concentrate on written propaganda.[66]

Federal officials in New York were anxious to move quickly to stop this activity and to capitalize on public hostility to such open critics of the war. United States Attorney for New York H. Snowden Marshall recommended strongly to Attorney General Gregory that such draft opponents be treated summarily; Federal Marshal Thomas McCarthy, stated publicly that he would "arrest this woman" if she organized more meetings.[67] Washington authorities, however, wanted to study shorthand accounts taken at the meetings before ordering arrest. Ultimately, they did both. McCarthy gleefully led a raid upon the offices of *Mother Earth*. When Goldman demanded to see his warrant, he replied that none was needed. He then proceeded to turn the offices upside down, throwing correspondence, books, pamphlets, and other personal possessions on the floor. Eventually, the raiders made off with a wagonload of materials, the *New York Times* noting with satisfaction that a "splendidly kept card index" of "reds" was captured which would greatly simplify the work of the Secret Service.[68] Goldman and Berkman were arrested and brought before United States Commissioner Samuel W. Hitchcock, charged under conscription statutes enacted during the Civil War and a provision of the Draft Act of May 18, 1917, with having formed a "conspiracy to induce persons not to register." Assistant United States Attorney Harold A. Content demanded high bail, and it was set at $25,000 each. Goldman and Berkman's attorney, Harry Weinberger, protested that the amount was unreasonable and violated the Eighth Amendment, but such arguments fell on deaf ears, and government officials made it clear that the bond had been set high so that neither defendant could go free on bail.[69]

66. Richard Drinnon, *Rebel in Paradise* (Chicago, 1961), p. 187.
67. Ibid., pp. 187–88.
68. *The New York Times,* June 16, 1917, p. 23.
69. Drinnon, *Rebel in Paradise,* p. 188.

When the case came up for argument, Content charged that the No Conscription League had misused funds; that German money was supporting the activities of Goldman and her cohorts; that they had advocated violence in their public meetings; and finally, that they had conspired to prevent registration. The first three charges, although persuasive to many, could not stand up in the face of legal challenge. The fourth, however, was relatively easy to demonstrate. Even so, Goldman successfully used the occasion to deal some telling blows against the government's wartime policy toward dissent. Categorizing herself and others who opposed wartime repression and conscription as "political criminals," she argued strongly that the policy of making criminal previously permissible actions such as dissent and protest and opposition to repressive policies flew in the face of the tradition of American liberty which encouraged constructive criticism of the nation's "social faults." [70] In pronouncing sentence, Judge Mayer took time to insist that the trial had nothing to do with political principles. "No issue of free speech was involved," he said. "No American worthy of the name believes in anything else than free speech." But, Mayer insisted, "free speech means, not license, not counseling disobedience of the law. Free speech means that frank, full, free, and orderly expression which every man or woman in the land, citizen or alien, may engage in, in lawful and orderly fashion. . . ." [71] As to the draft, Mayer ruled that before the registration act became law, everyone might speak vehemently against it, but once it became law," "then it became the duty of every person living under this Government to obey that law. Individual opinion might still be fully expressed, and proper agitation for the repeal of such a law continue, but the law itself thenceforth must be obeyed." [72] A patriotic jury took thirty-nine

70. Ibid., p. 191.
71. United States Supreme Court: Transcript of Record, October Term, 1917, No. 702. Emma Goldman and Alexander Berkman, Plaintiffs in Error, *v*. U.S. (S.D., N.Y.).
72. Ibid., p. 13.

minutes to return a verdict of guilty. Mayer promptly imposed the maximum penalty of two years in prison and a fine of $10,000.

To the surprise and anger of many, Justice Brandeis signed a writ of error, allowing an appeal to the Supreme Court. In this instance, as Richard Drinnon has written: "the government came close to outright intimidation in its efforts to keep its two hated adversaries behind bars." [73] Bail for both was increased, and surety companies were pressured to refuse to post bond for fear of being labeled unpatriotic. Simultaneously, the Post Office Department began moving on *Mother Earth* and another anarchist journal, *The Blast,* published from the same location, banning them from the mails. So adamant was the post office solicitor that the Chicago postmaster was instructed to "completely destroy" all issues that arrived in that city.[74]

By this time, Clarence Darrow was prepared to join attorney Weinberger on the brief which went to the Supreme Court. They argued that the trial had failed to bring out any evidence of guilt under the indictment, especially since the alleged "conspiracy" was overt, and there was no proof that these overt acts caused anyone to disobey the law. But the major part of the argument turned on a contention that the Draft Act was unconstitutional, since it violated the Thirteenth Amendment, which forbade slavery or involuntary servitude, violated the First Amendment, which forbade Congress from prohibiting free speech, violated the prohibition against the establishment of religion (by providing exemption only for certain religious objectors to war), and violated the Fifth Amendment due process clause. Supporting *amicus curiae* (friend of the court) briefs by constitutional law expert Hannis Taylor and National Civil Liberties Bureau attorney Walter Nelles made much the same argument. If the act itself was unconstitutional, these critics felt, a conviction for violating it could not be sustained.

Such arguments so offended Chief Justice White that he

73. Drinnon, *Rebel in Paradise*, p. 195.
74. Ibid., p. 197.

charged the attorney stating them with a disturbing lack of patriotism. This attitude emerged more clearly when on January 7, 1918, White declared the Draft Act constitutional in an opinion which characterized conscription as a "noble and supreme duty" owed the government by the citizen.[75]

One week later White again spoke for a unanimous court in holding that "a conspiracy to commit an offence, when followed by overt acts is punishable as a crime, whether the illegal end is accomplished or not." [76] There was no doubt that Goldman and Berkman were guilty of conspiring to induce others to refuse registration for the draft. The Chief Justice warned others who might be inclined to act similarly, by giving a sufficiently broad scope to the doctrine of criminal conspiracy to enable authorities to use it virtually indiscriminately to get at critics of that policy.[77] Goldman, having finally made bail, was on a speaking tour at the time that the decision was announced. She promptly began to organize a Political Prisoners Amnesty League in an attempt to secure the rights of those later charged as she was.

White's use of conspiracy doctrine was typical of the behavior of the federal courts during the wartime period. To the extent that there was received legal doctrine with which to handle wartime cases, the judges tended to use it in as broad a fashion as necessary to achieve the desired goal of coercing opponents of the war to conform. The same was true in the free speech area, a fact which became evident from the ultimate rule emerging from The *Masses* case and its general use.

With regard to procedural rights—especially the Fourth Amendment's protection against unreasonable search and seizure, false arrest, excessive bail, and the right to a fair and

75. Selective Draft Law Cases, 245 U.S. 366 (1918).
76. Goldman *v.* U.S., 245 U.S. 474, 477 (1918).
77. White ruled it "settled doctrine that an unlawful conspiracy . . . to bring about an illegal act and the doing of overt acts in furtherance of such conspiracy is in and of itself . . . a crime punishable as such irrespective of whether the result of the conspiracy has been to accomplish its illegal ends." Goldman *v.* U.S., 245 U.S. 474, 477 (1918).

impartial jury—the assurance that these would be extended to an unpopular client or that his attorney (when he could find one) might successfully plead any of these rights was varied, at best. No systematic study of this has been carried out: Attitudes toward general wartime instrumentalist doctrine must be inferred from the behavior of members of the legal community in select situations. With regard to state legal processes and officials, the ruling in the 1884 Hurtado case, proclaiming that the way that state courts conducted their business was not a federal concern, had been reinforced by the Twining rule of 1907 with regard to the responsibilities, or lack thereof, of the federal government in intervening in situations involving questionable due process at the state level.[78] There was no easy constitutional justification for such intervention (the Fourteenth Amendment, despite Justice Marshall Harlan's eloquent dissent in *Twining,* did not afford that justification). Thus, the Bill of Rights guarantees did not apply to the states in the procedural area, any more than they did in the substantive First Amendment area. As to procedure in the federal courts, the situation was probably reversed—but again there was a pattern of great diversity. Lacking precedents for applying the wartime statutes which moved the federal government into monitoring behavior previously not considered criminal, initial application depended heavily upon the judge's and the jury's perceptions of the seriousness of the alleged criminal behavior—and frequently upon the ethnicity, cultural status, political orientation, and class background of the person involved. Thus, no adherence to a consistent rule of law marked the application of either federal or state criminal sanctions in the wartime period.

The behavior of government lawyers further exposes the absence of any commitment to equal justice or uniform due process in the war years. An occasional weak protest was heard when government arbitrariness become too overt and excessive. Such was the rare exception rather than the rule. One example

78. Twining *v.* New Jersey, 211 U.S. 78 (1908). On local practices see Samuel Walker, *A Critical History of Police Reform* (Lexington, Mass., 1972), pp. 104–06.

involved early calls by certain of the more frenetic patriots for the use of martial law on the domestic front to manage the wartime crisis. Inspired by the actions of Austria, which transferred all offenses such as treason, sedition, espionage, and sabotage from the civil to the military courts, and by England's Defense of the Realm Act, which allowed both aliens and subjects accused of spying anywhere in the British Empire to be tried under military law, a number of politicians put pressure on the Wilson administration to emulate such practices. Two troubling situations seem to have given rise to such demands. A growing apprehension over spies and the alleged failure of the administration to deal with them effectively led many to suggest that this was a job for the Army. A deluge of letters to senators demanded that the military be given more control over spies in order to defend the country against espionage and sabotage.

Attorney General Gregory, anxious to stem this tide and convince critics that the Justice Department had the situation under control, turned to a department underling, Charles Warren, for advice as to how to proceed. Assistant Attorney General Warren approached the task with relish. A Harvard Law School graduate and scion of a distinguished New England family, Warren had long been a foe of subversive influences in the country, having been a founder of the influential Immigration Restriction League and a proponent of prosecuting persons charged with anti-British activities as early as the neutrality period. As Joan Jensen has written, "for a man working within the civil branch of the government, Warren had an amazing disdain for the judicial process when it came to disloyalty." [79] When Gregory asked him to develop a better program for the Justice Department, he declined, saying that he felt that the full matter of sabotage should be handled by the War Department. "One man shot after court-martial," he told Gregory, "is worth a hundred arrests by this Department." [80] Gregory then

79. Joan M. Jensen, *The Price of Vigilance* (Chicago, 1968), p. 107.
80. Charles Warren to Thomas W. Gregory, January 11, 1918, Justice Department Files. National Archives, Washington, D.C.

turned to another assistant, John W. Davis. Davis, who had successfully defended the Selective Draft Act of 1917 and represented the government in the Goldman case, had earlier assisted Warren in drawing up a presidential proclamation, based on an Act of 1798, authorizing internment of enemy aliens under certain conditions. He again lent support in the matter at hand. "I am with Mr. Warren," he told Gregory, "in believing that the trial and execution of a spy under one or the other of the statutes would be wholesome." [81] Ultimately, however, he sided with those who had serious doubts about turning civilians over into military hands.[82]

The second source of concern grew out of an increasing apprehension over the question of bail. According to past practice, bail was granted to all but the most serious offenders pending trial and appeal, so as to minimize the inconvenience suffered by persons accused but not finally convicted of crime.[83] In many ways, the need for granting bail was greater during the war than at other times because of the overloaded conditions of many dockets and the consequent delays. On the other hand, when persons accused of obstructing the conduct of the war were released on bail, it was often possible for them to continue the type of activity for which they were awaiting trial. A number of such cases spurred public indignation. One of the most famous, if not the most serious, was that of Victor Berger, editor of the Socialist *Milwaukee Leader,* who was indicted in February 1918 for conspiracy to violate the Espionage Act. Shortly after his indictment he became the Socialist candidate from Wisconsin for the United States Senate, and thereafter—while on bail—he carried on his campaign on a platform de-

81. John W. Davis to Thomas W. Gregory, January 18, 1919, Justice Department Files. National Archives, Washington, D.C.

82. William Harbaugh, *Lawyer's Lawyer: The Life of John W. Davis* (New York, 1973), p. 127.

83. Exceptions had grown in celebrated political cases involving such controversial public figures as the Haymarket principals, Eugene V. Debs in the Pullman strike situation, and labor radicals such as "Big Bill" Haywood in the Steunenberg case.

manding an immediate armistice and withdrawal of American troops from France.[84] The idea that a man on bail, and a foreign-born Jew at that, should be in a position to continue this kind of activity aroused many patriotic Americans. Again the possibility of turning to martial law, where bail was not available, seemed an efficient wartime alternative.

Yet protests were heard when Warren prepared a bill providing that persons accused of a wide range of offenses involving interference with the progress of the war should be turned over to the military for summary trial before military courts and the application of drastic penalties. Senator Frank B. Brandegee of Connecticut promptly condemned the measure on the Senate floor as "absolutely violative of every guarantee contained in the Constitution as to trial by jury and individual liberty." [85] He then demanded that it be submitted to the Senate Judiciary Committee, where, he was convinced, its "eighteen distinguished lawyers members" would find it unconstitutional. When Woodrow Wilson was asked about it, he replied, ". . . it would be a very serious mistake to put our own citizens under court martial, for I think it would make an impression with regard to the weakness of our ordinary tribunals which would not be justified." [86] As a result the bill was eventually withdrawn. Wilson was less sure about enemy aliens, however, and ultimately supported the Sedition Act amendment to the earlier Espionage Act, which afforded the Justice Department greater latitude in prosecuting men accused of "disloyalty" and allowed courts to inflict harsher penalties on those so convicted.

The outcome of the spy hysteria was predictable and unfortunate. With public figures such as Senator Warren G. Harding and ex-President William Howard Taft charging the administra-

---

84. Sally M. Miller, *Victor Berger and the Promise of Constructive Socialism* (Westport, Conn., 1973), pp. 198–201.

85. *Congressional Record* 56 (April 22, 1918): 5401–02. See also pp. 5471–72.

86. Ray Stannard Baker, *The Life and Letters of Woodrow Wilson* (New York, 1939), 7:517–18. See also Carl B. Swisher, *American Constitutional Development* (New York, 1954), pp. 617–18.

tion with weakness and urging that spies be shot, the prevailing atmosphere contributed to a number of vigilante episodes. As we have seen, the president responded to such incidents on one hand by publicly deploring such action and on the other hand by insisting that they showed the need for greater force by legitimate law enforcement agencies in rooting out disloyalty.

A similar ambivalence marked the government's attitudes toward the question of search and seizure, and with it the parallel issue of proper arrest. To the extent that there was a formal rule of law in this area which might guide the behavior of federal officials, it was the prewar Weeks case of 1912, in which the Supreme Court had suggested that the exclusion of illicitly obtained evidence was the only effective way of discouraging illegal searches.[87] Federal officials, the court ruled, must obtain warrants in order to legitimately seize individuals or their effects. They could not simply gather up material "under color of their office." Although the ruling was not directed to state officials—the court making clear that the Fourth Amendment was not directed at individual misconduct of local officers—the federal model, it was suggested, was one which might well be emulated. But if this was the rule of law on this point, its effectiveness was quickly vitiated as war hysteria led law officers to interpret its meaning in such a way as to flout it completely.

The thrust of the rule was that illegally seized evidence was inadmissible in court. The question, however, quickly came to turn on what was "illegally" seized evidence and as cases arose interpreting that phrase, it became clear that if evidence promised to demonstrate that the "wrong" people were trying to undermine the war effort, the government obviously had every right to seize it and its sponsors in order to protect the country against potential subversion.

The activities of the American Protective League provided a clear test of this new "rule of law" concerning the admissability of evidence. From the outset the attorney general's

87. Weeks *v.* U.S., 232 U.S. 383 (1914).

office was troubled by the legal dilemmas involved in utilizing the civil volunteers who were league operatives, all of whom were eager to enforce federal rules against "the disloyal." When the opportunity arose for such patriots to participate in "slacker raids"—searching out men who had not registered for the draft or citizens who had not bought bonds or otherwise supported the war effort and "holding" them for ultimate proper legal dispensation—Gregory was torn. If private citizens were to be given responsibility for locating delinquents, Gregory wanted the volunteers to remain under his control, but he did not want to trust them with authority to arrest. Even agents of the Bureau of Investigation had received no statutory right to arrest from Congress. Their authority came from Gregory as attorney general. Endowing volunteers with the same authority would undoubtedly raise questions from congressmen.

Legally, there was no easy way out of the dilemma. Under common law any citizen had a right to arrest a person committing a felony or breach of the peace; but a slacker was doing neither. Gregory finally attempted to resolve the dilemma by assigning to local draft boards the authority to "locate and cause to present themselves to the boards, or to the proper representatives of the Justice Department, any man who had failed to complete his questionnaire, had not reported for his physical, or who had not responded to his call of duty." League members who located a delinquent, however, operated under a different set of guidelines: Should they "find it impracticable to induce him to present himself to the proper authority, [they] should take the matter up immediately with the proper State or Federal officer, in order that the arrest might be effected in accordance with the law." [88]

This left open the question of how a league member could induce a young man who did not want to go to war to report to his draft board voluntarily. APL agents, however, read the fine print exactly the way they wished to. Having obtained evidence, frequently by highly dubious means, regarding the al-

88. Jensen, *Price of Vigilance,* p. 190.

leged presence of "slackers," they initiated "slacker raids" in major cities, beginning with Minneapolis in March 1918, in which league operatives deployed a dragnet through hotels in the lower-class lodging district, rounded up hundreds of men, and locked them in the local jail as "slackers." Those who challenged the authority of the APL found its members defended in court by United States attorneys. Bureau of Investigation agents, badly in need of support personnel, also ordered league members to "take" or "hold" men suspected of draft dodging, while being very careful, however, not to suggest to the APL operatives that this was the same as ordering an illegal arrest.

Such officers appeared to be totally oblivious to the principle of habeas corpus. Men were frequently "taken" illegally by civilians and held indefinitely while telegrams were sent to local draft boards to confirm their status. Sometimes, weeks passed before the draft boards replied and the suspects were released. Some special agents, a bit squeamish about holding men without warrants, filed complaints for violations of the Selective Service Act while the investigations were pending. Usually, however, the men were simply held upon no legal authority, and even when they were found to be real delinquents, no one was sure what to do with them because the draft regulations were not precise on this question.[89]

During the summer of 1918, the practice of detaining "slackers" spread through most major cities of the United States, eventually reaching the "slacker's paradise," New York City. In the process, questions arose. When United States Marshal for New York Thomas McCarthy (who had always been nervous about federal use of volunteer agents of the APL)[90] took away the badge of a league operative and released his eighty-five prisoners on the grounds that private citizens had no legal right to take draft "slackers" into custody, eyebrows began to

89. Ibid., pp. 192–93.
90. McCarthy had backed the attempt of the Secret Service to establish a central intelligence agency.

raise. However, Bruce Bielaski, head of the Bureau of Investigation, denounced McCarthy's behavior, announcing his complete support for the league's activities. When, in early September, the great New York raid occurred, followed by the illegal incarceration and detention of literally thousands of young men, the protests against such questionable actions, and the thorough lack of due process involved, began to reach Washington.

With a crucial off-year election coming up, a number of Republican Congressmen, in search of issues with which to lash the Wilson administration, assailed Wilson for undermining civil liberties by condoning this type of behavior. Critics pointed out that league operatives used in the raids had no official standing or warrants for arrest. Hiram Johnson of California charged that he had evidence that the New York raid had been staged at the direction of the attorney general with the approval of the provost marshal general and questioned their sensitivity for basic personal rights.[91] Even the *New York World,* a pro-Wilson newspaper, ran an editorial under the heading "Amateur Prussianism in New York," deploring the raid as a "rape of the law" and demanding an investigation.[92] Wilson promptly made a public statement calling for an investigation of the Justice Department. O'Brian was assigned to prepare a detailed report. The fact that he was a Republican with a reputation as a Progressive interested in civil liberties was highlighted by the department. In the meantime, Wilson and Gregory made bold public statements deploring APL excesses and reiterating their devotion to individual rights. As outrage mounted, considerable negative public comment emerged, with one New York lawyer, Charles Collman, writing to Gregory, "I know that we are living in extraordinary times, calling for unusual methods, but I do not believe it is the policy of our Government to put weapons of oppression in the hands of private organizations."[93] In the

91. *Congressional Record* 56 (September 5, 1918): 9979.

92. The *New York World,* September 6, 1918, p. 14. See also Arthur E. Ekirch, *The Civilian and the Military* (New York, 1956), p. 193.

93. Charles Collman to Thomas W. Gregory, September 6, 1918, Justice Department Files. National Archives, Washington, D.C.

meantime, Frank Cobb, a journalist and close friend of Wilson, called the raids a "shameful spectacle which I would not have believed could happen outside a conquered province under Prussian military control." [94] John Nevin Sayre (whose brother was the President's son-in-law), acting for the National Civil Liberties Bureau, visited Wilson to complain about the administration's general disregard for civil liberties.[95] *The Nation,* proclaiming "Civil Liberty Dead," blasted the administration for allowing arrests to be made by "irresponsible agents of a volunteer self-appointed protective (!) league." [96]

O'Brian, however, ultimately brought in a "whitewash" report generally commending APL members for their restraint. Gregory maintained publicly that the only aspect of the raids which was unlawful was the use of volunteers and military men by special agents of the Bureau of Investigation who made the arrests. This had been done, he insisted, solely upon the authority of the Bureau of Investigation without consulting him or any law officer of the Justice Department. He in turn prepared a statement deploring any actions "contrary to law," again apologizing for excesses but maintaining that no persons were known to have been assaulted or maltreated. Wilson, in releasing this statement to the press, indicated that he generally accepted such a view.[97]

But aspects of the issue lingered. Bielaski, attempting to smooth over the controversy, indicated publicly that the frequent charges of illegal arrest missed a subtle point of the law. His orders to league operatives to "hold" and "bring" men to justice really meant that they had no authority to arrest. This view was promptly subscribed to by O'Brian and Gregory. Yet such a position raised serious doubts as to the general commit-

94. Baker, *Life and Letters,* 8:385–86, 405.
95. Jensen, *Price of Vigilance,* p. 211.
96. "Civil Liberty is Dead," *The Nation* 107 (September 14, 1918): 282. See also "The One Thing Needful," *The Nation* 107 (September 14, 1918): 283.
97. Jensen, *Price of Vigilance,* p. 213.

ment of such legal leaders to any rule of law. Again, as Joan Jensen has perceptively observed:

Both O'Brian and Gregory were good lawyers, well trained in constitutional law. They knew arrest meant not only formal arrest by an officer but any restraint of an individual's freedom to be at large, and that "to hold" a person was to restrain his freedom to be at large. Yet they approved of the vague wording which legal clerks in the Justice Department had formulated. And they did it, evidently to escape the constitutional problem presented by the lack of legal authority for their subordinates.[98]

By the end of the war, APL raids had netted forty thousand delinquents for the War Department. Of the 3 million investigations made for the government by the league, the directors estimated that at least 2 million had involved the Selective Service system. Curiously, there were no legal cases testing the constitutionality of such action during the war period. It was only in the postwar years that the courts were called upon to decide whether civilians had a right to "hold" a person and whether their attempt to do so was an infringement of the due process clause of the Constitution. Finally, in 1922 the Circuit Court of Appeals for Northern California ruled that no such right could legitimately be claimed, awarding damages to an individual "held" by a draft board on the instructions of an agent of the Bureau of Investigation. Stating that the war did not automatically suspend due process of law and making clear that arrest without a warrant was unconstitutional, the court cited the Civil War decision of *ex parte* Milligan,[99] which held that

98. Ibid., pp. 214–15. *The New York Times* commented editorially at the time that leaguers, soldiers, and sailors could hardly have understood the "technical distinction laid down by the Attorney General." September 13, 1918, p. 10.

99. *Ex parte* Milligan, 4 Wallace 2 (1866). Early in the war Charles Warren had contended before the Committee on Military Affairs, that the Milligan case was irrelevant to World War I situations. For his argument see "Spies, and the Power of Congress to Subject Certain Classes of Civilians to Trial by Military Tribunals," *American Law Review* 53 (March–April 1919): 195 ff.

a person had the right to be at liberty until arrested in accordance with proper legal procedures.

On the basis of the as yet imperfectly processed record, the Justice Department's own behavior, and for that matter the behavior of federal and state officials at a number of levels, seems almost equally cavalier when it came to search and seizure and arrest patterns involving citizens other than alleged draft dodgers. Unlike league operatives, government officials were conscious in varying degrees of the need to project the appearance of legality in their public behavior. Certain rudimentary steps were taken in order to avoid the stigma of being charged with employing autocratic methods. But "get the spies and traitors at any cost" actions frequently enjoyed the public's sympathy and support, so minimal caution was normally sufficient.[100]

The massive raids conducted against the IWW by federal officials were a direct response to mounting public hysteria regarding that organization. Much of that hysteria had been contrived and manufactured by the nation's conservative press and was based upon allegations that the body's activities were designed to interfere with the war effort and destroy the nation's economy—allegations for which no sources were ever given. Such charges, however, had elicited mob violence against IWW members,[101] and had ultimately led President Wilson to appoint Judge J. Harry Covington of the District of Columbia court to investigate the organization. Upon the announcement of his appointment, IWW Secretary-Treasurer William D. Haywood had promptly invited the judge to visit IWW headquarters in Chicago, where "he would be given access to books, and papers and also given all the assistance possible in the inquiry."[102] Covington did not respond. Rather, he preferred to get his in-

100. See, for example, Homer Cummings and Carl McFarland, *Federal Justice* (New York, 1937), pp. 413–31.
101. Philip Taft, "The Federal Trials of the I.W.W.," *Labor History* 3 (Winter 1962): 59–60.
102. W. D. Haywood, "Preamble Still Nailed to Our Masthead," *Solidarity* (October 20, 1917).

formation through raids on IWW headquarters and forty-eight local halls conducted on the orders of Attorney General Thomas W. Gregory after he had received the report of Judge Covington. The raids produced "more than five tons of letters, documents, books, papers, pamphlets, supplies, equipment, furniture and fixtures." [103] The seized material was in turn presented to a grand jury during the September 1917 term of the United States District Court of Illinois, and it became the basis for the indictment of a large number of IWW leaders and members. This activity, which led to the Chicago IWW trials, had a partial counterpart in similar actions by the Justice Department in Sacramento and Wichita. In the Sacramento case, however, a temporary inconvenience intruded. A Justice Department special agent, Don S. Rathbun, became "obstructionist." After raids on local headquarters in Sacramento, Rathbun, after looking over the evidence in the hands of the local police, advised that there was not sufficient justification in it for holding any of the men arrested, other than three who had allegedly been involved in a dynamiting episode. Further, he could not undertake, in behalf of the department, to make further investigations or to order those picked up to be held. City officials then held those arrested while the governor of California, the local sheriff, and the chief of police protested to Washington against the "suspect" attitudes of agent Rathbun. The fifty-four men and one woman were shortly indicted by a federal grand jury on charges of violating the Espionage Act, with forty-six eventually convicted and sentenced to prison terms ranging from two months to ten years. [104]

In the Wichita raids special search warrants were obtained by the Department of Justice. Later charges leveled by Caroline A. Lowe, an attorney involved in the cases, however, suggested that the Wichita defendants were arrested "on John Doe warrants issued in Butler County, Kansas, at the suggestion of agents of the Carter Oil Company, the Sinclair Oil Company,

103. Taft, "Federal Trials of I.W.W.," p. 61.
104. Ibid., pp. 77–78.

Gypsy Oil Company, and other oil companies doing business in this section of the country." [105] In any event, thirty-four indictments were issued in March 1918.

Arrest practices in the case of others charged with violating wartime statutes followed a similar pattern. Jacob Abrams was a left-wing Jewish alien, charged in August 1918 with throwing handfuls of leaflets written in Yiddish from a factory window onto a New York street. The pamphlets called President Wilson a hypocrite and attacked the American intervention in Russian Siberia as a blow aimed at all workers.[106] They also called for a general strike to protest United States policy. Abrams's arrest was conducted by military intelligence police acting on allegations that the action violated the Sedition Act of 1918. Another case involved the editors of a small German-language newspaper, the *Philadelphia Tageblatt.* The government proceeded on material obtained when in November 1918 the paper's offices were raided by federal agents and the business manager was seized and pressured to reveal the journal's sinister intentions— even though he protested from the outset that he had no control over the paper's contents and no association with its point of view.[107] In yet another case, the arrest of Socialist leader Eugene V. Debs for sedition was the result of a vigorous and consistent campaign of surveillance on the part of the Justice Department, which sent agents around the country to monitor his public statements, apparently in the hope that some verbal utterances might warrant federal indictment. When the indictment came, as the result of a speech in Canton, Ohio, it was based upon the shorthand reports of a government stenographer, who had attempted to take down what had been said. Then the federal attorney's office in Cleveland, working through that record, found that statements within it violated the new Sedition Act

105. "Amnesty for Political Prisoners," Testimony of Caroline A. Lowe before the House Judiciary Committee on H. Res. 60, 67 Cong. 2d Sess., pp. 32, 37.

106. Chafee, *Free Speech,* pp. 109–12.

107. Lawrence, "Eclipse of Liberty," pp. 96–97.

on ten different counts, even though no effort was made to link any punishable action with the statements or even to charge that they constituted incitement.[108] Further, when Debs was arrested, the authorities refused to make arrangements for him to post bail, although twenty-three hours later they were disappointed and angered when a jailer awakened him with the news that he had been nominated for Congress by the Socialists of Terre Haute, Indiana, and that a Cleveland comrade, A. W. Moskowitz, had provided the $10,000 bond necessary to effect his release.[109]

At the state level only minor variations occurred. Minnesota authorities, conservative and Republican in their ideology, set out to assail, and tried to cripple, the leftist Non-Partisan League, along with more vocal antiwar German-Americans and Swedish-Americans with whom they hoped to link the league in the public mind. They thus fostered an atmosphere in which attacks on such individuals, especially leaders and spokesmen, were viewed as patriotic prowar activity. League speakers were arrested frequently by a variety of local authorities on the grounds that their statements violated the state's sedition act. Yet George Creel had indicated earlier that the Non-Partisan League's loyalty was beyond reproach, and other federal leaders had made clear at various points that they did not consider League publications or speeches to be seditious or disloyal. The local situation contributed to mounting antagonism toward the league. Pockets of Minnesota were ethnically strongly German. When the mayor and city attorney of the predominantly German community of New Ulm—a city in which league actions had occurred—organized a meeting to protest conscription, they were indicted by the State Commission on Public Safety for "malfeasance in the performance of the duties of their office" and were removed from those offices by the governor.[110] In

108. Ray Ginger, *The Bending Cross* (New Brunswick, N.J., 1949), pp. 343–53.
109. Ibid., p. 359.
110. Leota M. Kellet, *Early Brown County* (New Ulm, Minn., 1966), p. 17; *Brown County Journal* (December 8, 1917), p. 1.

such an atmosphere it came as no surprise when A. C. Townley and Joseph Gilbert, the league's principal officials and spokesmen, were jailed for critical public statements to the effect that the war was being fought for economic and class reasons and that wealth should be conscripted along with men. Local variations in this pattern of state enforcement occurred, but in the various states with criminal syndicalism and sedition statutes, the record shows few local officials respecting elementary fair procedures in search and arrest patterns regarding alleged violators.

Such behavior by both federal and state officials did produce some murmurs of protest. But such expression came from a handful of people, normally individuals not prepared to let wartime hysteria cloud their vision regarding the inequitable and arbitrary treatment of those with unpopular wartime views. On this score the controversial National Civil Liberties Bureau was particularly vulnerable, especially as its membership constantly sought to expose the dubious legality of such governmental action and to alert the broader public to the troubling implications of suppressing dissent and dissenters.[111] The raid by federal agents against the New York offices of the organization appears to have been a direct response to the bureau's criticism of the government's harrassment of other organizations.

Technically, the NCLB raid was the logical and legitimate culmination of an extended Justice Department investigation carried out in an attempt to confirm suspicions that the bureau had been propagandizing against the war. Although the raid was conducted with a warrant, organization officials objected strongly. Walter Nelles, civil liberties attorney then standing in for Roger Baldwin—who had resigned to fight his own draft call—examined the warrant carefully and proclaimed it invalid "for failure of the supporting affadavit to show probable cause"

111. Certain Justice Department officials, while scarcely condoning the NCLB, were sensitive to its potential influence. John Lord O'Brian especially held grudging respect for the organization. Donald Johnson, *The Challenge to American Freedoms* (Lexington, Ky., 1963), p. 76.

and on the grounds that it invaded the right of confidential communication which bureau officials properly had. Nelles quickly decided to cooperate, however, when Rayme Finch, the federal agent in charge, drew a revolver. He was further appalled when Union League operatives serving as dollar-a-year agents of the Justice Department (an assignment which exempted them from the draft) elected to seize not only organization material thought to indicate obstruction of the war, but everything in the office, including the private correspondence of NCLB officers. With files and correspondence thus confiscated, the only appropriate action for the body was to move quickly to avoid prosecution on the basis of this material. In this the organization was ultimately successful, and no indictments were returned. District Attorney Francis G. Caffey could hardly hide his disappointment at this outcome, noting that although the NCLB activities could apparently not be proven to be illegal, it was nonetheless "a thoroughly undesirable organization." [112]

When it came to inequities in actual trial procedures, even less protest was raised. The tendency was to overlook the fact that judges were anxious to display their loyalty by administering harsh sentences to those who seemed to be disloyal and that juries were equally anxious to convict such people. The highly

---

112. One dimension of the NCLB raids lends further insight into federal procedures of the time. Roger Baldwin was assigned, during his incarceration for draft evasion, to straighten out the NCLB files, which had been thoroughly mixed up during their confiscation. As Baldwin tells the story: "Working daily in the F.B.I. office, I got to know the insides of some shady operations. Finch, with great pride, showed me his telephone tapping equipment and asked if I wanted to listen in on any conversation; he'd put on anyone I named. I declined. He showed me also a whole setup for forming an I.W.W. local—forms, membership cards, literature. Thus the F.B.I. could catch the 'criminals' they made. I was disgusted and said so, but they laughed me off as naive. In the course of examining our files, I found inserted among the papers by error a report of the F.B.I. on me, headed 'Roger Baldwin, I.W.W. Agitator.' I handed it to Finch without comment. He looked a bit embarrassed for the first time and said, "We have to make it strong even if it isn't right.' " Roger Baldwin, "Reflections of a Life in Civil Liberties—I," *Civil Liberties Review* 2 (Spring 1975): 64.

decentralized nature of the American judicial system, the absence of uniform standards and court procedures, and the widely held belief that if people were getting trials at all they were getting justice were impediments to overt criticism. The war perverted the rule of law in the courts as fully and as unjustifiably as it had in the arrest process. Certain select examples are revealing.

When the IWW trials began in Chicago, attorneys for the organization sought to quash indictments on the grounds that the testimony of the agents of the Department of Justice before the grand jury had been based purely upon hearsay evidence. They further charged that the United States district attorney had submitted a variety of illegally seized data to the grand jury, in violation of the Fourth Amendment to the Constitution and of the Weeks precedent, and that the use of the papers, letters, documents, and property considered by the grand jury in their deliberations was in violation of the provisions of the Fifth Amendment to the Constitution and the rights of the defendants thereunder. Lastly, the defense claimed with considerable justification that the warrants were "fully void" because they failed to describe with any degree of particularity what was properly to be seized.[113] The demurrer was promptly overruled by Judge Kenesaw Mountain Landis before the case was tried, thus eliminating the possibility of pleading certain constitutional rights in court. Similar procedures were followed during the empaneling of the jury. When the defense insisted upon attempting to determine the views of prospective jurors, the judge objected strenuously. The jury which was ultimately seated was clearly made up of citizens whose class status and wealth virtually insured that their views would be hostile to the defendants.

The prosecuting attorney, Frank K. Nebeker, a corporation lawyer from Utah (the scene of bitter anti-Wobbly sentiment), however, took no chances. During the early parts of the trial, Nebeker went out of his way to introduce evidence designed to prejudice jury members against the organization and its past

113. Taft, "Federal Trials," p. 62.

actions, even though much of the material which he introduced related to statements and events antedating the period covered by the indictment.[114] Letters, journals, and pamphlets approving the use of sabotage, for example, were introduced, even though no specific proof of its practice was ever shown; information from the IWW headquarters was produced in which the war and the draft were discussed, the inference being that the body opposed both; the government presented evidence that several IWW branches had voted to resist the draft; material from the organization's newspaper, *Solidarity,* was also introduced, including an editorial which declared, ". . . capitalist wars are not worth fighting for . . . the duped workers foot the bills and the parasites get all the gains. . . ." When attorneys for the defense asked for an opportunity to reply, in order to show the reasons for this attitude or to indicate that other labor organizations also spoke out against certain wartime profiteering, the judge ruled such information out of order. When the defense tried another tack and sought to introduce information detailing the working conditions and economic atmosphere which had induced men to join the organization—including the *Report of the Commission on Industrial Relations,* a body appointed by Woodrow Wilson—Judge Landis held that "what is in that *Report* has not the slightest bearing on the case." [115]

Throughout the trial, the defense was hampered by the government's suppression of IWW publications—which, had they not been closed down, might have been able to inform the public of the IWW's side of the case (unlike the general press, which carried only hostile information)—and by the seizure of its mail, through which appeals for financial aid to finance the long trial could be made. This violation of freedom of the press and the mails in order to pervert justice so aroused a group of liberal writers and educators that they took ads in national

114. The defense attorneys attempted, in vain, to raise ex post facto objections to the process.

115. United States Supreme Court: Transcript of Record, October Term, 1918, Haywood *v.* U.S., IV, 245. See Taft, "Federal Trials," p. 69.

journals to call on the public to assist the defendants so that they might receive a fair trial. The appeal called attention especially to the expense of bringing witnesses long distances to testify, so that the defendant's case might be properly defended to the jury.[116] In his final summation, the prosecutor devoted his time to castigating the organization for its disloyalty and for its persistent attempts to destroy the capitalist system. The jury in turn took less than an hour to reach a verdict, finding each defendant guilty on four counts, a process which entailed making four hundred decisions on guilt or innocence in less than sixty minutes.

Appeals were immediately filed, with the convicted men in the meantime languishing in Leavenworth. A number were released on bail, but many were imprisoned not only during the war period but well into the 1920s. Subsequently, Alexander F. Lanier, a captain in the military intelligence division of the general staff of the Army, examined the forty-four thousand pages of typewritten record. He came to the conclusion that the evidence to convict was woefully inadequate. This information was subsequently reported to Congress.[117]

In the Jacob Abrams trial, courtroom justice clearly was affected not only by the defense's antiwar pronouncements but by anti-Semitic and anti-alien and anti-Bolshevik sentiments. The trial judge, Henry Clayton, had been called to New York City from the northern and middle districts of Alabama because of crowded court dockets. He was totally unfamiliar with conditions in the immigrant ghettoes, and his only acquaintance with Bolshevism was through the media. Clayton denied the

116. Among the signers were John Dewey, Carlton J. H. Hayes, James Harvey Robinson, Helen Keller, Thorstein Veblen, George P. West, Robert M. Bruere, John A. Fitch, Rev. Percy Stickney Grant, Inez Hayes Irvin, and Walter Weyl.
117. A similar pattern occurred in the IWW trial in Sacramento, California, where—again over the objection of defense lawyers—the court allowed the introduction of evidence antedating the period in which the alleged conspiracy took place. Despite the fact that defense attorneys pointed out the clearly prejudicial nature of this information, that fact was waived and the conviction of all indicted ensured.

defense the opportunity to produce evidence regarding the actual situation in Russia about which Abrams was protesting.[118] When the defense requested an instruction that actual intent must be shown in order to prove a violation of the Sedition Act, the judge refused to give it. As the trial proceeded he took over the questioning of witnesses, not only making queries but adding gratuitous statements that were highly prejudicial to the seven defendants. The court also excluded from the jury's consideration explanations by the defendants of their views and their reasons for writing the pamphlets, apparently preferring to derive an explanation of motives from less sympathetic sources. Thus, by the time the case went to the jury, the jurors had been amply exposed to the defendants' unpatriotic opinions and the judge's unconcealed indignation. Since no adequate instruction on the issue of "intent" was made, the jury was encouraged to convict on the basis of the defendants' beliefs alone. A guilty verdict was the predictable result. But at sentencing Justice Clayton added one final note. Announcing that he would tolerate no propaganda supporting these "miserable defendants," he then delivered a lengthy patriotic harangue attacking them for their misguided ideas.[119] When the case was appealed to a higher court, and ultimately the Supreme Court, the judge's prejudicial comments and questions before the jury were not challenged. Under such circumstances, especially given the fact that much of Judge Clayton's prejudice had reached the newspapers, one would have thought that the Supreme Court would have actively reviewed the trial transcript to be sure that prejudice and extrajudicial pressure on the lower court were not evident. However, the attitude of a majority of the justices toward dissenters and the war had the effect of insuring

118. The defense was not permitted to produce testimony by experts on Russian affairs—for example, evidence showing that the intervention was not a part of the war with Germany. It was therefore impossible to show that opposition to America's Russian policy was not a crime because it did not concern the war with Germany.

119. Chafee, *Free Speech,* p. 125.

that the scope of appellate review would be narrow and superficial on war-related issues.

In the Schaefer case, involving the editors of the *Philadelphia Tageblatt,* indictment turned upon the provision of the Espionage Act of 1917 making it a crime to "publish . . . false reports and statements." The question became one of proving falsity, since the material which had led to indictment had largely been editorials, news stories, and reports. The government ultimately argued that while such material printed by the paper was not in itself false, the editors, so poor financially that they were unable to afford telegraphic service, got their material from other newspapers and altered that material into stories slanted to support the German war effort. The charge, then, was that the material was false because it differed from the original and had been revised or mistranslated so as to bear a changed meaning. The trial judge in turn instructed the jury to determine whether, based upon their "fund of general information," the slant which the editors were giving stories they had pirated from other sources was accurate. The jury, well aware that an acquittal would have been the equivalent of a determination that these unpatriotic and pro-German sentiments were not false, promptly convicted. The decision was sustained at the Supreme Court level by Justice McKenna.[120] One interesting note did emerge from the high bench. Justice John H. Clarke, writing his only dissent in a wartime free speech case, took the occasion to contend sharply that the case involved a

flagrant mistrial, likely to result in disgrace and great injustice, probably in life imprisonment for two old men, because this court hesitates to exercise the power, which it undoubtedly possesses, to correct, in this calmer time, errors of law which would not have been committed but for the stress and strain of feeling prevailing in the early months of the late deplorable war. . . .[121]

120. Schaefer *v.* U.S., 251 U.S. 466 (1919). Brandeis and Holmes dissented. Brandeis criticized the verdict because it condemned men, "not merely for disloyal acts, but for a disloyal heart; provided only that the disloyal heart was evidenced by some utterance" (at 493).

121. 251 U.S. 466, 501 (1919).

The observation is remarkable, not only because it was accurate, but because it was unique coming from the Supreme Court during and after the war. No other justice in these years dissented so clearly on grounds that the trial under review had been so fundamentally unfair that justice not been done. This is in turn ironic, since the appellate courts' record was one of overlooking improper and prejudicial evidentiary rulings, jury instructions, and patriotic pre-sentence harangues which commonly occurred at almost all of these trials.

Finally, in the state-level trials of the Non-Partisan League leaders, the courts demonstrated that federal judges had no corner on patriotic wartime justice. When Joseph Gilbert came up for trial in Red Wing, Minnesota, following his indictment for sedition against the state of Minnesota, the judge barred all Non-Partisan League members from the jury. The result was that the jury was composed entirely of enemies of the league, since there were virtually no citizens in the area of Red Wing at the time who were not either strongly for or strongly against the league.[122] In the case involving the arrest of league head A. C. Townley for sedition against the state, the atmosphere at the trial was sharply affected by the pretrial issuance of a "Report of the Committee to Oppose Judicial Recall," by the American Bar Association, which contended that "the northwest has been honeycombed with the results of the insidious work of the so-called farmers' Non-Partisan League, a most dangerous organization." "The State of North Dakota," the report went on,

is still in the thralldom of this socialist movement. It already has become a strong political factor in Minnesota, and has spread into South Dakota, Iowa, Nebraska and other western states. Its creed and platform are based upon abrogating constitutional protection and eliminating the primary functions of courts of justice, whether state or national. In the west this movement is known as 'Townleyism,' from the name of the agitator who had been most prominent in its organization and work—a man . . . who stands indicted in

122. Morlan, *Political Prairie Fire,* p. 171.

the courts of Minnesota on a charge of disloyalty to his government in time of war.[123]

Townley's conviction thus became for the jurors another act of patriotic citizenship.

The Townley example affords another revealing wartime legal development. This involved the behavior of attorneys called upon to defend unpopular wartime clients. Here again, the literature is of necessity predominantly anecdotal, but case after case can be found in which attorneys either shrank from accepting such clients or incurred punitive professional sanctions for taking the cases. Jerold Auerbach has compiled a series of striking examples in this regard, and concluded that "lawyers permitted the dictates of patriotism to determine the contours of professionalism. Members of the profession seemed unaware that their patriotism intruded upon their professional obligations . . . Lawyers prejudged guilt, equated dissent with treason, and accepted the notion that by taking a case they committed themselves to the defense of a cause. Professional stature took precedence over professional responsibility." [124]

Despite all of these pressures and developments, however, there were still scattered voices within legal circles which deplored the scrapping of the rule of law for the war period. This was particularly true of certain legal figures who, unlike the vast majority of the bench and bar, saw—along with a number of prescient public figures—the undesirable implications of these pervasive developments. The influential Boston attorney, Moorfield Storey, reached a number of consciences when he consistently maintained during the war that "we cannot allow the law to be enforced by a casual collection of hoodlums." His forthright views on the Espionage Act also struck positive and responsive chords: "It has been a cover for many unjust prosecutions, and I know that a great many sentences which seem to me to be preposterous have been inflicted on men for very

123. "Report of the Committee to Oppose Judicial Recall," *American Bar Association Journal* 4 (1918): 404.
124. Auerbach, *Unequal Justice,* pp. 104–05.

trifling offenses." [125] Others, such as urban reformer Frederic C. Howe, stated the problem in more general terms. "I hated the new state, hated its brutalities, its ignorance, its unpatriotic patriotism, that made profit from our sacrifices, and used its power to suppress criticism of its acts. My attitude toward the state was changed. I have never been able to bring it back. I became distrustful of the state. It seemed to want to hurt people; it showed no concern for innocence; it aggrandized itself and protected its power by unscrupulous means. It was not my America, it was something else." [126] These men shared Gilbert Seldes's view that one hundred years of intellect, science, and creative force had been undone in ten by the insensitive power-wielding products of the new statism. Some apprehensive lawyers, sensitive to the implications of condoning arbitrariness and the setting of new and dangerous precedents which laid the basis for future emergency departures from the rule of law, recognized that these wartime developments had to be counter-manded. Many felt, as Brandeis was later to write, that such wartime experience "should teach us to be most on guard to protect liberty when governments' purposes are beneficent. Men born to freedom are naturally alert to repel invasion on their liberty by evil-minded rulers. The greatest dangers to liberty lurk in insidious encroachments by men of zeal, well-meaning, but without understanding." [127]

Such individuals also seemed aware, with Randolph Bourne, that majority will is not to be trusted in periods of patriotic emotionalism, especially when the modernized state is filled with new machinery with which to effect broad new patterns of social control. Those charged with running the state, particularly under wartime emergency conditions, will use such machinery

125. William B. Hixson, Jr., *Moorfield Storey and the Abolitionist Tradition* (New York, 1972), p. 178.

126. Federic C. Howe, *Confessions of a Reformer* (Chicago, 1967, pp. 279–82. See also Roy Lubove, "Frederic C. Howe and the Quest for Community in America," *The Historian* 39 (February 1977): 270–91.

127. Quoted in Robert A. Nisbet, *The New Despotism* (Menlo Park, N.J., 1976), p. 4.

with sensitivity chiefly to the emotional demands of the majority—'and hence with little restraint. In the late Progressive period, the new modern state had no instruments within its legal structure for sensitive discrimination in the application of broad policies, from prosecution of espionage and sedition to censorship and the treatment of dissident or even non-complying minorities. These lawyers, with the vision of precedent-oriented legalists, understood far better than most of their contemporaries the ominous implications of modernization.

The proposals of such individuals generally took two forms. To one group of legalists, a sensitive and careful new law of civil liberties was required which would provide a body of legal distinctions which courts could apply when Bill of Rights freedoms, particularly First Amendment rights, were abused. To another, a more fruitful response was a political approach, which entailed mobilizing support behind a pro–civil liberties policy and program.

The most prominent spokesman for the former view was Zechariah Chafee, who, along with civil liberties–oriented lawyers such as Hannis Taylor,[128] Walter Nelles,[129] and Albert De-Silver,[130] channeled his energies into refining civil liberties law— and in some cases virtually creating it. A ninth-generation New Englander and scion of a prominent and wealthy Providence, Rhode Island, family, Chafee had begun to explore the law of civil liberties as a Harvard Law School staff member in the immediate prewar period and found it at that time woefully thin, if not nonexistent. With the coming of war and the buffeting received by radicals, pacifists, and conscientious objectors, either by mob violence or by federal and state prosecution,

128. Taylor, former American minister to Spain, spoke out strongly against the wartime state, submitting a strong brief in the Selective Draft Law Cases and appearing in a number of the Espionage Act and Sedition Act cases as counsel for the defense.
129. Nelles was early counsel for the NCLB and later for the ACLU. See Peggy Lamson, *Roger Baldwin* (New York, 1976), pp. 74–75.
130. Walter Nelles, *A Liberal in Wartime: The Education of Albert DeSilver* (New York, 1940).

Chafee woke up to the fact that that void was rapidly being filled, that constitutional freedom of speech was being redefined, often very heavy-handedly, by judges called upon for early and often hasty interpretation. As he subsequently wrote: "I soon realized that it would be foolish for a scholar in this field to limit himself to old authorities, while new law was in the making." For Chafee this meant searching for new boundaries of freedom of expression, "so that speakers and writers may know how much they can properly say, and governments may be sure of how much they can lawfully and wisely suppress"; it meant hurdling Blackstone and the common law doctrine of "no prior restraint" [131] and attempting to evolve a set of legal guidelines more clearly reflecting a common sense view of the relations of state and citizen.

Chafee was far more impressed with Judge Learned Hand's "direct incitement to violent resistance" test from *The Masses* case than he was with Justice Oliver Wendell Holmes's "clear and present danger doctrine." Either was better than the new, restrictive wartime case law. In this regard, he gestured toward the reality of legal instrumentalism, hoping not only for a better and more sensitive law of civil liberties, but expressing his view that "channels outside the law" would also have to be mustered to produce greater tolerance in judges and jurors "so that when the next emergency arises we shall be better prepared." [132]

A new law had indeed emerged in the form of federal criminalization of wartime dissent aimed less at behavior or action than at ideas, expression, and association, subjects which, to him, should not be punishable. There was adequate language making unlawful acts punishable under the law of criminal attempts; sedition and anarchy laws were at best redundant

131. Blackstone's principle held that government could not designate in advance what could or could not be said or written, but it could administer subsequent punishment if the expression constituted a danger to the public interest. How the latter was to be determined constituted one of the more troubling ambiguities in the rule.

132. Zechariah Chafee, Jr., to Learned Hand, March 28, 1921. Chafee Mss. (Chafee Papers, Harvard Law School).

and at worst unconstitutional. When such laws punished language "for its own sake" without there being a probability of violence or revolution, "they are . . . thoroughly bad." [133] Chafee insisted that utterances, with the exception of false statements, were punishable only because "of their relation to specified acts. . . . Attempts and incitement . . . must come dangerously near success." For Chafee the problem was really one of social values. Punishment of expression was in itself dangerous, because it denied society the benefits of a free exchange of ideas on matters of general concern. [134] Nurtured on the nineteenth-century verities of morality, progress, and tradition, he regarded free expression as essential. [135] What these World War I measures had done so disturbingly was to release forces of persecution that violated the national tradition of open discussion which had hitherto held those forces in check. Chafee was convinced that postwar America had to revive and refine the libertarian traditions of an earlier day and adapt them to a modern context, and to a new set of modernized power relations.

But Chafee, ever the patrician and concerned both with the persuasiveness of his written argument and his own respectability (factors which counted if he was to make an impact upon a generally elitist bench and bar), was alert to the troubling implications of the politics of civil liberties which had emerged as a result of wartime suppression. To him the major freedom of expression issues during the war "arose from a left-wing critique of capitalist institutions." [136] The American left opposed the war on the grounds that it was a class war, with the masses compelled to fight to increase profits and preserve a reactionary

133. Zechariah Chafee, Jr., *Freedom of Speech* (New York, 1920), pp. 51–52.

134. Chafee did not go as far as some other civil libertarians did. David Starr Jordan, for example, argued at the time that there was no logical basis for any restrictions on speech, per se. Freedom of speech, to him, was virtually an absolute right. Edward M. Burns, *David Starr Jordon: Prophet of Freedom* (Stanford, 1953), pp. 45–47.

135. Jerold S. Auerbach, "The Patrician as Libertarian: Zechariah Chafee, Jr., and Freedom of Speech," *New England Quarterly* 42 (December 1969): 518.

136. Ragan, "Holmes and Chafee," p. 37.

international power balance. To disseminate this message widely, radicals and pacifists sought to wrap the protective veil of the First Amendment around their expression. For Chafee this constituted a questionable practice in turning abstract libertarian principles into antiestablishment expression, a use of freedom of expression which he considered unwarranted. Civil liberties, he was convinced, had validity in and of themselves, both as a body of traditional American values and as a practical way of conducting human relations for the achievement of justice and equality. To link civil libertarianism with radicalism was thus to him devious and unjustified. He went out of his way to separate his public posture on civil liberties from that of radical instrumentalists who would turn it into a device for assailing the behavior of the new wartime capitalist bureaucratic managers in charge of carrying out the nation's public policy.

Chafee undoubtedly did prick the consciences of a number of members of the more respectable legal community (although more often law school lawyers than practicing attorneys). After the war he turned his wartime articles into a book, *Freedom of Speech,* which became the seminal twentieth-century treatise on that subject, and one which guided a generation of civil liberties lawyers. Similarly, by the early 1930s Chafee views regarding proper free speech doctrine came to be embraced by the Supreme Court of the United States in the influential Stromberg and Near rulings,[137] wrapping new legal protection around freedom of speech and press. On the other hand, at the time of their publication, his articles and the book made Chafee persona non grata in a number of conservative legal circles. Those who did not share his assumption that censorship, illegal searches and seizures, dragnet arrests of radicals, and deportations endangered due process far more than radicals endangered the nation found him guilty by association with the radical cause he frankly despised.[138]

137. Paul L. Murphy, *The Meaning of Freedom of Speech* (Westport, Conn., 1972), pp. 244–47.

138. In the immediate postwar period, strong efforts were made to either "silence" Chafee or get him removed from the Harvard Law School faculty. Auerbach, "The Patrician as Libertarian," pp. 524–25.

To a second group of legalists, the new law of civil liberties, and the new bureaucratic structure determined to use it, could best be overcome by recasting unsuccessful wartime efforts to politicize civil liberties issues in ways that the public and government would find meaningful and compelling. Here the leadership of the National Civil Liberties Bureau, and particularly Roger Baldwin, became the key movers. During the war the Bureau engaged in a type of minoritarian politics which relied on the Constitution and Bill of Rights rather than on political influence for legitimacy and authority. That approach had been a conspicuous failure. Thus, if civil libertarian goals were to be achieved—protecting individual rights against the government; extending them by law to groups not having them; and developing new rights not previously protected against government infringement—a different type of politics of civil liberties would have to be evolved.[139] In this regard, Baldwin and those who shared his position viewed the situation quite differently from Chafee and his devotees.

Baldwin's disillusionment with the courts as an agency for restoring the rule of law was deep-seated and predictable in light of his own wartime contact with them. As he wrote in 1931, "the courts do not help much as protectors of rights, for judges write economics as well as law, and usually on the side of established property relationships."[140] He was equally jaundiced regarding the majority legal community, from the bar associations to the large body of working attorneys in and out of government. Relief from the government's deliberate policy of the criminal prosecution of ideas, expression, and association would have to come through the political processes, with the

139. Walter Nelles, *Espionage Act Cases* (New York, 1918), was quick and early in picking up the ominous and negative implications of what was happening to public law in areas from proximate causation, free speech, intent, conspiracy, bias, presumption of innocence, definition of espionage, to the mails. Regarding the latter, see also Dorothy G. Fowler, *Unmailable* (Athens, Ga., 1977), pp. 109–25.

140. Roger N. Baldwin, "The Myth of Law and Order," in Samuel D. Schmalhausen, *Behold America!* (New York, 1931), p. 664.

people making the civil liberties issue a public agenda item and demanding that they be the arbiters between permissible and punishable behavior. Only if a civil liberties constituency could be developed which would push the issue into the public consciousness and require leaders to take sides on it would the courts ever feel compelled to respond to civil libertarian demands.

Prior to World War I, freedom of expression was a private matter involving interpersonal relations, not government-to-citizen relations. When the government, as a result of the wartime crisis, began to develop prescriptive guidelines for citizen behavior, it made civil liberties a public policy question. The manner in which this government-to-citizen relationship was being enforced and extended by the new bureaucracy assigned to carry it out only served to exacerbate the broader issue of the desirability of such governmental action. Thus, whether it was the Socialists and Wobblies, the pacifists and the conscientious objectors, Teddy Roosevelt and his followers, or critical Republican congressmen, the question of civil liberties and government's right to manage them was creating public tensions and public sentiments which could be exploited and manipulated, despite the Wilson administration's protestations to the contrary. Thus, due to the dubious nature of the government's own actions, a politics of civil liberties was evolving.

Civil Liberties Bureau leaders felt that the people should have input into that political process. But first the larger public had to be made to see the ominous implications of the new war-related body of statue and case law for themselves and for the nation. With the pressures of the wartime crisis behind them, the bureau sought to articulate the issues to which concerned citizens should be addressing themselves. This meant providing lawyers, lobbyists, and publicists, to better enable citizens to get their views before appropriate agencies where they might be heard and considered. Only through such rallying of the public, NCLB leaders were convinced, could meaningful steps toward the restoration of a rule of law be taken; even then the fight would be a bitter one, since it would entail imposing legal restraints upon the powerful in American society, thereby forcing them to acknowledge that "little" people also had rights which had a claim equal to theirs for equitable legal protection. In this regard bureau leaders felt a further responsibility. Aware of the hostility that such actions would elicit from the nation's power brokers, they hoped to assist in building a countervailing force to the reinvigorated entrepreneurs and financiers moving back into positions of national power and the newly equipped power agents of government who were prepared to serve their peacetime ends. They could only hope that through these efforts to open the legal system to all, and thus to revitalize the concept of the rule of law, the legitimacy of their cause would ultimately be generally acknowledged.

Problems existed in persuading substantial segments of the American people that restoration of a rule of law was a desirable national goal in the immediate postwar period. To convince a dominant majority that their own self-interest would be better served by extending the rule of law uniformly to all citizens was a difficult assignment. A great deal of that difficulty lay in the ambivalences surrounding the meaning of the concept for different groups of Americans at the time. For many there had not been a departure from the rule of law during the wartime period, despite the claims of civil liberties legalists. To such citizens, including the president, his entourage, and a majority of the Congress and judiciary, the rule of law was rooted in a common religious and moral order. This inferred a clear relationship between law and community and a willingness on the part of citizens to subordinate selfish personal interests to the "common good." From this perspective, a rule of law meant adherence not solely to one's own individual rights, but to a concept of "common good" whereby the individual blended his rights and liberties with his own primary obligation to the community, attempting in the process to strike a balance whereby the exercise of those rights did not injure the communal group of which he was a part. In this view of the rule of law, individual sublimation to a broader national interest, particularly when that interest was pursuing moral ends and moral purposes (such as making the world safe for democracy), could be expected in the name of proper individual adherence to the principle of the rule of law. This attitude marked the pre–civil libertarian vision of the rule of law and has continued to have its adherents to the present time.[141]

Civil libertarians took a different view of the rule of law. To them it embodied the sanctity of procedure without which all contests became subject to the will of the strongest. It was a view that commitment to a uniform law and its processes was not only the best but the only route which would limit power in deference to the less powerful and to the principles of tolerance, decency, humanity, and right.[142] To these proponents the rule of law concerned itself less with community, national interest, and the "common good" than with the individual, his freedom, his conscience. They stressed the need for the state to recognize such individuality and self-determination, even if it meant temporarily impeding, in minor ways, the accomplishment of broad general public purposes. To sell such a view of the rule of law to a public largely raised upon an alternative one was no easy task.[143]

141. It enables a modern legal moralist to argue, for example, that Richard Nixon's offense was not his disobedience of the law, but his failure to present a plausible case for his violations of law as necessary to the broader public good, that is, national security. The same Princeton professor contends that few people would have cared about his illegalities had he made a persuasive case that he was simply sacrificing temporarily the need for adherence to "minor" legal procedures for the sake of the national good. Sanford Levinson, "The Specious Morality of the Law," *Harper's* 254 (May 1977): 42.

142. One of the earliest pamphlets of the National Civil Liberties Bureau, "The United States Supreme Court on War-Time Liberties" (New York, 1918) quoted from Justice David Davis's opinion in the *ex parte* Milligan case (4 Wallace 2 [1866]) to this effect.

143. For a good many Americans the realization of the importance of that view and the dangers inherent in a community-oriented one did not become clear until 1970s legalists such as Jeb Magruder and John Ehrlichman and comparable rationalizers of Watergate pointed out where they might lead.

7

Contemporary Perceptions of the Civil Liberties Issue and Its Postwar Future

THE HISTORIAN, sixty years removed, observes what was happening in the civil liberties area during World War I with a sense of impatience and annoyance. Contemporaries should have been far more alert to the implications of their actions and should have been aware of the necessity for dealing more resolutely with the repressive modernizing forces afoot at that time. Yet to pass such a judgment is to assume unrealistic clairvoyance on the part of earlier figures and to berate them unfairly for not realizing the ultimate implications of their behavior. On the other hand, such a posture is particularly tempting, given the uniqueness of what was taking place in those years.

The actions taken during World War I affecting civil liberties were unprecedented. For the first time a national policy of deliberate and massive mind control was adopted. Government manipulated and molded public opinion, stepped up Americanization, and criminalized "wrong" ideas, disloyal expression, and suspect association.[1] This in turn reflected a new concep-

1. I am drawing a deliberate distinction here between manipulation, wherein a person is conditioned or educated to a certain view, which may or may not interfere with freedom, and coercion, which clearly does. See J. Roland Pennock and John C. Chapmen, eds., *Coercion, NOMOS*

tion of the proper use of governmental authority vis-à-vis private power units. For the first time the leadership of the great entrepreneurial and financial interests (as well as the leadership of organized skilled labor) were prepared to let themselves be temporarily supplanted at the macroinstitutional level by a wartime directorate of governmental bureaucratic managers. Such individuals were ready to surrender the initiative in the public policy area, particularly regarding the coercion and repression of unpopular dissident elements. Previously, they had handled such people—Wobblies and labor agitators, generally, Socialists, agrarian radicals, and antimilitarists—through more informal means, either by intimidation or by sanctions applied by private or local governmental forces. Now the federal government was willing to suppress these groups in the name of wartime exigency. Private power groups, which had greatly distrusted burgeoning federal regulatory authority in the economic field (unless it could be successfully coopted to serve their interests), were eager to accept such federal activity when applied to stifling the ideas and expression of their perceived enemies. In fact, they were delighted to have the national government playing this new role, since federal authorities could rationalize such actions as essential to victory in a war to preserve international liberal capitalism without incurring the criticism and stigma which private power sources would have elicited had they attempted to crush their enemies in such fashion.

Government was playing a new coercive and repressive role. Its policies were pushed upon Congress with rationalizations which were not always totally persuasive. The reactions to this development were new, also. For the first time civil liberties became a central political issue debated in the nation's highest chambers and in the nation's press. Critics rejected the war emergency rationalization as a persuasive justification for

XIV (Chicago, 1972), pp. 7, 12, 117, and passim. See also Don S. Kirschner, "The Ambiguous Legacy: Social Justice and Social Control in the Progressive Era," *Historical Reflections* 2 (Summer 1975): 85.

such a radical departure in governmental policy—especially when their own former basic freedoms and supposedly inalienable rights were now being alienated in the claim that they were always expendable in a period of national crisis. They questioned the grounds for giving new federal agencies—from a Committee on Public Information and a Bureau of Investigation to the newly swollen Justice and Post Office Departments—discretionary power to sharply limit Americans' use of their individual freedom. Further, they deplored the absence of remedies for the innocent citizen whose rights were violated by the excessive zeal of agents of these organizations. How far, the critics asked, would this departure from prior assumptions regarding personal freedom be allowed to go; and if it went too far, what legitimate mechanisms could the American people turn to to call a halt to the process?

Such new concerns produced interesting if, at times, somewhat simplistic responses. To one group of citizens, this unique situation signaled the necessity for a rapid updating of American law to provide the essential new answers to such new problems. But for a larger group of concerned civil libertarians, the appropriate reaction was to assess the political dimensions of the situation and develop essentially political strategies to cope with it. This meant exposing the fact that power wielders were not about to turn away from this new politics of repression, which served their interests nicely. It meant refuting the arguments of establishment spokesmen that the civil liberties issue was a bogus one contrived by people with devious motives to serve their own disruptive ends. It further meant establishing the legitimacy of assertive wartime dissent as a valid and defensible action for loyal Americans.[2]

Such a position meant developing new and unfamiliar ar-

2. "I am charged with radicalism for opposing government repression," said Senator William E. Borah, "but it is radicalism which consists in the attack principally upon those who use the Constitution of the United States when it protects them, and trample upon it when it comes in their way." Claudius O. Johnson, *Borah of Idaho* (Seattle, 1967), p. 214.

guments regarding the role and validity of Bill of Rights freedoms and then persuading others of the merits of their stand. Ways had to be found to demonstrate the irony of destroying democracy at home in the name of an international struggle to preserve and extend it abroad. A persuasive rationale had to be evolved which would bring home to naïve Americans the fact that precedents for repressing personal freedom could be turned against them. And above all, large numbers of people had to be persuaded that civil liberties questions were too important to leave simply to government officials and the legal community—that the people themselves had a clear self-interest in involving themselves with the preservation of their own basic rights.

The challenge was in some ways monumental. The inability of any substantial number of Americans to perceive accurately the immediate and long-range implications of what was taking place was strongly conditioned by contemporary attitudes, values, and particular situational factors, as well as by the immediate goals and ambitions of the active participants. An overview of the perceptions of certain definable groups and individuals affords partial explanation of their myopia.

The view from the White House and other divisions of the executive branch was shaped by an urgent sense of the need to attain an early victory in the struggle with Germany. President Wilson, a thorough convert to the idea of the validity and utility of the modern state, had long believed that government agents and bureaus at all levels of the federal system should take on new roles and functions in order to rationalize the desirable competitive struggles which capitalism inspired. By lessening the strains of that struggle, government would help to insure the survival of political democracy and economic capitalism against the socialistic criticism that was gaining currency in Europe and at home. When the war came it was a simple matter for the president to add other functions to the government's role. Among those was the organizing and mustering of public opinion behind the war effort and, conversely, the containment of actions and expression which might unduly hinder it. This would further maximize the efficiency of that effort. Since this action was being taken to aid a high moral cause, the temporary sacrifices it would necessitate when people were forced to give up some individual freedoms were perfectly justifiable.[3]

When protests against the arbitrariness of the government's behavior arose, Wilson's response was a bit more complex. Temporary repression carried out in a positive spirit (which meant making people see the value of their sacrifice and reassuring them that their freedom would be restored once victory was assured) was neither indefensible nor unrealistic.[4] Repression carried out in a "mean" spirit by insensitive officials or self-appointed local patriots against unpopular groups was to be deplored. Individuals who would pervert the intent of legitimate repressive legislation, especially by turning it into an excuse for working off hostilities against those whose views, values, and accents they did not like, were to be discouraged. In this regard Wilson would not seem to be an early version of Joseph McCarthy or Richard Nixon. His aim was not to use the loyalty issue for partisan political reasons, to destroy his opponents by tarring them with accusations of disloyalty. Rather, he wished to minimize that dissonance which might actually impede the accomplishment of the higher mission of making the world safe for democracy and preserving modern Western capitalism.

3. There were other human rights aspects to the war in the minds of certain of its supporters. To James M. Gray, dean of the Moody Bible Institute, World War I was a divine judgment upon the world's sins: "Belgium, whose sorrows we deplore, is reaping what she sowed in the atrocities of the Congo . . . Russia is receiving of the Lord's hand for the persecution of the Jew, and Turkey for her treatment of the Armenian. . . ." Quoted in Paul L. Carter, *Another Part of the Twenties* (New York, 1977), p. 43.

4. Such a view is embraced by one school of political philosophers who believe that if a public program contains a promise of benefit, it is not coercive. Only if it involves denial, with no commensurate gain— that is, only if the incentive or sanction is negative—is it a true threat to liberty. Pennock and Chapman, *Coercion,* pp. 5–6.

Such a view emerges from his attitudes toward vigilantism. When the local militant majority took the law into its own hands during the war period and applied informal social controls to disloyalists, dissenters, and those suspected of not supporting the war effort totally, the president took every opportunity to deplore such excessive local and, in some instances, state action (especially in states where that action was carried out by clearly identifiable local Republicans). In so doing, he frequently proclaimed his commitment to fundamental American liberty and due process, but he pointed out also that disloyal elements were menaces. Disloyal activity should be taken care of legitimately and formally by the proper agencies of the federal government.

Wilson, however, carefully ignored the fact that the hysteria which led to local vigilantism had been partially manufactured by federal agencies such as Creel's Committee on Public Information. He also conveniently overlooked the behavior of federal officials—particularly those at lower levels—who, in their suppression of individual freedom in the name of a legitimate national policy were often as heavy-handed, insensitive, and destructive of individual rights as irate private citizens. Yet Wilson seemed compelled to project federal repressive policy as respectable and ethical. He wanted such policies to be conducted in such a way that the government's new bureaucracy could be viewed as a benign and paternalistic force, and not an enemy either of the people or of their rights.

Wilson's perception of dissenters is less easy to pinpoint. From his youthful days as an instructor at Bryn Mawr College, he had taken the public position that "homogeneity of race and community thought and purpose among the people" are essential if the state is to act as an effective organic body. Such homogeniety was the "the first requisite for a nation that would be democratic," even if it had to be forced by the governing body.[5] Throughout World War I he issued periodic warnings

5. Arthur S. Link, ed., *The Papers of Woodrow Wilson* (Princeton, 1968), 5:74–75.

against hyphenate disloyalty, especially in a period of grave national emergency. His motivations for repressive policies harbored certain ethnocultural perceptions and assumptions regarding both the expected behavior of minority groups and their potential for failing to perform as good Americans in an emergency circumstance. On the other hand, his perception of economic minorities was considerably more benign. Wilson never forgot that he was a Democratic president and a friend of labor, the farmer, and the less affluent within American society. He perceived less need for governmental harrassment of people with controversial economic and class views, preferring, as in the case of the Non-Partisan League in the Middle West, to work with such groups in the hope of pulling them behind a war effort which, he insisted, was essentially designed to advance liberal purposes.

The fate of civil liberties in the postwar era seem to have concerned Wilson not at all. With the war's end the necessity for further repression would largely be past. Just as he had sought during the war period to suggest strongly and publicly that the temporary sacrifice of civil liberties should not be a debatable, partisan political issue, so he seemed to hope that the issue would disappear in peacetime. The nation could then return to the road toward collective liberal progressive accomplishment on the domestic front from which it had been diverted by the war.

Wilson's underlings shared many of his views but departed from others. Liberals such as Creel and O'Brian followed largely in their leader's footsteps. So also did Secretary of Labor William Wilson. Gregory, Burleson, and Bielaski perceived the situation in a slightly different light. Frequently displaying the "mean" spirit which Wilson deplored, they viewed their wartime role as not only coercive but, frequently, punitive. They drew no distinctions—ethnocultural as opposed to those based on economics or social class—of the kind that Wilson saw. Rather, they seemed to take a certain devious delight in harrassing Socialists, Wobblies, and dissenters of all kinds—

particularly antimilitarists, pacifists, and conscientious objectors. These men were never as quick to deplore vigilante action as was the president. If vigilantism could be harnessed to the war effort, and its spirit turned into a device for coercing the unpopular, so much the better. Such a view reflected a differing perception than the president's of those who opposed the war. Wilson viewed such citizens as strayed sheep to be led to a salvation which he understood better than they—thus saving them from their own frailties and misguided beliefs. To Gregory, Burleson, and Bielaski, and to the men of action and decision whose patriotic activity they condoned, pacifism and any reluctance to embrace violence in a period when it was legitimized by war and the war spirit was a symbol of decadence, if not cowardice. Men who deliberately shunned active involvement obviously lacked not only patriotism but virility and should be exposed and humiliated in the most direct, public fashion possible. This at times caused unique problems, such as in the case of the Wobblies, whose frequent roughhouse tactics in the name of pacifism then had to be confronted with rougher ones.[6]

There was also contrast between the president and such underlings regarding the justification for punishing questionable expression and opinion as well as behavior. Wilson's perception of the government's proper role in this area generally focused upon curtailing disruptive action. Some of his subordinates had no such reservations and set out to link expression to illegal action. Realizing that deviant expression was seldom dangerous, per se, they applied the concept of constructive intent, which argued that if the motives of the individual taking the controversial position were designed to foment questionable action, public speech by that person was instantly punishable in and of itself. They further believed that the validity of reasonable restrictions on civil liberties should not terminate with the armis-

6. On violence and the suppression of pacifism, see Elwin H. Powell, *The Design of Discord* (New York, 1970), p. 165, and Irving L. Horowitz, *Radicalism and the Revolt against Reason* (New York, 1961), pp. 118–19.

tice. Having erected bureaucracies and mechanisms with which to harrass and otherwise clamp down on the activities and actions of radicals and dissenters generally, they hoped to be able to extend the process into the postwar years and simultaneously to capitalize upon it in order to advance their own political careers and the futures of their agencies.

Members of the Congress, and a variety of other public figures in the political arena, perceived civil liberties in political terms from the outset. For Republicans such as Theodore Roosevelt, Henry Cabot Lodge, and Charles Evans Hughes, Wilson's policies of wartime suppression were made-to-order issues affording the Republican opposition welcome ammunition with which to charge the president—a chance to accuse him of wartime dictatorial tendencies and insensitivity toward fundamental American rights such as freedom of speech and of the press. But their perception of the issue went little further. Roosevelt had little patience with ethnic diversity, even less with dissent on the part of radicals and militant, lower-class working people. Freedom of speech and of the press were for responsible national patriots like Roosevelt himself and certainly were not to be bandied about and abused by Socialists and Wobblies. As to his perception of the proper postwar future of civil liberties, nothing in his writings indicates any concern on this score. The issue, in other words, was a convenient wartime one with which to whip a hated adversary. Beyond that its utility diminished sharply.

For more sensitive figures (Senators Ashurst, Borah, France, Gore, Hardwick, Hiram Johnson, LaFollette, Norris, Shields, and Underwood and Representatives Browne, Cary, Chandler, Huddleston, London, Mondell and Wood) the issue was far more than a partisan political question. Such men deplored the passage of the espionage legislation, censorship generally, and the worst anti–civil liberties manifestations of centralization on the floor of Congress at the time such issues were being debated. They raised serious questions about aspects of the government's wartime programs.[7] They were concerned about the corruption of democratic processes and the dangerous precedents which they feared would permit such corruption to reoccur during a future national emergency. While their perception of the state was a quasi-paternalistic one—most had supported child labor laws, pure food and drug acts, and other regulatory measures—most had a healthy skepticism regarding the government's permissible role in coercing conformity of opinion, attitudes, and people's general associations and legitimate organizing actions. They viewed the end of the war not only as a time for repealing emergency wartime espionage and sedition acts, but as a period of essential retrenchment for bureaucracy, with an especially clear need to curtail the authority of bureaus and agencies with mandates to suppress individual freedom.

The other segment of the power elite, big business and conservative labor, perceived the situation in similar terms but with important variations. While business was happy to have the government suppressing its enemies during the war period, it was suspicious of that process once the war was over. For large segments of the business community, the end of the war ideally meant an end to big government generally. This entailed dismantling much of the wartime bureaucratic structure and returning control of the nation's public policy matters to Wall Street rather than Washington. While the suppression of radicals was certainly desirable to business, business preferred to return to an older system whereby such individuals were either handled by non-government coercion,[8] or through the state and local governments, which were normally more compliant to the demands of business and could take care of issues more subtly

7. See *Congressional Record,* vols. 55, 56, passim.

8. By this term I mean economic, political, civic, educational, professional, and social organizations and processes which impose types of social control on the behavior of individuals and groups. Problems exist here, however. See William A. Muraskin, "The Social Control Theory in American History: A Critique," *Journal of Social History 9* (Summer 1976): 559–68.

and quietly. Similarly, conservative labor, while it was happy to have its radical opponents contained by forms of repression,[9] was cognizant of the possibility that such instruments of repression could be employed against the activities of respectable labor organizations. They preferred to have the wartime bureaucracy dismantled and management-labor relations conducted on a private basis, without fear of federal intervention which would almost certainly favor property interests.

The perception of the victims of wartime repression varied, depending upon whether they had been singled out for repression due to ethnocultural status, or on the basis of their politico-economic condition. For many recent immigrants and hyphenates, particularly German-Americans and Irish-Americans, the whole wartime pattern of persecution was a bitter and ironic development in itself. A whole generation or two of immigrants had sought refuge in the United States as a way of getting away from government—government restraints, government officials, conscription, Prussian statism, state religion, and all of the other coercive elements which the European state represented. With American entry into the war in April 1917, they found themselves subjected to forms of state hostility and coercion not unlike those which they had fled, particularly if they sought to maintain their ethnic and cultural integrity.

As early as 1915 the president had publicly begun denounceing hyphenism. "Very loud and very clamorous voices," he warned the Manhattan Club in New York, "have been raised in recent months which profess to be the voices of Americans, . . . but which really 'spoke alien sympathies.' " Such voices were "partisans of other causes than that of America," the president contended, "and it was high time the nation should call [them] to a reckoning." [10] Such a reckoning came with American entry. Hyphenate groups and individuals found

9. See Frank L. Grubbs, Jr., *The Struggle for Labor Loyalty: Gompers, the A.F. of L., and the Pacifists, 1917–1920* (Durham, N.C., 1968).

10. Ray S. Baker and William E. Dodd, *The Public Papers of Woodrow Wilson* (New York, 1925–27): 3:390–91.

themselves assailed as "immigrants of divided loyalties," a category sufficiently vague to include any German-Americans who dissented from majority opinion and a number of other hyphenate groups as well.[11] Loyal citizens were subjected to sinister tales of espionage and sabotage which suggested that they were the advanced agents of some German conspiracy, the willing tools of the kaiser, or subverters of national solidarity. The president fueled these flames in his Flag Day speech of June 14, 1917, copies of which the Commiteee of Public Information distributed to nearly 7 million Americans. In it, he sought to intensify spy hysteria and to weaken concern for civil liberties generally. The many immigrants and immigrant leaders who viewed this as unfair were even more distressed at their inability to refute such charges. They were confronting not only a hostile public, but the fact that increasingly the organs through which they communicated were also under fire, with many closed down by wartime censors. By and large, their response was marked by confusion, frustration, and sullen resignation. To protest too strongly or to invoke their claim to basic liberties which native Americans were also being called upon to sacrifice would merely afford the government a further excuse for more vigorous kinds of repression.[12] Significantly, no hyphenate organization made any deliberate effort to fight for the civil liberties of its members, much less the civil liberties of immigrants in general, in either the war period or immediate postwar period.

There were, however, some strong individual voices who refused to accept humiliation so benignly. Oswald Garrison

11. H. C. Peterson and Gilbert C. Fite, *Opponents of War, 1917–1918* (Madison, Wis., 1957), pp. 82 ff.

12. A highly revealing case involved the German community of New Ulm, Minnesota, where the State Commission of Public Safety removed all of the city officials in the town for their alleged pro-German views. The local response was one of "deep-seated, but frustrated resentment." Nicholas N. Nierengarten, "Free Speech in World War I: A Case Study in the Suppression of Rights" (Senior honors thesis, University of Minnesota, 1976), pp. 47, 56–57.

Villard, German-American in his ancestry and pacifist in his leanings, preferred to carry the battle to the government, despite ominous odds.[13] A respected prewar journalist and the grandson of abolitionist William Lloyd Garrison, Villard, writing in the *New York Evening Post* in late April 1917, charged that "Prussianism is coming to this country," contending that "those who preach the complete subordination of the individal to the state are the real Prussians and are more to be feared than a careless editor, or any commander of a Prussian U-boat." [14] "I believe the American Constitutional right of free speech should never be abridged," he maintained vigorously in a public statement against government heavy-handedness. "It is the cornerstone of our liberty and of democratic self control. The right to criticize the government is never more vital than in wartime." [15] But if any large number of hyphenates embraced such a view, they normally did so quietly and privately, hoping that peace would relax the pressures upon them, would bring a retrenchment in state action, and would create an atmosphere of tolerance in which they could once again proclaim their views without fear of public hostility and governmental suppression.

Socialists, Wobblies, and to a certain extent Non-Partisan Leaguers, frequently victims of politicoeconomic hostility and harrassment for their class views, were less restrained. Given the growing hostility which such groups generated as a result of both their growth in membership and their increasingly outspoken assaults upon vulnerable aspects of the capitalist system, they found the government's wartime behavior predictable

13. As Villard's antiwar position became more widely known, he was personally harrassed, his children were jeered at in school, his dachshund pup stoned, and he was referred to as "the Kaiser" by his neighbors. Oswald Garrison Villard, *Fighting Years: Memoirs of a Liberal Editor* (New York, 1939), pp. 329–31.

14. The *New York Evening Post,* April 21, 1917: 6. See also "Bryce on the Real Prussian Menace," *The Nation* 104 (April 26, 1917): 481–82.

15. Michael Wreszin, *Oswald Garrison Villard: Pacifist at War* (Bloomington, Ind., 1965), pp. 78–79.

and not entirely unfortunate. Such action lent a certain cre-
dence to radical charges about the repressiveness of the capitalist establishment. It encouraged spokesmen for such groups to
invoke the Bill of Rights and portray themselves as martyrs in
its behalf, as a means of gaining sympathy for their cause. They
hoped that the propaganda value of their stance would enable
them to continue their general programs. In this respect civil
liberties became a useful instrument for the further accomplishment of radical objectives. This assumed that the radicals were
free to use civil liberties to serve their cause, and not either in-
carcerated by government or brutalized by hostile groups intent upon keeping them from "abusing basic American rights."
But generally these radical groups doubted the wisdom of turning civil liberties into a cause in and of itself. To them, crusades for free speech and freedom of expression diverted
attention from the real issues of industrial and political control
and fooled people into thinking that the restoration of lost
liberties was more important than ultimate triumph in a class
struggle for workers' emancipation. While such individuals
could see some utility for turning to the civil liberties argument
as a diversionary ploy to fend off further persecution during
the war period, few, if any, saw it as a peacetime device for
advancing the cause of social reconstruction and industrial
democracy.

Activist libertarians, who sought to counter the repressionist aspects of the new statism, came at the politics of repression
from different directions. The handful of legalists led by
Zechariah Chafee were principally concerned with the manner
in which such government behavior was corrupting the abstract
values underlying democratic processes—freedom of speech and
discussion—and the inability of unpopular minorities to have
their views aired in the marketplace. Chafee had no illusions
regarding the withering away of the wartime state. Rather, he
was convinced that federal controls of the kind imposed in
wartime would undoubtedly be continued into the postwar
period. Therefore, it was essential to incorporate reasonable

restrictions and restraints on such government into the nation's constitutional law.[16]

The war had raised a troubling list of questions for which current legal rules had no adequate answer. Walter Nelles, who shared many of Chafee's views, designated them as follows:

What rights have citizens to criticize the conduct of the war, war legislation, and public officials?

What legal rights have they to express opposition to war in general, or this war in particular, and to advocate peace?

May they even express sympathy with the enemy without going beyond their constitutional rights?

Have the police the right to enter private meetings held on private property?

Have they the right to break up orderly public meetings on private property?

Have the police the right to break up meetings held on the streets, or stop the distribution of literature in public places?

Have the police the right to prevent a man from speaking on the ground that what he proposes to say, judging from announcements in advance, is "treasonable" or likely to incite a riot?

What authority have prosecuting officials to interfere with meetings, distribution of literature or public utterances? [17]

Before sensitive and sensible answers could be evolved to these general questions, the courts and legal community generally would have to set forth new and more precise rules regarding such legal topics as proximate causation, intent, conspiracy, bias, presumption of innocence, the legitimate limits of espionage legislation, and the legal status of the mails. Nelles was convinced that lawyers concerned with civil liberties matters would have to devote extensive time and energy to this task in the postwar period.[18] His perception of the new law which the

16. Zechariah Chafee, Jr., "Freedom of Speech in War Time," *Harvard Law Review* 32 (June 1919): 943–44.

17. National Civil Liberties Bureau, *Constitutional Rights in War Time* (New York, 1917), pp. 1–2.

18. Walter Nelles, *Espionage Act Cases* (New York, 1918), pp. i–vii.

war had made, and the necessity for promptly refining it, was considerably broader than that of Chafee.

Chafee and those who shared his concerns had little time for the victims of wartime repression or their views. The behavior of many of the radicals whose cases wound up in the Supreme Court—Schenck, Abrams, Debs, Frohwerk, Schaefer, and the others—horrified Chafee, who feared that linking the defense of civil liberties with the defense of radicalism would cloud the broader issue and undermine the integrity of civil liberties as an end in and of itself. "I am not an atheist," he wrote at the beginning of his 1920 book, *Freedom of Speech,* "neither am I a pacifist or an anarchist, or a Socialist or a Bolshevik. I have no sympathy myself with the views of most of the men who have been imprisoned since the war began for speaking out." [19] Yet in classical liberal style Chafee was prepared to defend to the death the ability of an unpopular speaker to have his say. Freedom of speech did have a social justification and was deeply rooted in basic democratic theory. Further, this was simply a matter of fair play. If the ruling class used its power to deny the rights of the minority and skewed the law to prevent that fact from being brought to the public's attention, the remedies which the system had to undermine the excessive abuse of authority would be greatly jeopardized. The job of good men was to preserve the process in light of the new conditions which the war had produced. In this regard Chafee, and others like him, saw the Supreme Court as benighted on the subject of civil liberties and set out to instruct its leading members on the utility and sanctity of freedom of expression.

Roger Baldwin, and those who shared his views, had no quarrel with Chafee's desire to preserve basic Bill of Rights freedoms. Although not sharing his elitist views, Baldwin was in many ways a classic nineteenth-century liberal embracing many of the values which shaped Chafee's position. To him society must be organized to maximize the freedom of all in-

19. Zechariah Chafee, Jr., *Freedom of Speech* (New York, 1920), p. 2.

dividuals. Such a view stemmed from other more fundamental beliefs: The individual was the basic unit of society, whose integrity was sanctioned and commended by natural law, by "Nature and Nature's God," as Jefferson put it; further, the individual's self-actualization was thought to be the primary engine of human and social progress. It followed that liberalism's commands centered around the rational and mechanical design of a system of restraints on those social forces that might work to undermine the individual's ability to develop him or herself, always consistent with the notion that the individual is never totally unrestrained by social imperatives. Through the nineteenth century and into the early twentieth, liberal theorists devoted themselves to the creation of an ideal milieu for fostering this kind of development. This thinking pervaded Baldwin's approach to the civil liberties issue in World War I.

Progressivism was to him antiliberal in its statist manifestations, in its emphasis upon social conformity and upon the welfare of the group before that of the individual. In contrast to Wilson's perception, therefore, the state was the enemy unless it performed such a classical liberal function. When the state failed to perform this function, concerned citizens bore a responsibility to take corrective measures. Eventually, the people of the country would have to be mustered behind a political campaign to preserve traditional liberal values through resuscitating and extending civil liberties to all. In fact, Baldwin placed high value upon bringing the "have-nots" of American society into that process. He deplored wartime excesses, on the grounds that the government was assailing the individuality of defenseless lower-class people who were essentially outside the system. His concern for such individuals, unlike Chafee's, was real and sincere. This concern for wartime victims went beyond the fact that they were frequently members of unpopular ethnic groups and that they were being harrassed for their cultural views or their radicalism. The crucial element was that they were "have-nots" who should be in the system: Baldwin believed that if they could be brought into the system and en-

couraged to use its mechanisms—particularly their civil liberties
—they would not only improve their own circumstances, but
would also contribute to the realization of a truly liberal state.
For Baldwin and his followers, this was not simply a late wartime tactic, a norm restoring activity, or an exercise in regime
maintenance. It was the revitalization and extension of traditional American political culture based upon a classical
Lockean consensus, a task which had to become a high-priority
agenda item for the nation in the immediate postwar years.[20]

There also were tactical considerations to which Baldwin
and National Civil Liberties Bureau leaders were alert. Their
desire to see repressive federal restraints and bureaucratic activities curtailed did not mean that they wanted society simply
returned to prewar conditions under which a private power elite
applied informal sanctions against dissident individuals. Rather,
the road ahead had to involve not only breaking federal power
but breaking the stranglehold of private power on millions of
vulnerable Americans as well. They hoped to be able to make
it more difficult for private power to use informal controls to
suppress those "have-nots" in American society who had to be
able to manage their own destiny if they were ever to achieve
any improvement of their economic or political condition. To
do so they had to be free to exercise their civil liberties without
interference from repressive forces outside the government or
from those elements of local government and law who served
as the willing instruments for private power sources.[21] In this
regard Baldwin and his associates were operating out of a classical tradition which Plato had recognized and deplored in *The*

20. On the ongoing nature of the Lockean consensus as the basis
of American political culture, see Donald J. Devine, *The Political Culture of the United States* (Boston, 1972), pp. 135 ff., especially pp.
190–200. Ronald Formisano and Kathleen S. Kutolowski, "Anti-Masonry
and Masonry: The Genesis of Protest," *American Quarterly* 29 (Summer
1977): 139–65, stress the centrality of the concept of equality before
the law in American development.

21. Paul L. Murphy, *The Meaning of Freedom of Speech: First
Amendment Freedoms From Wilson to FDR* (Westport, Conn., 1972),
pp. 30–32.

Republic. In his case against Justice, Thrasymachus maintained that law always represents "the interests of the stronger," otherwise those strong enough to make the laws would not enact them. The act of guaranteeing civil liberties to American "have-nots" promised to open the way to the achievement of power and, as a result, access to the lawmaking process.

Finally, and centrally, the perception of the Justices of the Supreme Court of the civil liberties issue stood to affect its future development. Generally, the justices viewed the issue casually and searched for legal and doctrinal ways to condone the government's wartime actions. In the immediate postwar Espionage and Sedition Act cases, which grew out of the heavy-handed application of wartime restraints, the majority of the high bench sought legal rationalizations with which to sustain the conviction of unpopular antiwar protesters. But to Justices Holmes and Brandeis the issue was too complex and important to simply be wrapped up with a note of casual judicial acquiescence.

Holmes's first opportunity to assess judicially wartime developments in the civil liberties area came early in 1919, when the cases of *Schenck* v. *U.S.*,[22] *Frohwerk* v. *U.S.*,[23] and *Debs* v. *U.S.*[24] reached the high tribunal. In those cases Holmes joined a majority which in effect assumed the traditional Blackstonian posture wherein conviction was upheld on the grounds that the indicted parties had violated the common-law crime of seditious libel. Setting forth his famous "clear and present danger" test in his majority opinion in the Schenck case, Holmes drew the limits of permissible expression almost solely along lines of individual interest: "When a nation is at war, many things that might be said in times of peace are such a hindrance to its effort that their utterance will not be endured so long as men still fight." [25] When individual expression was a clear threat to

22. 249 U.S. 47 (1919).
23. 249 U.S. 204 (1919).
24. 249 U.S. 211 (1919).
25. 249 U.S. 47, 52 (1919).

the national interest during a war period, it should clearly give way to that national interest. This view lacked any well-developed conception that speech might serve broader social interests, interests which would be disadvantaged if denied the ideas which such speech contained.

In the interim between these decisions and the Abrams case, decided by the Supreme Court in November 1919, Holmes's civil liberties consciousness was raised sharply and dramatically by men who set out (and were able) to educate him on the subject.[26] Learned Hand denounced the insensitivity of Holmes's free speech ruling in the Debs case. Ernst Freund, of the University of Chicago Law School also deplored his Debs posture as one which would authorize the needless punishment of utterances in the future. In addition, Freund called for tolerance for adverse opinion, implying that Holmes's ruling had fostered intolerance. "Tolerance of adverse opinion is not a matter of generosity," he wrote in *The New Republic* in May 1919, "but of political prudence."[27] And finally, Zechariah Chafee took Holmes to task for his position so vigorously and persuasively that Holmes, now smarting from liberal charges of his insensitivity in the civil liberties area, agreed to allow Harold Laski to arrange a meeting with Chafee at tea. Holmes emerged from this discussion convinced that the First Amendment established a national policy favoring a search for truth, while balancing social interests and individual interests.[28] In the Abrams case Holmes embraced this position and strongly urged toleration in a ringing dissent.[29] With this dissent, he began reconstructing the "clear and present danger" formula as a device to protect rather than restrict future civil liberties.

26. Fred D. Ragan, "Justice Oliver Wendell Holmes, Jr., Zechariah Chafee, Jr., and the Clear and Present Danger Test for Free Speech: The First Year, 1919," *Journal of American History* 58 (June 1971): 39–43.

27. Ernest Freund, "The Debs Case and Freedom of Speech," *New Republic* 19 (May 3, 1919): 13; Ernest Freund, "The Debs Case," *New Republic* 19 (May 31, 1919): 152.

28. Ragan, "Holmes and Chafee," p. 43.

29. Abrams *v.* U.S., 250 U.S. 616 (1919).

Brandeis's concern for social interest in the civil liberties area had manifested itself much earlier than that of Holmes. Handicapped by the controversy surrounding his appointment, he had not been able to strike out on a leadership path, however. He thus had little choice but to acquiesce in Holmes's Schenck opinion, even though it had dealt inadequately with the issue of speech serving a social purpose. He thus joined Holmes happily in his Abrams dissent, feeling that it was an important step toward a more permissive evaluation of the role of free speech in a democratic society. But Brandeis, willing to innovate in an effort to evolve pragmatic ways to confront social evils, saw the curse which bigness had produced during the war period as questionable both at the national and state level. Thus, when a state case, *Gilbert* v. *Minnesota,*[30] involving the arrest for sedition of a Non-Partisan League leader, reached the high bench, Brandeis was anxious to use it as a vehicle for pointing out inequities and omissions in the law which had contributed to high levels of intolerance and civil liberties denial in the war period. One of the principal problems of the victims of local wartime repression had been the absence of any federal legal remedies. Despite strong arguments by advanced legalists such as John Marshall Harlan,[31] that the Fourteenth Amendment had provided the machinery to apply the Bill of Rights to the states, the Supreme Court had not moved that way. Rather, it had consistently embraced the position that a citizen who felt his/her rights were being denied, either by state authorities or private individuals, should rely solely on state courts for remedies. So, for example, arrests under state sedition and criminal syndicalism laws had produced cases which were not normally considered appealable to the federal courts. The result was that minority rights would be respected only if an occasional state judge was prepared to inject considerations of tolerance into the controversy. In his Gilbert dissent, Brandeis insisted that when Bill of Rights guar-

30. 254 U.S. 325 (1920).
31. Twining *v.* New Jersey, 211 U.S. 78 (1908).

antees were denied to United States citizens by state action, federal review and concern was warranted. He understood well that the main repressive forces in American society in the pre-war period had been either private power or state governments acting at the behest of private power. Realizing that in the immediate postwar period many states had rushed peacetime sedition and criminal syndicalism laws onto their statute books,[32] Brandeis saw the need for devising new legal protections for the rights of citizens who were vulnerable under those laws. His faliure to make his point in his Gilbert dissent, while significant and reflective of the climate of the immediate post–Red Scare era (the case reached the court in the fall of 1920), was ultimately not as important as the fact that his Gilbert dissent was subsequently embraced by the Court, beginning in 1925 in the Gitlow case,[33] as a legal device to get at state abuse of civil liberties.

Such perceptions shaped future civil liberties development in the United States. While Wilson assumed that the civil liberties issue would disappear with the war's end, he did not count on the legacy of the war period. Wartime harrassment of liberals, radicals, and pacifists actually turned out to have been politically counterproductive. Most of these people would have supported the president during the war period and after, had they not been branded as disloyal, or silenced by vehement bureaucrats such as Gregory and Burleson. But in suppressing liberal groups and individuals, and thus leaving only conservatives and reactionaries uncensored, the Wilson government left the latter groups in excellent positions to criticize and undermine general Wilsonianism in the postwar period.[34] It was they who

32. Eldridge F. Dowell, "A History of the Enactment of Criminal Syndicalism Legislation in the United States" (Ph.D. dissertation, Johns Hopkins University, 1936), 2 vols.

33. Gitlow *v.* New York, 268 U.S. 562 (1925).

34. George Creel commented on this at the time, writing to Wilson: "All the radical or liberal friends of your anti-imperialist war policy were either silenced or intimidated. The Department of Justice and Post-Office were allowed to silence or intimidate them. There was no voice left to argue for your sort of peace. When we came to this election [1918] the

led a great wave of reaction against the president, killing much of his domestic and foreign program and ultimately plunging the nation into the great postwar Red Scare of 1919 and 1920.

A second legacy of the wartime abridgement of civil liberties involved the concept of civil liberties as a public policy question. Those who sought most vigorously to make it a major issue during the war period lost much of their leverage with the armistice. Ostensibly the government no longer had excuses for suppressing individual freedom as a wartime necessity and matter of national survival. To such outspoken anti-Wilsonians as Theodore Roosevelt, the issue did die in November 1918. But for a great many other Americans it did not die except in this kind of official form. Postwar leaders such as Burleson, Gregory, and especially Gregory's successor, A. Mitchell Palmer, meant to extend the politics of repression and campaigned vigorously in the immediate postwar years for federal peacetime sedition and espionage laws to replace the wartime legislation.[35] National Civil Liberties Bureau members and sympathizers, however, who wished to pursue a positive politics of civil liberties, had not only to fight this process, but they also had to try to keep the issue alive as a question of the permissible limits of private power or state power—both of which, they contended vigorously, constituted fully as great a threat to individual freedom as did any federal wartime program. For such activist libertarians the years ahead involved maintaining a vigilant eye on federal officials out to renew repression, while attempting to alert a segment of concerned American society to the civil liberties implications of heavy-handed corporate authority, union

---

reactionary Republicans had a clean record of anti-Hun imperialistic patriotism. Their opponents, your friends, were often either besmirched or obscure." George Creel, *The War, the World, and Wilson* (New York, 1920), pp. 145–46.

35.   Stanley Coben, *A. Mitchell Palmer: Politician* (New York, 1963), pp. 241–45; Murphy, *Meaning of Freedom of Speech,* pp. 59–100, passim.

busting, and the use of labor spies, informers, and labor injunctions.[36]

In a broader sense the assault on civil liberties in the First World War marked the beginning of a modern and accelerating process. The kind of repression which characterized the World War I era was not generally based upon fears of a revolutionary international communist conspiracy or even, for that matter, serious fears of a German takeover and overthrow of American capitalism. There was much hostility to the kaiser and Prussian militarism. But defeat of the kaiser was generally assumed from the outset of American entry, and to the extent that massive assaults were launched against German-Americans in this country during the war period, these were not attacks on such hyphenates because they were traitors, spies, or an economic threat. Rather, the war was used as an excuse to eradicate ethnocultural traits and behavior which many prewar native-born Americans found abrasive and undesirable.[37] When it came to Socialists, Wobblies, and Non-Partisan League members (to say nothing of militant pacifists), again the curtailment of civil liberties was not carried out to frustrate some international revolutionary threat to Western capitalism. The assault was really directed at these people, who were dubbed trouble-makers and nonconformists, because their prewar activity had disrupted normal, efficient capitalist-democratic development in America.

Thus, as the 1920s and early 1930s wore on, a good many Americans came to see that domestic radicals and hyphenates were not the threat that they had been painted by the Wilson government and its propaganda agencies during the World War I period. A basis existed for liberalizing the law regarding civil

36. The primary concern of postwar civil liberties activists with the rights of labor have been chronicled elsewhere. See Alan Reitman, *The Pulse of Freedom* (New York, 1975), pp. 28 ff. Jerold S. Auerbach, *Labor and Liberty* (Indianapolis, 1966).

37. Frederick C. Luebke, *Bonds of Loyalty: German-Americans and World War I* (DeKalb, Ill. 1974), pp. 310–11.

liberties, and particularly First Amendment freedoms, as soon as the traditional and misguided hysteria about these people subsided and was widely rejected.[38]

However, this growing awareness of the dynamics of the World War I era failed to provide a viable base for opposing the repression of the late 1930s. When Franklin Roosevelt, the F.B.I., and the House Un-American Activities Committee began taking actions against groups ranging from the Nazi-American Bund and the Silver Shirts to domestic communists, they labored to establish a more effective and durable link in the public mind between such individuals and some sort of international conspiracy than the one Wilson had forged for domestic war opponents in 1917 and 1918.[39] Thus, the more recent process of big government's taking up the cudgel against disloyalists, subversives, and other enemies of national security gained its particular modern form, and especially its anticommunist character, long after the controversies of World War I had been thoroughly resolved. Once that new climate had been created, it was not difficult to revitalize, strengthen, and expand the various federal agencies of repression which arose during the First World War and to use them as devices for managing civil liberties over the next fifty years.

38. Emphasis upon the manufacture and manipulation of intolerance is deliberate, representing a view in contrast to scholars who argue that intolerance is a function of internal behavioral factors. See Bruce C. Flack, "Dynamics of Intolerance: Internal and External Models in the Study of Intolerance in the United States during the 1920's," *Illinois Quarterly* 39 (Winter 1976): 47–64.

39. This linkage did not diminish appreciably until the Depression years. The execution of Sacco and Vanzetti, in August 1927, reflected once again the breakdown of the rule of law under anti-alien and anti-radical pressure and the willingness of the legal profession to acquiesce in that process. See Eric Foner, "Sacco and Vanzetti: The Men and the Symbols," *The Nation* 225 (August 20–27, 1977): 141.

Index